Beyond Their Years

Five Native Women's Stories

John Steckley

Canadian Scholars' Press Inc.   Toronto   1999

Beyond Their Years
John Steckley

First published in 1999 by
Canadian Scholars' Press Inc.
180 Bloor Street West, Ste. 1202
Toronto, Ontario
M5S 2V6

We acknowledge the financial support of the Government of Canada through the Book Publishing Industry Development Programme for our publishing activities.

Canadian Cataloguing in Publication Data

Steckley, John 1949-
　　Beyond their years: five Native women's stories

Includes bibliographical references and index.
ISBN 1-55130-150-4

1. Indian women—Canada—Biography. 2. Indian women—Canada—History. I. Title.

E78.C2S685 1999　　　305.48'897071　　　C99-931973-6

Third Printing

Page layout and cover design by Brad Horning

Dedication

To Angelika (Angie), my wife, a generous soul who put up with a great deal so that I could write this book. Every home we have ever had she has had to share with the five women in this book.

Table of Contents

Introduction

In 1971, in his *Portrait from the Plains*, Grant MacEwan wrote that Native women "... were their husbands' slaves and in tribal legends and stories they rarely rated high enough to be mentioned by name" (MacEwan 1971:45).[1] That was not true. Such women only existed in the then-dominant portrayals of Canadian Native women composed by those ignorant of the respected place of women in Native society. In the words of Chipewyan writer Cora J. Voyageur: "In contrast to what was written about Indian women, indigenous customs held women in high regard; they were powerful within their communities" (Voyageur 1996:98).

Since around the time of MacEwan's work, contemporary Native women in Canada have made a good beginning in ensuring that they are not ignored in written works. During the 1970s, a number of autobiographies were published, the best known of which are the excellent and still timely works by Maria Campbell (*Halfbreed*) and Jane Willis (*Geniesh: An Indian Girlhood*).[2] In the 1990s, we can learn about such women from a broader selection of material, including Cora Voyageur's above cited chapter on "Contemporary Native Women" (Voyageur 1996), Patricia Monture-Angus' autobiographical *Thunder in My Soul: A Mohawk Woman Speaks* (Monture-Angus 1995), the stirring Native vignettes included in *Sharing Our Experiences* (Mukherjee 1993), and in Lee Maracle's novel *Sundogs* (Maracle 1992) or her more recent scholarly work, *I am Woman: A Native Perspective on Society and Feminism* (Maracle 1996), to mention just a few enlightening sources.

Two Stereotypes

However, most of what Canadians read about in novels and see on television and in the movies are modern expressions of two familiar old stereotypes: the Indian Princess and the Squaw. Who is the Indian Princess?[3] In the United States, she is an integral part of the American story of how their country was formed. She is the beautiful Pocahontas, of Disney's world view, saving the handsome John Smith from certain death and in the process abandoning the best interests of her Powhatan nation for those of the incoming white people. She is the somewhat mysterious Sacajawea, the Shoshone woman who aids the Lewis and Clark expedition from 1804 to 1806, helping to open the West to civilization and the eventual reservation entrapment of the Shoshone and other Plains peoples. They are seen as heroines that helped to build American society. But, while those women truly existed, their stories have been altered so much for so long that they have served as imperfect models for understanding—cartoon characters contributing to a one-sided, happy ending.

The Indian Princess is not part of the founding myths of Canada, as she is neither French nor English. Still the image, like so many others, has been borrowed from the US and is found scattered in faint copies here and there in Canadian writing. For example, Emily Pauline Johnson, popular Mohawk poet, novelist and stage entertainer of the late nineteenth and early twentieth centuries, was frequently referred to as 'The Mohawk Princess' by Canadian press and public alike.[4] Catharine Sutton, whose biography makes up one of the chapters of this book, has long had the unofficial title "the Indian Princess" attached to her name.

What is a squaw? Let's begin with the etymology of the word. It had a respectable beginning, coming from a Massachusett word meaning female.[5] Cognates (related terms) appear in related languages.[6] The following examples of the use of the cognate -**kwe**-[7] in the construction of words in the related language of Ojibwe present a good sense of how the word was traditionally used:

Chief's wife, **ogimakwe**. I am the chief's wife, or a female chief,
   nind ogimakwew. (Baraga 1878: English-Ojibwe p. 48)
Ikkwe. Woman; pl. **-wag**
Ikkwe-aiaa. Female being, female, (of animals;) pl.**-wag**
Ikkwe-bebejigoganji. Mare; pl. **-g**...
Ikkwe-pijiki. Cow; pl. **-wag**

Ikkwesens. Little girl...
Ikkwesensike, (nind) or **nind ikkweke**. I give birth to a girl...
Ikkwesensiw, (nind) I am a little girl...
Ikkwew, (nind) I am a woman." (Baraga 1878: Ojibwe-English,
    p. 151)

"Squaw" became degraded once the term entered the English language and the characterization became a well-established part of non-Native mythology about Native people, negatively influencing people's perception of Native women. The demeaning nature of this more-fiction-than-fact figure is well-described by Klein and Ackerman in the introduction to their *Women and Power in Native North America*:

> The concept of "squaw" belittles the lives of Native men and women alike. The squaw is a drudge who is forced to endure hard work while her husband swaps hunting stories with his friends....[T]he Native woman appears to have no social input, no choice in spouses, and no respect. She is an inferior to her husband and necessary only for her labor and for her sexual and reproductive duties. Her sexual favors can be sold by her husband while she meekly acquiesces. (Klein and Ackerman 1995:5)

In Smits's insightful paper, "The 'Squaw Drudge': A Prime Index of Savagism" (Smits 1982), he speaks of the squaw as a figure or symbol used by white writers (including two American presidents Thomas Jefferson and Theodore Roosevelt) as a sign that Natives were "savages" and as ample justification for colonial expansion across the continent. Native culture was portrayed as brutal and barbaric because lazy, abusive Native men exploited their wives, sisters, mothers and daughters. Colonialism was needed to better the lot of Native women. This use of a distorted depiction of the lives of Native women to justify colonialism is clearly illustrated in the following passage from the writing of Methodist missionary Egerton R. Young, who worked with Natives in the Prairie provinces during the latter half of the nineteenth century:

> Marvelous were the changes wrought among these Indians when they became Christians. And in no way was the change greater or more visible than in the

improved conditions of woman. In paganism she has not the life of a dog. She is kicked and cuffed and maltreated continually. She is the beast of burden and has to do all the heavy work.... Very quickly after they become Christians does all this change. Ten happy homes begin. Mother and wife and sister and daughter are loved and kindly cared for. (Young 1970:148-9)

The squaw is a figure more familiar in Canadian works than is her more seductive royal sister. Speaking of the Blackfoot, John McLean, a well-educated and prolific nineteenth-century commentator on Canadian Native culture, wrote:

Amongst the Blackfeet, marriage is simply a bargain between the suitor and the young woman's father, for a certain number of horses. If she is fair and beautiful, a greater number of horses must be paid for the intended bride. From two to twenty horses have been paid for a wife by young men. In the good old days when the buffalo were abundant, the more wives a man possessed, the richer he became, as the greater number of robes dressed by them soon proved. When the husband became angry his wife, he beat her with impunity; when he wished her no longer, he sold her, and when found guilty of adultery, her nose was cut off. (McLean 1970:26)

A similar characterization appears in the influential writings of twentieth-century anthropologist Diamond Jenness. Witness his depiction of what he felt it was like, historically, to be a woman in the culture of the Gwich'in, a Dene people of the Yukon:

Their own women received no gentle treatment; they performed nearly all the hard work in camp, transported all the family possessions, ate only after the men had eaten, and had no voice in family or tribal affairs except the one prerogative of selecting husbands for their daughters. Mothers often killed their girl babies to spare them the hardships they themselves had undergone.... (Jenness 1932:403)

What images of Native women do Canadians receive today? Beyond the stereotypes of Pocahontas and her no-name-nation sisters presented in what appears to be a growing industry of Native theme romance novels, there are some encouraging signs. There is the developing literature on contemporary Native women mentioned above. Further, in the television shows North of 60 and The Rez, we have seen Native women who expand Canadian perception of what these women can be like.

Still, what is missing are non-fiction stories of historical Native women who lived in Canada. Even partial knowledge of their existence is as fragmented geographically, ethnically and geographically. Take the women whose lives will be discussed in this book. Devout Catholics may know of Kateri Tegakwatha, at least a little, as the saintly Lily of the Mohawks. Thanadelthur is familiar as a respected folk hero to her Chipewyan people. Most Newfoundlanders learn in elementary school classes that Shanawdithit was the last of the Beothuk. People living in the Georgian Bay harbour town of Owen Sound, Ontario, often know something of Catharine Sutton, especially if they have spent any time at the Grey County Museum there. Recently a Windsor museum featured a small presentation on Mary McKee, but outside those museum walls, her story is barely known.

Without the knowledge of the lives of Native women such as these, readers of novels and filmgoers have little by which to judge accuracy. Distortions and the perpetuation of stereotypes such as the Indian Princess or the Squaw can easily continue unchecked. They seem right because they are familiar. Repeat a lie often enough and it begins to sound like the truth. What I want is for readers of this book to realize that historically Native women were as diverse in personality and life history as were the women, or men, of any culture in the world.

Approach Taken in Writing the Book

For the readers both to understand and assess this book, I must outline my approach to writing it. My primary goal is to reach a particular audience, one that has a different cultural background from that or those of the women discussed. To teach people from one culture (the audience) about people from another culture (the subjects) is to build an intellectual bridge that traverses an often tumultuous river of difference. Good bridges have their supports planted firmly on both sides of the river. Good teachers and writers must as well. Of course, extending the analogy a little, the ones designing and constructing such bridges typically have spent more time on one side of the river, potentially giving them greater access to the world view held by inhabitants of that side. I would argue that both sides give valid access points for effective communication across cultural divides. Voice is an important concern in intercultural communication, but so is having an interpreter that knows what the audience will listen to and can understand.

As a teacher, I believe strongly in having a good sense of audience. I have two particular audiences in mind for this book. I teach in a community college in Toronto. Students there come from a broad variety of cultural backgrounds; some were born in different countries and have learned English as a second language. Most were raised in a modern urban environment, typically in the greater Toronto area. A majority of these students take my courses as electives, not directly as part of their career path.[8] Many intend to work in technical fields. They have little or no background or interest in complex social scientific theories. Generally speaking, they know little about Native culture or history, but are eager to learn more. I very much want them to have a greater understanding of Native women. I feel I know (most of the time) what works in communicating ideas to them.

My other main audience is Native. My first year teaching was in the winter of 1980, at Memorial University of Newfoundland. Among my students was a small group of young Innu from Labrador. For two years (1992-1994) I taught mostly Native students at the Univerisity of Sudbury. Each year during my teaching career at Humber College (1983 to date), I have had a number of Native students. I can safely say that I have learned a great deal from these students, of their intense desire to gain back the history that has been denied them by generations of schools and teachers, of their no-nonsense approach to how that history is taught by anyone, Native or non-Native.

An approach that takes serious heed of the characteristics of these two audiences will be more likely to succeed than would one which presumes greater reading knowledge and which tries to fit these stories snugly into tight theoretical agendas. What does this mean in terms of how I have written this book? For one thing, each chapter begins with a cultural, historical introduction, which helps establish the necessary knowledge base—the context for better understanding the biography to follow. Another aspect of the book that reflects my audience-targeted approach is to have the biographies spiced up with the occasional dash of the dramatic. The intent is to engage the imagination of the reader, making the biographies appear more like stories on a screen rather than just studies on paper. If at least some of the readers come away from the book with a few vivid pictures that have leapt across time and culture to impress images in their minds, then I believe I have succeeded more than if I had pursued a path of greater theoretical tidiness or if I had managed to make a few key dates and places stick in the readers' minds.

I look forward to reading what others of different backgrounds and approaches write about these women in the future. They need to be spoken of by a variety of different voices that bring to their stories a choir of different-toned understanding. They deserve no less. One voice speaking, no matter how articulate, well-informed or culturally placed, is a monologue that has its limitations as to how much it can express. Like seeing with one eye, it can lack perspective. This is true no matter who possesses that one voice. Comfortable, self-serving stereotypes about Native women can come from both Native and non-Native, female and male writers.

Choice of Biographies for the Book

Why did I choose these women from the many that have earned the right to be read about and known? In part, the choice was made for me. The written record does not provide much information about many historic Native women. A single statistic can illustrate something of the problem. The *Jesuit Relations* are annual reports about what Jesuit missionaries were doing in New France. They supply most of the contemporary written information we have about Natives in seventeenth-century Canada. The Jesuits wrote often of the Huron, as their missions with that people stretched from the 1620s to 1781. Of the 301 Huron names appearing in the *Jesuit Relations*, only 34 are the names of women (Steckley 1998:1)—around 11 percent.

Another reason relates back to the audience focus of this book. All of the stories had proven themselves engaging when told to a variety of audiences: primary school, secondary school, college and university level, Native and non-Native.

Perhaps the main reason, however, that I chose these women relates to the title of the book, *Beyond Their Years*. All of these women lived beyond their years. Kateri Tegakwitha, Thanadelthur and Catharine Sutton, despite dying in their twenties, lived on as inspirational role models to their people. Shanawdithit and Mary McKee lived on primarily by being bearers of culture, passing on the ways of their people to a broader world.

Story of the Stories

The writing of each biography has a story as well, which tells something about why the individuals were chosen and something about my biases. The biography of Kateri Tegakwitha was the hardest for me to write. Partially that difficulty stems from trying to learn about her by looking through the dark glasses of religious and cultural bias that shaded the writings of the Jesuits who originally recorded her story and of their counterparts of the same faith who authored works in the nineteenth and twentieth centuries. I am not anti-Jesuit. While Protestant in my upbringing and beliefs, I have had years of good working relationships with Jesuit scholars, through my connection with Sainte-Marie Among the Hurons in Midland and through my employment at the University of Sudbury, which is administered by Jesuits. They have earned my respect.

For the most part, though, the difficulty I have encountered in writing about Kateri Tegakwitha comes from my confusion concerning her motivation for what she did. My first reaction to her was that of bewilderment concerning why she seemed to destroy her life so willingly. Some ten years ago I began investigating her story and wrote a short biography of her for a Catholic magazine (Steckley 1987). I wrote her story because I hoped that would help me to understand her. Writing the chapter in this book has increased my comprehension of that originally mysterious woman.

I have long been intrigued by Thanadelthur. I first put together a version of her life when I was teaching a Native history by biography course at a seniors' centre in Agincourt during the early 1980s. Later I told her story to a group in Grade 2 as part of a general presentation about Native culture. Asked to write about what was their favourite part of my presentation, almost all of the children stated that it was the story of the Indian lady. For years I have been looking for an opportunity to write about Thanadelthur. I have also long wanted to see her biography as the subject of a movie, but I dread to think how Hollywood would distort her character.

As a graduate student in anthropology at Memorial University of Newfoundland I soon became very aware of the Beothuk and their tragic tale. For years later I have taught their story in my own classes. In the fall of 1994, in a lecture in a class in Native Studies at the University of Sudbury (a college of Laurentian University), I used the strategy of telling their story through the medium of Shawnadithit's life. At the end of the lecture I was asked if I could recommend any written version of that life. I could not. Several of the Native students in the class then asked me (actually told me) that I should write such a story. I took that to heart and began this project a few weeks later.

Catharine Sutton's biography has a very different story although it was chosen largely because of the same group of students. Working with Nishnabe (more commonly known as Ojibwa) students in the Department of Native Studies at the University of Sudbury for two years, I wanted to write the story of a Nishnabe woman. After a long, frustrating time looking through the *Dictionary of Canadian Biographies*, where almost all the Natives referred to are male, I finally came across her name and her determined quest to buy land. I felt that it was important that future Nishnabe students knew who she was and what she had accomplished.

A major part of the story of this biography is the work of historian Donald Smith. Over the years he has amassed a great deal of often obscure and hard to obtain information concerning her life. This biography could not have been written without his efforts. I feel a little guilty in this regard. I have long been a fan of his writing, particularly of his work on the Mississauga. I cannot thank him enough for his generosity in sharing his research. I was constantly looking for ways to pay him back with linguistic tidbits that would aid him in producing his version of her biography as part of a collection of biographies on Mississauga of the nineteenth century. I encourage my readers to buy a copy of his book.

I have likewise piggybacked my biography of Mary McKee on the meticulous work of another scholar, my good friend (and best man at my wedding) Charles Garrad. His encyclopaedic knowledge of Petun archaeology and of Wyandot culture and history made my work on this biography so much easier. Many times I have gone to Charlie's place and seen the picture of Mary McKee looking down at me from inside his hall. I could not help but wonder what her story was.

Being for more than 25 years a student of Huron/Wyandot culture, and particularly the language, I wanted to write the biography of one of the people who had given me my Indian name, "Hechon" (first given to Father Jean de Brébeuf), and who have recently presented me with a pipe. Knowing only a little bit about Mary McKee, I asked

Charlie whether there was enough material on her life to write a biography. He said there was, so I proceeded. At first, it was an act of faith that enough material would somehow appear. Thanks to Charlie's diligent pursuit of such information, that material was eventually forthcoming. Again, I cannot thank him enough for the work that he has done to make my chapter on Mary McKee that much more thorough.

Also to be noted for helping me write this chapter is Darren English (Chihoatenhwa), the Kansas Wyandot who has worked to make the Kansas Wyandot website a good source of information and primary documents.

Editorial Note

To get the flavour of the original texts, as well as to avoid the intrusive use of *sic*, wherever possible I have kept to the original spelling and grammar, no matter how far it departs from modern grammatical and spelling conventions.

Notes

[1] MacEwan's book *Portraits from the Plains* illustrates the neglect of presentation of Native women in Canada. It includes the biographies of 33 different Native people. Only one of those biographies was of a Native woman, and it was entitled "A Lady Warrior: Nameless Heroine." It contained two partial biographies.

[2] There were also such books as *I am Nokomis, Too: The Biography of Verna Patronella Johnston* (Vanderburgh 1977) and *Forbidden Voice: Reflections of a Mohawk Indian* (Greene 1997).

[3] The Indian Princess type is well described under the name "Pocahontas trope" in the following quote from Carol Douglas Sparks:

> The Pocahontas trope was especially popular in early nineteenth-century descriptions of Navajo women.... Pocahontas was invariably young and beautiful, yet still untouched. An erotic virgin. Pocahontas invited and welcomed the white male adventurer, rejecting her own culture and heritage as inferior. Symbolically, the land she represented surrendered itself to the redeeming touch of the white male colonizer. The Pocahontas trope riddled factual documents, indicating the extent of the myth in shaping perception. Trappers and traders...described

Navajo women as the epitome of the Cult of True
Womanhood: not only physically attractive and very white,
these paragons of domestic virtue made wonderful wives,
mothers and lovers...Industrious, loyal, generous and
welcoming—these desert madonnas recognized the
superiority of the American male. (Sparks 1995:139-40)

[4] A biography of Pauline Johnson, published in 1931, and often referred
to in encyclopaedia entries about her, was entitled "The Mohawk
Princess, Being Some Account of the Life of Tekahionwake."

[5] There is no truth to the false etymology that the word "squaw" is based
on a Mohawk word referring to female genitals.

[6] See Hewson 1993:50, 92, 215 and 227 for cognates in related languages.
For a Delaware parallel, see O'Meara 1996:211-2.

[7] See this as -qua- and -equa- on pages 149 and 155 respectively.

[8] I often argue long and hard that learning about different peoples in an
elective will benefit their career and the rest of their lives as well, but
that is not the issue here.

BIBLIOGRAPHY

Baraga Frederick. 1878. *A Dictionary of the Otchipwe Language.* Montreal:
Beauchemin Valois.

Campbell, Maria. 1973. *Halfbreed.* Toronto: McClelland & Stewart.

Greene, Alma. 1997. *Forbidden Voice: Reflections of a Mohawk Indian* (orig.
1972). Toronto: Green Dragon Press

Hewson, John. 1981. "Beothuck Language," in the *Encyclopedia of
Newfoundland and Labrador* vol. 1, ed. by J.R. Smallwood and
R.D.W. Pitt. St. John's: Newfoundland Book Publishers (1967),
pp. 181-2.

Hewson, John. 1993. *A Computer-Generated Dictionary of Proto-Algonquian.*
Canadian Ethnology Service, Mercury Series Paper 125. Hull:
Canadian Museum of Civilization.

Jenness, Diamond. 1932. *The Indians of Canada.* Ottawa: King's Printer.

Kidwell, Clara Sue. 1992. "Indian Women as Cultural Mediators," in
Ethnohistory 39: 97-107.

Klein, Laura F. and Ackerman, Lillian A. 1995. "Introduction," in *Woman
and Power in Native North America.* Norman, Oklahoma and London:
Univ. of Oklahoma Press, pp. 3-16.

MacEwan, J. W. Grant. 1971. *Portrait From The Plains.* Toronto: McGraw-
Hill.

Maracle, Lee. 1992. *Sundogs.* Penticton: Theytus Books Ltd.

Maracle, Lee. 1996. *I am Woman: A Native Perspective on Society and Feminism.*
Vancouver: Press Gang Publishing.

McLean, John. 1970. *The Indians of Canada: Their Manners and Customs* (orig. 1889). Toronto: Coles Publishing.

Monture-Angus, Patricia. 1995. *Thunder in My Soul: A Mohawk Woman Speaks.* Halifax: Fernwood Publishing.

O'Meara, John. 1996. *Delaware-English/English-Delaware Dictionary.* Toronto: Univ. of Toronto Press.

Mukherjee, Arun, ed. 1993. *Sharing Our Experiences.* Ottawa, Canadian Advisory Council on the Status of Women: Mutual Press.

Shoemaker, Nancy. 1995. "Introduction," in *Negotiators of Change: Historical Perspectives on Native American Women.* New York: Routledge, pp. 1-25.

Smits, David D. 1982. "The 'Squaw Drudge': A Prime Index of Savagism," in *Ethnohistory* 29 (4):281-30.

Sparks, Carol Douglas. 1995. "The Land Incarnate: Navajo Women and the Dialogue of Colonialism, 1821-1870," in *Negotiators of Change,* pp. 135-156.

Steckley, John L. 1987. "Our saintly maid among the Mohawks." *The Canadian Messenger* pp. 8-9.

Steckley, John L. 1998. *Wendat Names in the Jesuit Relations,* Research Bulletin #18. Petun Research Institute.

Vanderburgh, R.M. 1977. *I Am Nokomis,Too: The Biography of Verna Patronella Johnston.* Don Mills: General Publishing.

Voyageur, Cora J. 1996. "Contemporary Indian Women," in *Visions of the Heart: Canadian Aboriginal Issues,* ed. by David A. Long and Olive P. Dickason. Toronto: Harcourt Brace & Co., pp. 93-115.

Willis, Jane. 1973. *Geniesh: An Indian Girlhood.* Toronto: New Press.

Young, Egerton Ryerson. 1970. *Stories from Indian Wigwams and Northern Campfires* (orig. 1893). Toronto: Coles Publishing Ltd.

1

Kateri Tegakwitha[1]

"CATHERINE TEKAKWITHA, who are you? Are you (1656-1680)? Is that enough? Are you the Iroquois Virgin? Are you the Lily of the Shores of the Mohawk River?" (Leonard Cohen, *Beautiful Losers*, 1991:3)

"And what if there is a plastic reproduction of your little body on the dashboard of every Montréal taxi?" (op. cit., p5)

Kateri Tegakwitha (pronounced Teh-gah-kweet-ha) has been a source of spiritual inspiration for Catholics, Native and non-Native, since her premature death over 300 years ago. From shortly after that spring day in 1680, miraculous cures have been attributed to her intervention with God on behalf of the afflicted. Pilgrimages to her grave began when the earth was still newly placed on top of her simple wooden coffin. In the eighteenth century, Jesuit historian Father François-Xavier de Charlevoix wrote that Tegakwitha was the "New Star in the New World" because of her shining, positive influence on the faithful. Still today, large numbers journey regularly to the places of her birth and of her death. On June 22, 1980, she was beatified by Pope John Paul II, earning her the much esteemed right to be called Blessed. This places her one short step from being proclaimed a saint, the first Native to be so honoured.

The Bias of the Source Material

Establishing the facts about Kateri Tegakwitha is not an easy process. She has been interpreted so much as a symbol, the person has not had much of a chance to be seen. One major difficulty lies in the bias of the sources of information. Almost from the beginning, the Jesuit missionary contemporaries who compiled her life story were intending to make her a saint. As two modern scholars have commented (Koppedrayer 1993 and Shoemaker 1995), the priests wrote her story based as much on the model of the Lives of the Saints as on what actually took place during her life. Further, the vast majority of the nineteenth- and twentieth-century works about her, including virtually all of the more than 50 book-length biographies, are authored by people, usually Jesuits, dedicated to the cause of her eventual sainthood. One, Father Henri Béchard, bore the title of Canadian Vice-Postulator for the Cause of the Venerable Kateri Tegakwitha. Cited in most encyclopaedia entries on Tegakwitha is a work by Maria Buehrle (see Appendix A), an author who had earlier published the life story of an Italian child martyr. Buehrle's book was clearly meant to help lay the foundation for Kateri's eventual sainthood. Drawing upon such sources made determining what is illuminating fact and what glorifying fiction a challenging task at times.

Another major source of bias, to be discussed further at the end of this chapter, is that Kateri Tegakwitha was part Mohawk. French writers from her time up until fairly recently have tended to be very condemning of the Mohawk (see Appendix B). She has often been portrayed as a Christian rose among Mohawk thorns.

Tegakwitha's People

a) The Mohawk

Tegakwitha was of mixed heritage. Her mother was Algonquin, however, she was born also of a Mohawk father, a leader of his people, in a Mohawk village, Ossernenon, near present day Auriesville, New York. Her name is Mohawk, rather prophetically meaning **'She Moves Things'** (Michelson 1973:75).[2] Who are the Mohawk? They are a people who must once have had a significant town or sacred site called 'Kanyenke' ('At the Flint'), as their name for themselves has long been **'Kanyenkehaka'** or 'People of Kanyenke.' This was represented by the seventeenth-century Jesuits by the short form 'Agnie' or 'Anie.' They are a nation whose ancestral home as far back as can be remembered is in what is now New York State. They lived south of the St. Lawrence and southeast of Lake Ontario, and were the eastern most of the original five nations who joined together to form the **Rotinnonhsionni** ('They Make a House'), the Confederacy of the Iroquois.

The Iroquois Confederacy was formed in response to the message and efforts of the Peacemaker. Raised somewhere along the eastern part of the north shore of Lake Ontario, from his childhood he had visions of peace. At some point in time long before contact (dates vary, but the 1400s to 1500s seem the most likely time) he made his presence felt among five feuding nations. Some say he was a Huron-Wendat, for their ancestors lived in that area around that time. A Mohawk leader, Hiawatha, helped his people become the first to accept what the Peacemaker had to say. Some stories tell us that Hiawatha originated the use of wampum as an instrument of sending important messages. The Algonquian word **'wampum'**[3] refers to the beautiful and hard-to-manufacture shell beads used for making necklaces and bracelets. More importantly, since at least Hiawatha's time, they have been used to form the belts of peace linking the Iroquois with other nations.

The Peacemaker's message, along with the story of its origin and acceptance, is known as the **Kayanerenkowa**[4] or the Great Law of Peace. The heart of the message was that the linguistically and culturally related neighbours, the Mohawk, Oneida, Onondaga, Cayuga and Seneca, had more to gain from mutual peace than from the destructive warfare that had featured so prominently in their past relationships. In 1722 or 1723, the Tuscarora, also Iroquoian speakers, were offered refuge in the Confederacy house from the devastating attacks of American settlers and their soldiers, and thus became the sixth nation of the Confederacy.

b) The Mohawk and the Algonquin

This Iroquoian peace did not extend to nations, such as the Algonquin, who spoke languages belonging to the unrelated Algonquian family. The negative nature of Mohawk interaction with these peoples can be seen in the derivation of the word **Mohawk**,[5] from an Algonquian term for "'they eat (animate) things,' hence 'man eaters'" (Hewitt in Hodge 1971:307).

The name given to the Mohawk and their fellow Confederacy members by the Algonquin was hardly more complimentary. It was **Naadawe**, a word making an unflattering reference to snakes. A different Algonquian language version of this name, taken in the plural, contains the 'Sioux' that gave another non-Algonquian nation its best known name.[6]

The word '**Algonquin**' is said to be derived from the Maliseet term '**elakomkwik**,' meaning 'they are relatives or allies.' Tegakwitha's mother's people lived up to this name by being both the linguistic and cultural relatives and sometime allies of the nearby Nipissing, Ojibwa, Odawa, Montagnais, Maliseet and Micmac. They were also allies of the Iroquoian-speaking Huron-Wendat.

But the Algonquin were far from being allies of the Mohawk. In the early seventeenth century they lived along the Ottawa River and some of its tributaries both east and west. The Mohawk lived and hunted southeast of the Algonquin by the St. Lawrence River. Seventeenth-century French sources record only a few periods of peace between the two peoples, including a short time during the 1620s, in 1634 and 1645. None lasted long. The dynamics of the time, with the French and English slowly pressing west, would not allow it. In 1646, the Mohawk scored a decisive victory over the Algonquin. This severely disturbed the Algonquin world, sending some of them to seek French protection. Included in their number was Tegakwitha's mother.

She was captured in 1653 outside the town of Trois Rivieres, the place of her baptism. From there, she was taken to the Mohawk community of Ossernenon, on the shores of the Mohawk River, some 40 miles from present-day Albany. The Mohawk adopted her into their society. Later, she married Tegakwitha's father. Unlike her, he was not a Christian. Three years later, in 1656, they had a little girl, their first child.

c) The Mohawk and the French

The French and the Mohawk had a similarly antagonistic relationship during the seventeenth century. As the eastern door of the Confederacy house, the Mohawk were the first to experience warfare with the French. In 1609, the 'Father of New France,' Samuel de Champlain, decided to strengthen the French connection with their

Native allies, the Montagnais, Algonquin and Huron-Wendat, by attacking the common enemy of all three of these allies, the Mohawk. It would be easy to think of Champlain as a warmonger in this instance. That is perhaps unfair, judging more by the effects of his decision[7] than by his reasoning. There was a logic to the move that would have made sense to Champlain at the time. These Native nations had helped the French, and military assistance was what they had requested in return. Prior to Champlain's decision, the Mohawk had no significant contact with the French.

In July, 1609, Champlain approached the south end of the large, outstretched lake that now bears his name. He was deep in Mohawk country. Accompanied by two well-armed compatriots and 60 Montagnais, Algonquin and Huron, Champlain attacked a Mohawk war party. The guns of the French determined the victory, blowing large holes in their target's heretofore effective wooden, slat armour. This caught the Mohawk by surprise. They had not been in a fight against such weapons before. Fifty warriors, including two chiefs, were killed; ten to twelve were taken prisoner. The next year, along the Richelieu River that connects Lake Champlain with the St. Lawrence, 100 Mohawk warriors were likewise attacked and beaten in their own country. Fifteen were captured, the rest killed.

'Who hit whom first' has long been remembered by the Mohawk, although this conflict-initiating fact has not often been pointed out in history books until fairly recently. Thus began a smouldering conflict between Mohawk and French that would occasionally flare up into some nasty brushfires during the rest of the seventeenth century. The tension, battles, close calls and threats between the two peoples would be stressed by historians and other writers of the nineteenth and most of the twentieth century to the extent that more positive events, relationships and feelings shared between the two would be less likely to be remembered well. The telling of Tegakwitha's story would suffer in the process.

Ignored or simply not seen was that both Mohawk and French societies were divided as to how to best deal with the other. Not everyone on either side wanted the conflict to continue. Both peoples had their peace and war factions, their doves and their hawks. This can be seen concerning the death of Jesuit Father Isaac Jogues. Traditionally, history textbooks have made much of the fact that the Mohawk killed him. Less stressed was that this murder was committed against the will of the clan that had adopted him, the Wolf clan, some of whom felt quite close to their adoptive nephew, son and brother. Members of the Wolf and the Turtle clans seemed to have been more pro-French, or at least more inclined to peace with the French, than those young men of the Bear clan who executed Jogues as a sorcerer. Rumour had it that Jogues had caused worms to infest their corn and make the people sick.

Tegakwitha's Early Life

As stated earlier, Tegakwitha was born in 1656. She hadn't lived long before she first experienced tragedy. It came in the form of one of several European-borne killer diseases then crossing the Atlantic. In 1660, when she was a mere child of four, smallpox struck her community. That was not the first time the lethal invader had hit the Mohawk. The initial outbreak had been in 1633. It has been estimated that by the early 1640s the Mohawk had lost up to 75 percent of their number to European diseases (Richter 1992:59 and 312-3 fn18). That was one major reason why the Mohawk were anxious to adopt prisoners captured from other societies.

Soon the smallpox entered Tegakwitha's longhouse. She developed a high fever. For ten days her fate swung back and forth between life and death. When she finally recovered, she had suffered losses both physical and emotional. Her face was scarred with pock marks; her eyes were also affected. According to Father Pierre Cholenec, writing in 1715:

> The small-pox had injured her eyes, and this infirmity having rendered her incapable of enduring the glare of light, she remained during whole days shut up in her [longhouse]. By degrees she began to love this seclusion, and at length that became her taste which she had at first endured only from necessity. (Kip 1873:82)

Her early biographers tell us that she was self-conscious about both her facial scars and her weak eyes, causing her to cover her face with a blanket, not the usual practice of Iroquois women. Interestingly and somewhat prophetically, this practice was not unlike wearing the veil of a nun. These same biographers discerned divine providence in her surviving the smallpox and also in the fact that its effects kept her away from others and rendered her less desirable to members of the opposite sex who might have led her astray.

To the foreign slaying hand of smallpox Tegakwitha lost her parents and her younger brother, whose names are unknown to us (but see Appendix A). However, she was not truly orphaned in the sense that we would think of in present-day Western society. A deep commitment to extended family pervaded and still characterizes Mohawk culture. Everyone belonged to one of the three clans. Her home community of Ossernenon was predominantly Turtle clan, while other major villages were more Wolf or Bear. Although Iroquois clan membership is determined matrilineally, that is, along the mother's side, Tegakwitha would probably have belonged to her father's clan, which is unknown. That clan would be responsible for her welfare.

Further, she had another father. In Mohawk, the respectful term of reference **'rakeniha,'** meaning 'he is my father,' was used when speaking of one's father, father's brothers and the husbands of one's father's sisters.[8] There was no other expression for the relationship. A mother's brother was something else. A rakeniha quickly adopted Tegakwitha when her parents died. Apparently he was the husband of one of her father's sisters. However distant that relation might seem to most twentieth-century Canadians, both before and after the adoption this Mohawk leader would have addressed and referred to Tegakwitha as his child.

Catholic biographers of Tegakwitha, especially those of the twentieth century, tend to vilify this man. Buehrle in particular portrays a more Dickensian evil stepfather than a Mohawk rakeniha. She portrays his wife and her sister (also Tegakwitha's aunt) as figures more like Cinderella's nasty stepsisters than they probably were. Buehrle was not really a student of Mohawk culture. Not surprisingly, then, she seems to draw her images of Tegakwitha's family more from familiar European depictions than from anything rooted in Mohawk culture.

There is not much that we know about Tegakwitha's uncle. He was the leading political figure in Ossernenon, and thus may have had attached to his position a Native leader's traditional responsibility for orphans. While he seems not to have had any children of his own, he adopted two girls, Tegakwitha and, later, an older girl. There is not much else concerning this man that we know for certain. It is evident, however, that he objected vehemently to his people, especially his adopted daughters, leaving Mohawk country and taking up residence under the authority of French missionaries. That part of the story will be picked up later.

As a young Mohawk girl, Tegakwitha would have worked with and for her aunts. While there is some question in this regard,[9] it is likely that she would have addressed them as '**agrahak**' (Bruyas 1970:97), a term referring just to father's sisters, and one bearing respect similar to that of rakeniha (see Steckley 1993). We can learn something about the nature of an agrahak in the following passage in which Father Isaac Jogues speaks about the relationship between him and his Mohawk aunt:

> ... I said to a good old woman,—who, by reason of her age, and the care that she had for me, and the compassion that she felt toward me, called me her nephew, and I called her my aunt,—I then said to her: "My aunt, I would much like to return to our Cabin; I grow weary here."... That good woman said to me: "Go then, my nephew, since thou art weary here; take something to eat on the way." (*JR* 25:45)

Cholenec outlined the work that Tegakwitha would have shared with her agrahak:

> [S]he occupied herself at home in rendering to her aunts all those services of which she was capable, and which were in accordance with her sex. She ground the corn, went in search of water, and carried the wood; for such, among these Indians, are the ordinary employments of females. The rest of her time she spent in the manufacture of little articles, for which she possessed an extraordinary skill. (Kip 1873:82-3)

A French attack on her people was to disturb these peaceful activities and to have major repercussions in Tegakwitha's life. In the fall of 1666, Alexandre de Prouville de Tracy led a 1000-plus invasion force made up for the most part of the crack troops of the Carignan-Salieres regiment. They were directing their offensive at the very heart of Mohawk country. De Tracy's intent was to crush the Mohawk's infuriating capacity to send deadly efficient raiding parties into territory that the French were claiming was theirs. This was the third of three attempts to achieve that end that year; the first two had been unsuccessful. Luckily, when the French army approached, the 300 to

400 Mohawk warriors, along with numerous women and children, easily eluded their less woods-wise antagonists. Unfortunately, however, the French torched the Mohawk villages, fields and much of their crucial winter supplies of food, mostly corn. After the French left, Tegakwitha's home town of Ossernenon was rebuilt across the Mohawk River and was renamed **Gandaouague**[10] ('At the River, Rapids').

The Jesuit Mission in Mohawk Country

The Mohawk would also feel another effect of their being the closest member of the Confederacy to the French: the presence of black-robed missionaries in their midst. Jesuit Father, later Saint Isaac Jogues, was the first. He had a somewhat limited impact as he was a prisoner when he lived with the Mohawk from 1642 to 1644. Tegakwitha's first Christian mentors were not French missionaries, however. She initially heard the stories and tenets of Christianity from the substantial number of people in Gandaouague who were Christian Algonquin and Huron. The Jesuits claimed, probably a slight exaggeration, that these former captives made up two-thirds of Gandaouague's population. Her first direct contact with missionaries occurred in 1667, when she was eleven. After De Tracy's punishing expedition, the Mohawk were forced to accept missionaries as part of the ensuing peace treaty in 1667. Although they would stay for only three days at Gandaouague, their impact on and remembrance of Tegakwitha appears to have been long term. When Jesuit Fathers Jacques Bruyas, Jacques Fremin and Jean Pierron came for their short visit, they stayed at Tegakwitha's longhouse as her adoptive father was a prominent figure in the community. They were reported as being impressed by the quiet manner and what they felt was the natural piety of the bashful, preteen girl who served them so dutifully during their stay.

Without doubting the obvious sincerity of her faith during later years, one cannot help but wonder whether there might also have been an anti-social shyness in the young Tegakwitha that could have been interpreted by the Jesuits as piety. In their eyes, Native children were at their religious best when silent and controlled, rather than filled with the energy and outgoing activity of normal youth. Tegakwitha was not as strong, as clear-sighted, nor as pretty as the other girls who hadn't had to fight the deadly smallpox. Perhaps this led her to have early chosen a quiet, reclusive life away from members of the opposite gender and from the more rowdy elements of her own sex. This may have been one factor in her apparently early decision not to marry.

After their brief stop at Gandaouague, Fathers Fremin and Pierron went to **Tionnontoguen** ('Between the Hills'), which was deemed the Mohawk capital. There they set up the mission of Sainte Marie Among the Iroquois at Agnie (i.e., Kanyenke). Father Bruyas set up his mission among the Oneida, the Mohawk's neighbours to the west.

The Tionnontoguen mission seems to have fared reasonably well. By 1669, Fathers Fremin and Pierron claimed to have had a baptism head count of 251, then at least 53 the next year, 80 the next. Tegakwitha was not in their number. It should be remembered, however, that the Jesuits baptized mainly those Mohawk who were about to die, especially the very young and the very old. They could be assured of winning souls for heaven in that way. The chances of backsliding would be low. The Jesuits were not too trusting of Iroquois who professed that they had been converted—they had been burned a few times before.

As the years passed, Tegakwitha would have had ample opportunity to hear about Christianity from these missionaries. Gandaouague was only a short four leagues (fewer than 20 kilometres) away from the Jesuit mission. By at least 1670, Father Fremin was travelling to the villages close to Tionnontoguen every week. In the *Jesuit Relation* of 1673, we get the first reference in that series of mission records to the "Mission of Gandaouague, or of Sainte Pierre in the Country of Agnie" (*JR* 56:89). Other sources suggest that it had been set up in 1670 by Father François Boniface. Despite the exposure she had to Christianity, first through the Algonquin, Huron-Wendat and Mohawk converts, then through the French missionaries, it was not until 1676 that Tegakwitha became 'struck with water' (i.e., baptized). Why is this? I see her late baptism as a combination of Jesuit reluctance to baptize Mohawk that were not about to die, Tegakwitha's shyness and some measure of opposition on her father's part. Also possible is that Cholenec's statement that she "burned with an intense desire to embrace the Christian faith" (in Koppedrayer 1993:283) wasn't exactly an accurate appraisal of Tegakwitha's attitude during that whole several year period. That desire may have been exaggerated by those intent upon making a saint of Tegakwitha in telling her story after the fact.

A change came in 1675 with a new arrival to Gandaouague. In French he was Pere Jacques de Lamberville, but his Huron-given name would have been more recognized and perhaps respected by the Mohawk. It was **Ondesonk**, 'Hawk,' a Huron-Wendat leader's name first borne by a Frenchman in the person of the martyred Father Isaac Jogues. Just as the Huron-Wendat and the Iroquois had their valued names passed down through the clan, so the names they gave the priests and other significant Europeans were inherited in succession. French governors, for example, were always called **Onnontio** ('It is a Great Mountain'). This was initially a translation of a governor's name, Montmagny. In being a Jesuit coming to live at Gandaouague, Father Lamberville inherited the name of Ondesonk.

There are two versions in the early writing of how Ondesonk and Tegakwitha met. One comes from Father Lamberville himself:

> I was there some years without knowing her until one day, having found her in her cabin where, on account of a foot injury, she was kept in, I conversed with her about Christianity and I found her so docile that I exhorted her to be instructed and to frequent the chapel, which she did with remarkable regularity once she was healed; as I saw her so steadfast, I inquired about her habits, everyone spoke well of her. Indeed, I noted that she had none of the vices of the girls of her age, that encouraged me to teach her henceforth. (Koppedrayer 1993:284)

That was written in 1677, before the saint-making mythology of Tegakwitha had truly begun. Almost 40 years later, Father Cholenec added a sanctifying touch to the same story:

> It was in summer, she was alone, occupied with work in the cabin while the savages worked in the fields. The missionary, following his rounds in the afternoon, and, thinking that no one was in the dwelling of Catherine, had already passed over it, when he suddenly felt inspired to trace back his steps and enter the cabin. And, as he avowed later, he was, at first sight, taken with this young girl, so much did one see her appearance shine with modesty and virtue. On her part, she was overcome with the joy of

having found the chance she so desired to embrace
the Christian religion. (Koppedrayer 1993:284)

Not long after first listening to him speak in his self-admitted
bad Mohawk, Tegakwitha asked to be baptized. In seven to eight
months, actually a rather short period of instruction for neophytes in
the Jesuits' Iroquois missions, she was baptized on Easter, April 18,
1676. On that occasion, she was presented with the Christian name
of Catherine or Kateri.

As Nancy Shoemaker noted in her insightful article "Kateri
Tegakwitha's Tortuous Path to Sainthood," there was something
familiar to an Iroquois woman about receiving a new name in such a
ceremony (Shoemaker 1995:60-61). The Iroquois had the ritual of
Requickening in which a person received the name of someone
important who had died. The person so-named was in a sense the
reincarnation of the previous holders of the name, spiritually
connected with them and expected to possess their better qualities.

Father Claude Chauchetière stated that in his opinion "The spirit
of Saint Katherine of Sienna and of other saints of this name, was
revived in her" (Shoemaker 1995:61). Kateri would repeatedly hear
the story of and be expected to live up to the standard of Catharine of
Sienna—meaning vowing never to marry.

Kateri wanted to leave. There are several reasons that would
have helped to create this desire. Gandaouague was not always a
safe home for the gentle Tegakwitha. As the Mohawk community
furthest to the east, Gandaouague sometimes took on the
characteristics of a frontier town. Outside of the French raids, there
were the attacks by the typically underestimated Mohicans, referred
to as the Loups or Wolves, a translation of the name Mohican. The
Relation of 1670 reports that on August 18, 1669, some 300 Mohican,
armed with muskets, stormed the village. While the Mohawk
eventually triumphed, their death toll was between 13 (the Mohawk
estimate) and 50 (the Mohican figure). Unfortunately, once peace was
established between the two warring nations, the path was cleared
for the people of Gandaouague to have much freer access to the brandy
of the English towns, with predictable results.

Then there was the threat, in Kateri's eyes, of marriage. Probably
owing to the prominence of her uncle, she had been engaged at eight
to a boy of the same age. Nothing came of that. However, as she grew
older, Tegakwitha's family repeatedly tried to set her up with potential
husbands, all of whom she refused. Buehrle claims, with no cited

source of information, that there were six. We do know that on at least one occasion, when a prospective suitor from a prominent family was brought to her longhouse, Tegakwitha ran outside and hid until he went away. As would be expected, the Jesuit missionary biographer Father Cholenec made much of her family's negative reaction to her turning down this marriage. Less predictably found in his writing, and therefore more likely to be true, is his documentation of their eventual acceptance of her reluctance to marry, typical Mohawk respect for the independence of an individual. Cholenec wrote that, "By degrees, her relatives were softened, restored to her their kind feelings, and did not further molest her in regard to the course she had adopted" (Kip 1873:87).

In traditional Mohawk society, during more normal times, Kateri would probably have married eventually. It is not so much that she would have been forced into marriage against her will. It is more that her desire to remain single would have had no positive purpose or meaning attached to it without the great significance given virginity by the Catholic church at that time. One wonders which came first, her reluctance to marry for personal reasons, possibly relating to her withdrawn nature and self-consciousness about her appearance, or her desire to remain a virgin for Christian reasons. The two types of influence probably went hand in hand to produce in Tegakwitha a genuine abhorrence of sex and marriage. Interestingly, in his seventeenth-century Mohawk dictionary, Father Bruyas recorded this noun, appearing as **Ganna°k8a**, as referring equally to marriage, spouse and the act of having sex.[11] Context would tell the listener which of the three meanings the speaker was referring to specifically. When Tegakwitha would hear someone speaking of a possible spouse for her, she would hear the word meaning the sexual act.

Another possible reason for Kateri's wanting to leave Gandaouague was that her adoptive father's wife felt some animosity towards her. Perhaps this was in part because Kateri would not work in the fields with the other women on Sundays, something for which she was chastised. There is also the possibility of jealousy. Kateri's aunt had not given birth to any children, and Kateri was a potential child-bearer in her late teens. One day, in the spring of 1677, the aunt claimed she heard Kateri refer to her adoptive father by his personal name rather than by the more usual respectful term rakeniha. Supposedly, the aunt interpreted this as some kind of indication that there might be some physical intimacy between Kateri and her husband. She took these alleged suspicions to Father Lamberville, saying, "Well!... so Catherine whom you esteem so virtuous, is notwithstanding a hypocrite who deceives you. Even in my presence she solicited my husband to sin" (Kip 1873:94). Lamberville seems to have trusted Kateri well enough not to believe any such accusation.

At the heart of this kind of suspicion of Kateri is the fact that the Iroquois had a hard enough time believing that the French priests and nuns, let alone one of their own young people, would ever decide to completely refrain from sex. As a single woman, Kateri would sometimes be the subject of mistrust, even when she lived in the mission community of Caughnawaga in later years (see below). The main reason given by all sources, traditional and modern, saint-creating and more purely academic, for Kateri's wanting to leave Gandaouague was religious persecution. There were, after all, reports of Kateri being threatened by a young man with a tomahawk (a spurned suitor perhaps?) and at least one incident of someone throwing stones at her. People sometimes addressed her and referred to her in derision as the Christian. I do not doubt that a number of Mohawk did not like the fact that she was a Christian and did not hide that dislike. However, I do not believe that it was for primarily religious reasons that opposition existed among the Mohawk to their people being converted. Even Father Cholenec seems to have admitted that her family did not oppose her religious practices when he stated that, "Even her relations did not seem to disapprove of the new course of life which she was leading" (Kip 1873:89).

This opposition was probably more political than religious in nature, a form of Mohawk resistance to the very real threat of outsiders trying to run their lives. The Mohawk did not want to share the fate of the Huron-Wendat, who made their home in French-controlled territory rather than in the land of their ancestors.

Their fears would be made concrete with the existence and growth of the mission community Father Lamberville suggested that Tegakwitha flee to, should she get the opportunity. This community had been founded in 1667, the same year as the two missions in the country of the Iroquois. Jesuit Father Pierre Raffeix, feeling that De Tracy had pacified the Mohawk, encouraged half a dozen Oneida who had been visiting the Montreal area to winter at Prairie-de-la-Madelaine on the south shore of the St. Lawrence. Wheels were turning in the minds of the more calculating of the French political and religious leaders. A community of Christian Iroquois close by might serve as a buffer against attacks by the more independent and traditional-minded Iroquois and maybe even by the English.

The mission, named St. François-Xavier, would early become a success, owing in no small part to the strength of character, the abilities and the devotion of some of its first recruits. Foremost of these was another Catherine—**Catherine Gandeactua**—called by one biographer the "foundress" of the mission (Béchard 1976:322). She was an Erie ('It Has a Long Tail', i.e., a cougar), a member of an Iroquoian-speaking nation that since their devastating defeat at the hands of the Iroquois in 1654 had formally ceased to exist as a people. Adopted by the Oneida, she married François-Xavier Tonsahoten, a Christian Huron who likewise had become an Oneida. From 1667 until her death in 1673, she was the leading figure in making the mission a physical, emotional and spiritual home for the mixed population of several Native nations, primarily Iroquois, that chose to live there.

Catherine Gandeactua seems almost to have passed a baton to another capable religious runner that year. For in June of 1673, a new convert named **Joseph Togouiroui**, usually referred to in the writing of the time as the Great Mohawk, brought 42 of his people from Gandaouague and nearby Gannagaro to the mission. This really unnerved the leaders of the Mohawk, including Tegakwitha's father. Their startled reaction was recorded in the *Jesuit Relation* of 1673 as follows:

> A resolution so quickly taken and so promptly carried out aroused astonishment in the savages. The agniez of Tionnontoguen, who are not yet fully inclined toward the faith, expressed to Father Bruyas their resentment, and the reason they had for complaining of the black gowns, who seemed intent upon making a desert of their country and completely ruining their villages. (*JR* 57:109)

The response Bruyas gave was politically polished. He asserted that one of their own Mohawk warriors had initiated the odyssey, not a French priest. He claimed that such a move would benefit the Iroquois, as those living directly under the protection of Onnontio, the French governor, would prosper and grow in number. Bruyas did not say from whom they would be protected, but the implied threat was clearly communicated. Further, he threw back in their faces the probably similarly smooth line of an earlier Mohawk ambassador who had said that "the french and the agniez were like two bodies animated by one soul, or like two brothers who acknowledge the same father" (*JR* 57:111).

Clearly, the Jesuits wished to plant their own domestic spiritual garden of Mohawk in French territory, and they weren't averse to uprooting and transplanting all the patches of wild Mohawk to achieve this end. This can be seen in the obviously pleased words of the Jesuit writer recording the incident that:

> We are further assured that the other agniez, who in very small number have remained in the two villages of Gandaouague and Gannagaro are so dismayed by this departure that there is no doubt that they will soon follow the example of their countrymen. (*JR* 57:111)

Three years later, the very day of Tegakwitha's baptism, Togouiroui arrived at the mission of St. François-Xavier with 30 more Mohawk. Why did Tegakwitha not travel with either of the two parties leaving the country with the Great Mohawk? Highly plausible are the surprisingly sympathetic sounding words of Father Pierre Cholenec, who in 1715 stated that she:

> ... would very willingly have followed him, but she depended... on her uncle, who could only look with sorrow on the depopulation of his village, and who openly declared himself the enemy of those who thought of going to live among the French. (Béchard 1976:84)

While fear of the man's reaction may have been a factor in Kateri's not leaving, there are other possibilities. Kateri's uncle had lost one adopted daughter when that woman had left with Togouiroui in 1673. He would not want to have another taken from him. Perhaps, despite the attraction of living in a more peaceful and completely Christian community, Kateri still felt in 1676 that she should stay. Perhaps she felt compelled by a sense of duty to or felt some love for the man who had adopted her and who had already lost one adopted daughter. Then, maybe these feelings were overcome when she encountered antagonism after she was baptized. Perhaps the jealous accusation of her aunt proved to be the final straw. By 1677, she definitely wanted out.

Kateri's 'Escape'

That year plans were being made at the François-Xavier mission to effect Kateri's escape. Involved with the plan were her adopted sister, that woman's Mohawk husband, an unnamed Huron-Wendat man and one of the most dynamic Iroquois Christians of the seventeenth century—an Oneida known initially to the historical record as **Ogenheratarihens**, in French, *La Poudre Chaud*, (i.e., in both languages, 'Warm or Hot Ashes or Powder'). This might well have been a name with traditional religious significance as hot ashes are used in certain ceremonies (see Steckley 1988). Maybe the bearer of the name had ceremonial responsibilities. That could be why, when he was baptized, he acquired not only a Christian first name, Louis, but another Iroquois name as well, **Garonhiague** ('In the Sky'). This new name looks to have religious significance as well, this time Christian. His conversion seems to have changed his political allegiance as well as his religion, for he died in 1687, fighting alongside French troops in their attack on Seneca villages.

Here is what the conspirators planned to do. Louis Garonhiague was going to travel to the country of the Oneida to preach to his people. On the way, he and his two male companions would stop off at Gandaouague to begin his mission work. Then they would split up, Louis heading on to the Oneida. Tegakwitha, her brother-in-law and the Huron-Wendat would escape back along the 300-some kilometre canoe route to the mission. Their main worry was to do this without Kateri's adoptive father finding out. He would not want to lose his remaining daughter to the religious pied pipers of the French.

Before they arrived at Gandaouague, they hid their canoe at nearby Lake George. When they reached the Mohawk town, Louis was approached by the elders and invited to speak in council. When he began to speak of nothing but what the French missionaries had said before, the elders apparently left, while some others remained to listen. Meanwhile, the other two went to Father Lamberville's longhouse to quickly arrange with him and Kateri the details of her getaway. Kateri's unsuspecting adoptive father had left for the trading post of Fort Orange (Albany). But he wouldn't be unsuspecting for long. When Tegakwitha was noticed missing, a fleet runner was dispatched to find her father; so began a race for time.

According to Father Chauchetière, who in 1685 wrote the first biography of Kateri, her brother-in-law got the idea to head to the trading post to get some bread for their long journey. Obviously, he did not know about the dispatched runner. He left the other two behind, probably a gesture of caution. Meanwhile, Kateri's uncle had been notified. Chauchetière, and Cholenec after him, both stressed that when the Mohawk leader discovered his daughter had disappeared, he loaded up his musket with three balls. It is extremely unlikely that he intended to shoot his daughter along with the others, as seems to be implied. If there were any particular plan to this number, it would have been to shoot the three who were taking his daughter away. He would not have known about the split in the visiting party.

According to Chauchetière (known in Huron as **Horonhiayehte** or 'He Bears the Sky'), there was one path that both Tegakwitha's uncle and her brother-in-law had to follow. They were fated to encounter each other somewhere on the trail. Chauchetière describes their meeting as follows:

> Catherine's brother-in-law perceived the old man, but too close to have any way of avoiding him without being spotted. Thus he continued on his way, but Catherine's uncle did not recognize the one he was searching for and continued on along his side of the path. (Chauchetière 1887:78, translation mine)

When he returned to Kateri and the Huron-Wendat man, Tegakwitha's brother-in-law told them his amazing story. They were able to travel to the mission undetected.

In 1715, Cholenec told another version of this story. He claimed that Kateri's uncle:

> ... made such haste that in a very short time he came up with them. The two Indians, who had known beforehand that he would not fail to pursue them, had concealed the neophyte [Kateri] in a thick wood, and had stopped as if to take a little repose. The old man was very much astonished at not finding his niece with them, and after a moment's conversation, coming to the conclusion that he had credited too easily the first rumor which had been spread, he retraced his footsteps to the village. (Kip 1873:94-5)

Whatever actually happened, the Mohawk leader had lost another daughter.

Kateri's Life in the Mission Community

When Kateri arrived at her new home in the fall of 1677, the village had been moved up river to Sault St. Louis (the Lachine Rapids). The community had become known as Caughnawaga (i.e., Gandaouague), named both for the location and after the Mohawk town that was its greatest single contributor of citizens. As was standard Iroquois practice, the 21-year-old woman was soon placed within a family. She was adopted by and went to live in the longhouse of Anastasie **Tegonhatsiongo** (or Tegonatsenhongo), whose name possibly meant 'Across the Hearth.' Anastasie, a widow who had originally come north from Gandaouague with Joseph Togouiroui, had been a friend of Kateri's biological mother and had known Kateri as well. She also had been one of the first healthy adult Iroquois to be baptized. According to Father Chauchetière, she had "*un talent rare pour instruire*" (Chauchetière 1887:103).

The instruction would begin early. Not long after the two began living together, Anastasie saw Kateri stringing beautiful shell beads into her long, dark hair. She asked her new daughter whether she was ready to do without such pretty ornaments in order to honour the Blessed Virgin Mary. This was a tough test. Those bright beads were difficult to make, expensive to trade for and were prized like gold among her people. Kateri quickly undid the beads from her hair and reputedly never wore them again.

You do not have to be a devout Catholic to see that there was a strength of belief, a spiritual determination in Kateri that belied her often sickly body and quiet ways. One day she was cutting down a tree. It fell closer to her than she had anticipated. One of the larger branches hit her head and knocked her out. Friends rushed to gather around the unconscious, barely breathing Kateri. Some thought she might be dead or dying. Then she woke up, saying, "My Jesus, I thank you for having preserved me in this accident" (Chauchetière 1887:108, translation mine).

Anastasie was impressed. She soon sponsored Kateri in the highly respected *Confrérie de la Sainte-Famille*, a priest-run religious society that stressed personal dedication to charity and purity of body and soul. The organization had been introduced to the mission by Father

Philippe Pierson in 1671. After the relatively short (for the Iroquois mission) waiting period of seven to eight months, Kateri was formally accepted into the *confrérie*.

But there would arise one important area of conflict between the two women—marriage. Even in this Christian community, Kateri's desire to remain single and a virgin were considered odd, even suspicious. One time, during a winter hunt, a man came to the camp during the night after tracking a moose. Exhausted, he lay down in the first open place he could find in the longhouse. That just happened to be right beside the sleeping Kateri. The next morning his wife, apparently not a very trusting soul, noticed this sleeping arrangement. She thought about how Kateri would sometimes disappear into the woods for no apparent reason—she was praying in front of a tree upon which she had placed a cross—and would then return without bringing back any food or medicine. Her suspicions were further raised when later that day her husband asked for a woman to help him repair his canoe. He directed his appeal especially to Kateri, who was skilled in such crafts. When they arrived back at the mission, the suspicious woman went to speak with one of the Jesuit priests there. He did not know what to think. Kateri was known to be virtuous, but the couple had a reputation as good Christians. As soon as he spoke with Kateri, he could tell from her calm, assured response that she must be innocent.

In the summer of 1678, Kateri's adopted sister suggested that the 22-year-old maiden should get married. As reported by Father Pierre Cholenec, Kateri's confessor, the suggestion was couched in terms of the young woman's welfare and of the needs of the family:

> All the young girls among us take this course; you are of an age to act as they do, and you are bound to do so even more particularly than others, either to shun the occasions of sin, or to supply the necessities of life. It is true that it is a source of great pleasure to us, both to your brother-in-law and myself, to furnish these things for you, but you know that he is in the decline of life, and that we are charged with the care of a large family. If you were to be deprived of us, to whom could you have recourse? Think of these things, Catherine; provide for yourself a refuge from the evils which accompany poverty; and determine as soon as possible to prepare to avoid

them, while you can do it so easily, and in a way so advantageous both to yourself and to our family. (Kip 1873:103)

Kateri refused. According to Cholenec, "she thanked her for this advice, but the step was of great consequence and she would think of it seriously" (ibid). Kateri then went to Cholenec, her confessor, "to complain bitterly of these importunate solicitations of her sister" (ibid). The priest then, testing her resolve to remain a virgin, discussed with her some reasons why it would be good that she marry. Her response was the following:

Ah, my father... I am not any longer my own. I have given myself entirely to Jesus Christ; and it is not possible for me to change masters. The poverty with which I am threatened gives me no uneasiness. So little is requisite to supply the necessities of this wretched life, that my labor can furnish this, and I can always find some miserable rags to cover me. (Kip 1873:103-4)

He recommended that she think on the matter further. When she returned home, she was greeted by an unpleasant surprise. Her sister had gone to Anastasie, who also put forward the notion that it would be practical for Kateri to get married.

For Kateri this must have felt like a kind of betrayal. According to Cholenec's 1696 biography of Kateri, she negatively replied "in a voice that rang more than usually firm" (Béchard 1976:70). Emotionally wounded by one close to her, Kateri responded with what sounds like a hurtful comment. She asked her adopted mother if she thought so much of marriage, why didn't she remarry. Buehrle mistakenly asserts that Kateri said this "with the sudden light of fun darting into her eyes" (Buehrle 1954:135). Kateri was a very serious young lady. There is no evidence that she had much of a sense of humour, particularly concerning a subject on which she held such strong views.

Not accustomed to such a lack of respect from Kateri, Anastasie took the matter up with Father Cholenec (whose Iroquoian name was **Onnonkwahiuten**, 'Gentle Nature'). After he told her to think carefully for three days about her decision not to get married, as reported in one of his writings of 1715, Kateri said to him:

I have deliberated enough. For a long time my decision on what I will do has been made. I have consecrated myself entirely to Jesus, son of Mary, I have chosen Him for husband and He alone will take me for wife. (Koppedrayer 1993:287)[12]

Cholenec talked to Anastasie in support of Kateri's decision, saying:

Far from objecting, if she had any faith, she would esteem Kateri all the more, and feel happy and honoured herself because God had chosen a young girl from her long house to raise the banner of virginity among the Indians, and to teach them this sublime virtue which makes men like angels. (Béchard 1976:71)

Anastasie came to support this decision. However, while there was no formal break between Kateri and Anastasie, Kateri began more and more to spend her time with a small group of younger women with similar passions to her own. There was the Oneida widow **Marie-Therese Tegaiaguenta**, 12 years older than Kateri. In Cholenec's words, compared with Anastasie, Marie-Therese "was more zealous, had more fire, and was able to help her more" (Béchard 1976:168). Kateri and Marie-Therese met in the spring of 1678. Cholenec later wrote about this first meeting, telling us something about both the nature of the conversations the two Iroquois women would have and, as well, of Kateri's deep sense of personal guilt. They were both looking at the construction of the new church at the mission:

They saluted each other for the first time, and entering into conversation, Catherine asked her, which portion of the Church was to be set apart for the females. Therese pointed out the place which she thought would be appropriated to them. "Alas!" answered Catherine, with a sigh, "it is not in this material temple that God most loves to dwell. It is within ourselves that He wishes to take up His abode. Our hearts are the Temple which is most agreeable to Him. But, miserable being that I am, how many times have I forced Him to abandon this heart in

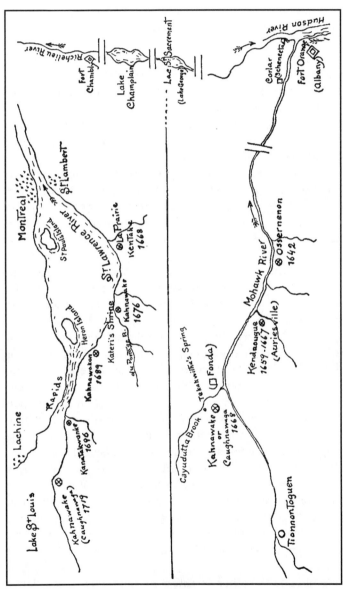

Above: Iroquois Missions on the shores of the St. Lawrence.
Below: Iroquois Missions on the banks of the Mohawk.

From Lecompte, Ed. s.j. 1927. *Kateri Tekakwitha: The Lily of the Mohawks*. Montreal: The Messenger Press.

> which He should reign alone! And do I not deserve,
> that to punish me for my ingratitude, they should
> forever exclude me from this temple which they are
> raising to His glory? (Kip 1873:101)

The two women quickly became close friends, sharing their joys and sorrows and an intense desire to do what was right in the Christian faith. In the language of the time, they also endeavoured to correct each other's spiritual mistakes.

Soon to join them was a Huron-Wendat woman, **Marie Skarichions**. She was a few years older than Kateri, possibly being born in 1650. Marie was also somewhat more experienced than the other two in mission life, coming from the Huron-Wendat mission community just outside of Quebec. Marie Skarichions seems to have been the one who first suggested that the three women form a religious society, setting up a convent on nearby Heron Island. She had seen the nuns in Quebec and had learned something about their vows and how they lived. The three women felt that a nun's vocation would be ideal for them. They sent the eldest of the trio, Marie-Therese, to ask Father Fremin's permission to form a society of nuns.

For traditional Iroquoian as well as new Christian reasons, this earnest request, made in 1678, should not be considered unusual. Women played time-honoured roles in the religious practices within Iroquoian culture. Among the Iroquois, for example, they often ran or were involved at important levels within key religious organizations. They could become Faith Keepers, those who organize and conduct the major ceremonies of the Iroquois and who were often called upon to speak on spiritual matters of significance. They still do. Spiritual societies dedicated to such important matters as healing and the fertility of crops could have female members and officials. Some such societies, such as the Society of Otters and the Towissas or Women's Ritual Society (associated with the three main crops of corn, beans and squash) were entirely made up of women. As females raised in Iroquois culture, Tegakwitha and Tegaiaguenta would have learned by example that women could play such roles in whatever cultural context a person might live. Learning about nuns would have just confirmed that.

Father Fremin and the other Jesuits were not ready to give Native women that much religious independence. Fremin stated that he was worried about the distance from the mission of their place of seclusion, and about the possibility that men could visit them there. As a member of an order that required long years of rigorous religious training, he felt that these relatively new Christians were 'too young in the faith' to go out on their own in the manner that they were suggesting. Further, as a European, he would probably not have had sufficient respect for Native organizational capacity to be able to trust Native Christians to run a small society of nuns, even under supervision.

He would be supported in this lack of trust by the leaders of the convents then in New France. They were very reluctant during this period to have sufficient faith in Native women to permit them to become nuns. This can be seen clearly in the case of **Geneviefve Skandharoua**, the Huron-Wendat girl of 15 who became the first nun of Native birth on November 33, 1657. In the *Jesuit Relations* we read about religious officials making statements about Skandharoua that appear positive on the surface. However, in some passages it is not hard for the reader to detect a distinct undercurrent of distrust of her commitment. Too often it was said that Native youth were not usually like her. In the patronizing words of one writer, "Little chickens fear the kite, little lambs run from the wolf, and little Savages abhor restraint" (*JR* 44:259). The Mother Superior in charge of Skandharoua tested the young Huron-Wendat in ways that stepped close to the border of emotional abuse. The following documents one example of this:

> ... one day,—rather to try her, than to punish her for any fault committed,—she was summoned to the refectory before all the Community, and after a rather severe reproof, was given her choice between leaving the Convent and taking the discipline [i.e., being hit by a small whip]. That poor innocent had no sooner heard the word 'leave,' than big tears started from her eyes; and, joining her hands, she begged us not to send her away, declaring that she was ready to receive such punishment as we should choose. At the same time she began to undress, but we took care not to proceed farther. It is a very rare thing among the Savages to upbraid their children, and still more to beat them. They do not know what it is to oppose them in anything; whence it can be seen that it required a very remarkable grace in this innocent

> soul to induce her to submit to what she by nature
> very greatly feared. (*JR* 44:265)

And when Skandharoua was dying, the Mother Superior literally waited until the last moment before permitting her to take her vows. She seemed not to want to take chances.

That appears to have been the position taken by the missionaries at Caughnawaga. Kateri's band (which is what they came to be called) had to be satisfied with being permitted to set up a special society of devotion within the tightly controlled *Confrérie de la Sainte Famille*. On March 25, 1679, on the Feast of Annunciation, Kateri alone was granted the special privilege of taking a vow of perpetual chastity. The vow was taken in private, perhaps a sign that the Jesuits did not trust others who might want to follow Kateri's lead.

The Lineage of the Baptized

Why did Kateri, and a growing number of her band, want so much to be nuns and not mothers? For a Mohawk woman, the attendant loss of family would be especially heartbreaking. As stated above, family was and is a key component of Mohawk culture. Such a loss might particularly be sad for Tegakwitha. She had lost her parents and brother while very young and had left her second set of parents back at Gandaouague when she went to the mission of Caughnawaga. In a way, the Jesuits had that drawback covered. We can see that in a text entitled *De Religione*. This recently translated work was written by Jesuit Father Philippe Pierson sometime during the early 1670s. Although this piece was composed in Huron-Wendat, it was directed towards the Iroquois specifically. In *De Religione*, Father Pierson presented baptism as being a form of adoption into the **-hwatsir-** or matrilineage of the family of Christians. Everyone in Iroquois society had to be placed into a lineage. Prisoners obtained through raids, even those who were to be tortured, were adopted into a lineage. According to Pierson in *De Religione*, the Jesuits, although celibate, could form a family in this same way. By extension, so could a Mohawk woman who wanted to be a nun. Maybe Kateri could not baptize anyone, but she could have many baptized brothers, sisters, nephews and nieces.

The following lines from *De Religione* come as an answer to the hypothetical question of what the Jesuits had to gain from baptizing people, a question that often occurred to those Iroquois who noticed that so many people died not long after being baptized:

> Admire, my brothers, that they will be a lineage in the sky, those who are Jesuits.[13] There they will adopt as their children in the sky the group they will have baptized.
>
> Would it be a trifling matter that I rejoice that one hundred people I baptized would arrive in the sky when they die? They would form a group there, those I adopted as my children. I would thus form my lineage, my large lineage.
>
> It is not insignificant that it is pleasing that parents and children exist together in the sky. They will be good to look at, a beautiful lineage that I engender. They are pleasing to me, the several hundred I baptized, as I will find in the sky those I adopted as children when I baptized them. There they would form a group. My lineage would surround me. I would not leave any out. They would not break their word to honour my name. I would live with my beautiful lineage. They would be pleasing to me. We would praise each other as parents and children forever. We would not abandon or separate from each other. (Steckley 1992:499-500)

These are words that Kateri Tegakwitha would have heard. They may have offered her some much needed comfort.

Chastity and the Catechism of Fear

Why was Kateri so opposed to sex? As suggested earlier, one reason might have been her shy nature. Another partial explanation might come from the traditional Iroquois respect for chastity. Iroquois culture is noted in the historical record for having respect for a woman's right to say no to sex.[14] The early French Jesuit historian, Charlevoix, for example, stressed that "the Iroquois in particular had the reputation for chastity" (in Spittal 1990:38). Repeatedly heard is that female prisoners of the Iroquois through the centuries were sexually untouched before they consented to be married. In one early-nineteenth-century case, this waiting period lasted for two years.

Respect for a woman's chastity is different, however, from a woman wanting never to engage in sex. This was new, largely the result of Kateri and her band being taught Christianity exclusively by people who had made a vow of celibacy themselves, people who had a great deal of power over their mission charges. Imagine the situation. You are told that certain practices could lead you to hell, that place that the missionaries stressed (as we will see) was frightful even to contemplate. What practices are these? They are sins. Now sin is not a Mohawk word. There was no equivalent in the language. The term that came to be used for sin can be translated literally as 'being mistaken in important matters.' The priests and nuns had a monopoly on knowing for sure what those mistakes were. Having that information gave them power.

Kateri and the others were given an overwhelming message that virginity was the right path to take and that no other sexual trail, even the one that involved getting married, could compare. The Jesuits taught love for and worship of the Blessed Virgin Mary. They demonstrated through the examples of their own lives that the very religious, those who were especially assured of salvation, lived a life of celibacy.

The Jesuits created a fear-and-guilt-charged environment in seventeenth-century New France when it came to anything sexual. We can observe this in the *Jesuit Relation* of 1644, reporting on the mission to the Montagnais. The Jesuits and their most devoted followers deemed dangerous situations which traditional Montagnais and we today would call reasonably innocent, fairly normal interaction between young men and women. But in the missions it was taught that damnation lurked behind every sexually tinged word, deed, thought or feeling, like an enemy behind a seemingly innocuous tree or bend of a river. Extreme measures had to be taken.

There was, for example, an older Montagnais woman who Jesuit Father Vimont wrote "manifests admirable zeal for the purity of the girls" (*JR* 25:185). How did she earn such praise?

> When the young men come back from war, she carefully
> assembles all the girls and locks them in at night, or
> shuts them up in the houses that we have built for
> them in the manner of the French, or in the granaries

where they keep their provisions. One night, while
we were reciting the prayers in our chapel, she
suddenly entered and hurried us out. We found that
she called us to help her against some young men,
who were walking about near a house in which some
girls were shut up. This was enough to drive them
from Sillery [the name of the mission], *where the
slightest suspicion on this head* [i.e., *en cette maniere—*
in this manner] *is criminal.* (*JR* 25:185; emphasis and
additions mine)

Speaking of the young Montagnais women of this community,
Vimont wrote:

There are many who accuse themselves, as of a
grievous sin, that some young men have spoken to
them of marriage,—although they have coldly
answered to this that the matter did not depend upon
them, but upon their parents.... One night a band of
young girls came to our door and called out: "My
Father, have pity on us." We asked what was the
matter. "We are afraid," they said, "of some young
men who are not well behaved. We are not safe in
our cabins; lock us up in one of those small houses."
There are some who, in giving an account of their
consciences, accuse themselves, as of a grievous sin,
of greatly hating a man who had spoken too freely to
them. Such scruples are pardonable in girls, and show
in what esteem purity is held here, where formerly
its name was hardly known. (*JR* 25:185-7)

We can read from the circumstances of the Sillery mission, where
people could be banished from their community for flirting and where
a proposal of marriage was sometimes perceived as threatening the
fate of one's everlasting life, that the Jesuit missionaries held great
discretionary power. Although most of them seem to me to be people
of some compassion, some abused their power. The following is a
case in point from Sillery. It is nothing short of spiritual bullying.
Unfortunately, this is not the only case of such bullying being reported
with slight amusement by writers quoted in the *Jesuit Relations*. While

Sillery was a place where missionary control was taken to extremes, the situation at Caughnawaga would not have been significantly different.

> One of our Fathers told a very innocent girl, in consequence of some remarks and reports, that he feared something affecting her honor, and advised her to be on her guard. She began to cry and withdrew to her cabin, where she related to her parents the cause of her tears. All began to weep with her, and passed the whole night in tears, until, on the following day, the Father, who had heard what had happened, consoled them and assured them that he did not doubt the girl's innocence; but what he had said was merely for the purpose of making her dread still more whatever might harm her purity. (*JR* 25:185)

Much of the power of the missionaries came from fear. Fear was a significant component in the mission message. In 1632, Father Paul Le Jeune, when he was the Superior of the Jesuit Order in New France, stated that "fear is the forerunner of faith" (*JR* 11:89). Fear of hell, created both through graphic pictures and through rich verbal imagery, was a major Jesuit weapon in the fight to win over the souls of the Iroquois. This weapon was wielded not only by French missionaries but by Iroquois Christians such as Louis Garonhiague and Anastasie Tegonhatsiongo. It would cut deep into a people already experiencing the hell on earth of deadly new diseases and punishing raids by the French.

We can learn the specific, horrific images the Jesuits were instilling into Kateri's impressionable young mind through the previously cited *De Religione*. We read in this text that the Jesuit missionaries focused especially on trying to convince the stoic Iroquois that what they would have to endure in hell if they were not good Christians before they died was much worse than any torture that any prisoner on earth could ever receive. One difference between the two situations was that the fire used to inflict pain inside the earth (i.e., in hell) could never be extinguished:

> The fire we burn with gets extinguished. Even if the flames are high, it would still be put out if we threw

a lot of water on it. But when it burns inside the earth, if we threw down enough water for an entire lake, would burning still be perceived? It would be like increasing the size of an already large hearth. And if several mountains of snow fell inside the earth, would it diminish the burning? It would not be extinguished. Give up any such hopes. The mountain of snow would burn. The lake would burn. (Steckley 1992:490)

Imagine when you read the next passage the effect this description might have had on Tegakwitha as a child. She had seen prisoners being tortured and had returned to a home torched by the French:

The fire inside the earth is not like the fire you burn prisoners with. Your fire burns intensely only where it is applied. It is not such a fire, the one that burns inside the earth. It is a piercing fire.
Your fire slowly eats the flesh, first eating the skin from the outside. Shortly afterwards, the fire would enter the inside of the body. Piece by piece it proceeds, this fire. First it cooks the flesh, then it eats through it. The flesh will not be consumed. One is covered with fire, and then it slowly advances, gradually penetrating inside.
But the fire that burns inside the earth immediately goes all over the body and into every bone. At the moment when the fire is placed for it to travel down and spread all over your body and to completely penetrate you. Inside, no place will be missed. You burn all over equally, inside and out. (Steckley 1992:490)

The body would not be alone in feeling the pain of burning. It would have company in its misery—the soul. Pierson wrote of the reunion of the body and the soul after death and of the resultant doubling of the pain that people would feel because of that reunion (Steckley 1992:481). More than just physical pain would be felt. There would be the agony of social isolation as well. The damned souls in hell would not be admired or praised for their withstanding torture, unlike prisoners here on earth who could be respected when they bravely endure what their enemy inflicted on them. The prisoners of the demons of hell would be universally hated:

> When someone is on a war party, he resolves to endure being tortured with fire for a long time. You know it is not a long time that humans are tortured with fire. You think, "My bravery will be admired. I will not cry out, and my name will be praised forever." Would you be so sure if you were in the fire inside the earth? You would not be consumed by the fire or be praised.... [L]ost inside the earth is admiration and praise. Would you be praised for being hated by the master [i.e., God]? Wherever you dwell now you will sink into the earth, where contempt, anger and hatred will continue....
>
> The people will be one in insulting and shaming you. It will not be possible for you to hide your face. You will hear the whole affair or what they say against you. It will be filled with shame. It will not only be those you know that will quarrel with your badness. Every person from every country will hit you again concerning all your many offences [i.e., sins]. They will wound you by saying, "Look at his badness. He is a murderer." They will say, "He should fall inside the earth as he is a good-for-nothing...."
>
> You will be held in contempt. You will see people insult you, stick out their tongues at you and shame you. No one is missing. They will all hate you and rejoice in your bad fortune. (Steckley 1992.492 and 492-93)

The Jesuits gave the Iroquois a great deal to think about.

Mortification

Perhaps this atmosphere of fear can best explain another feature of Kateri's Christianity, one that went deeper than the physical scars it inflicted. She practised a severe mortification, the deliberate seeking of personal pain for religious purposes. Mortification was then common among devout Catholics. Typically, the acts creating the pain were self-administered, but sometimes assistance was sought. Several reasons were usually given at that time to justify the practice. It served to reinforce the lesson that the body is of little importance relative to the soul, just as this temporary material life on earth is unimportant relative to the everlasting spiritual life that can be obtained in heaven. Some thought of it as a sharing in a vicarious way of the pain that Jesus suffered on the cross. Mortification could be, and often was, a form of penance, a punishment for sins committed or for the Original Sin that caused the fall from the Garden of Eden.

It is easy for the modern reader to make the connection between the practices about to be described and sadomasochistic sexual activities. A strict Freudian psychoanalyst might look at her mortification, her traumatic childhood and her near pathological opposition to marriage and come up with a diagnosis that Kateri was not psychologically healthy. However, it would be inaccurate, and not a little unfair, to thus apply twentieth-century standards in this area to a seventeenth-century person. I tend to side with the Catholic writers who look more to her purity of intent, her strength and her courage in their judgment of Kateri. However, unlike those writers, I question the sanity of the idea itself and the morality of those in authority who indirectly encouraged and knowingly permitted a frail young woman to contribute in this way to her own untimely death.

It should be pointed out that self-inflicted pain was not new to the Iroquois. They imposed physical hardships on themselves, both to prepare their bodies for the trials of life ahead and to aid in seeking communication with the spirit world. Young warriors-to-be were encouraged to bathe daily in cold water, to gash themselves on the shins with stones and to burn themselves as well, toughening themselves for combat and potential capture. The ideal was that they would be then able to sing their death songs and heap scorn on their captors while being burned and cut with sharp blades. Spirit seekers sought to make themselves appear worthy of spiritual mercy or favour. Raised as a Mohawk, Kateri would have been taught respect for such physical courage and spiritual dedication.

Kateri engaged in several forms of mortification. They ranged from small matters, such as mixing ashes in her food so that it wouldn't have a pleasant taste, to the use of fire. One night, after hearing

Anastasie talk to her about the fires of hell, she asked the older woman what she considered to be the severest penance to offer to Jesus as proof one one's devotion. Probably not realizing that the zealous Kateri would actually do this to herself, Anastasie replied that she believed that there was nothing more painful than being burned by fire. According to Father Chauchetière, Kateri that night was struck with a deep sense of her own sins. She waited until she was alone and burned herself from toe to knee with a live coal.

Kateri and her best friend Marie-Therese Tegaiaguenta encouraged each other in their mortification. One day the two women decided to place a hot coal between their big and second toes while reciting the Ave Maria. According to Jesuit Father Henri Béchard, the Canadian Vice Postulator for the Cause of the (then) Venerable Kateri Tegakwitha, writing in the 1970s:

> Marie-Therese... enjoyed good health, yet after having endured the pain for half a Hail Mary, she felt quite faint. Despite her debilitated condition, Kateri endured the fiery hot coal much longer. Marie-Therese never doubted that this prolonged penance suffered by Kateri belonged to the domain of the miraculous. (Béchard 1976:169)

This particular incident became somewhat mythologized over the years. When Chauchetière wrote of the incident in 1685, he spoke of how Marie-Therese was greatly affected by the sight of the large hole she saw in Kateri's foot the next day. By 1696, however, Cholenec had added somewhat to the legend of Kateri by declaring that, "The marvel was still greater, however, when the following morning there was no mark of the burn on her foot" (Béchard 1976:169).

Kateri and Marie-Therese can be considered to be partners in mortification, in part because Kateri lacked the strength to whip herself hard enough to satisfy her stringent standards. In 1683, Chauchetière wrote that Kateri:

> ... had made an agreement with... [Marie-Therese] to make each other suffer, because she was too weak to do so by herself, owing to her continual illness. She had begged her companion to do her the charity of severely chastising her with blows from a whip.

> This they did for a year, without anyone knowing it,
> and for that purpose they withdrew, every Sunday,
> into a cabin in the middle of the cemetery; and thence,
> taking in their hands willow shoots, they mingled
> prayers with penance. Finally, when ... [Marie-
> Therese] saw that her companion had fallen sick at
> the end of the year, she was pressed by scruples to
> reveal the matter, and to ask whether she had not
> sinned in what she had done. (*JR* 62:177-9)

The whipping regularly drew blood, but Kateri often complained that her friend did not hit her hard enough.

Kateri seems regularly to have outdone Marie-Therese in mortification. When she went on the winter hunt, she walked over the jagged ice of a pond barefoot. In February, she stood naked from toe to knee encased in snow as she said her Ave Maria. Kateri often wore a studded cincture, an iron belt with pain-inflicting points directed inwards. One winter's day, while carrying a heavy load of wood and wearing her cincture, she fell down. The fall must have hurt Kateri terribly. Yet, when Marie-Therese offered to carry Kateri's load for her, the younger woman just laughed and continued on with her work.

Not surprisingly, all of this took a definite toll on Kateri's health. Possibly the most deadly practice she engaged in began in January, 1680. Father Cholenec had spoken to her of how St. Aloysius Gonzaga had slept on a bed of thorns as an act of penance. Inspired, Kateri went out to gather the sharpest thorns she could find and made a spiny bed of them. For four painful nights, Kateri slept on this bed. She told no one of what she was doing. Some people noticed that she was looking particularly pale, but as she was never very healthy they did not think much more on the subject. Marie-Therese, however, suspected that Kateri was doing something extra in her mortification. She confronted Kateri. The increasingly pale and fragile young woman admitted to what she was doing and said that she would continue the practice until she died. For Marie-Therese, this was going too far. She replied to Kateri's declaration by saying, "[D]o you know that you offend God by undertaking this sort of excess without the permission of your confessor?" (Béchard 1976:170-1)

Kateri went to Father Cholenec, her confessor, and told him about how she had been imitating the saint mentioned in his stories. While according to his own written words he inwardly admired her action, he "pretended to be displeased and reprimanded her for her imprudence" (Béchard 1976:171). Cholenec could see what Kateri's mortification had cost her health. He wrote that "her face resembled that of a dead person" (Béchard 1976:173).

Not long after that, while carrying supplies in the cold heart of winter, Kateri contracted a fever. It was the beginning of the end.

Kateri was not much of a talker. We have few of her words recorded to remember her by. On her last days, from her death bed were remembered two statements that speak volumes about that young woman's life and her approach to Christianity.

One of these statements was made to **Marguerite Gagouithon**, a 20-year-old Onondaga woman, one of two who were keeping Kateri's death vigil. The year before she had married a much older man, an aging war leader, probably because she belonged to a prominent lineage. Owing largely to the difference in age between Marguerite and her husband, she had a sexual fling with a man her own age. Encouraged by the teachings of the missionaries, she came to feel the crushing emotional weight of a heavy burden of guilt. Consequently, she was probably the Iroquois Christian who employed on herself the discipline or scourge (i.e., the willow whip) most frequently and the one who took this practice to the most physically damaging extreme. A twentieth-century admirer of hers, Jesuit historian Father Henri Béchard, proclaimed his unqualified praise for her pain-inflicting actions by saying, "Marguerite Gagouithon, a seventeenth century Indian, was made of sterner stuff than what today generally produces" (Béchard 1976:195).

Early on the evening before Kateri's death, Marguerite asked permission to go out into the woods to whip herself on her already scarred shoulders. Marguerite wanted in this way to try to obtain the favour from God of a peaceful death and a short purgatory for Kateri. The priest gave this wish his blessing. Marguerite then went outside on that cold spring night, exposed her shoulders and beat them until she bled profusely. Kateri somehow found out about what she was doing and asked for the young Onondaga to be brought to her bedside. When Marguerite arrived, bleeding but happy that she was helping her dear friend, Kateri said:

> Come here, sister, so that I may say a few words to you.... Be of good cheer, my dear sister, continue with

the same fervor with which you have so well begun.... Sister, I know well what I say. I even know the place from which you have come, and I can assure you that whatever you do is well done and is most agreeable to our Lord. Be of good cheer, persevere, and fervently pray for me at my death, so that I may be released from purgatory as soon as possible. I will make it up to you, believe me! (Béchard 1976:192)

Her last words to her best friend, Marie-Therese Tegaiaguenta, were like her Christianity, determined and harsh:

I am leaving you... I am about to die. Always remember what we have done together, since we knew each other; if you change, I will accuse you before the tribunal of God. Take courage, despise the conversations of those who have no faith, and who wish you to marry; listen only to the priest. If you cannot serve God here, go to the Lorette Mission. Never give up mortification. I will love you in heaven; I will pray for you: I will assist you. (Béchard 1976:171-172)

Interestingly, in Buehrle's reporting of the speech, the part about possibly accusing Marie-Therese was left out.

Finally, on the afternoon of April 17, 1680, Kateri Tegakwitha died. Her impact after death was immediate and strong. Within a week, her adopted mother Anastasie had a vivid vision of Kateri accompanied by a dazzlingly bright cross. A few months later, she likewise appeared to Father Chauchetière. More than a year later she was seen in a dream by Marie-Therese. Kateri's band of devout women flourished and grew. Her example inspired women to practice mortification, to give up fancy clothing, makeup and jewellery, and to work to help the needy.

Miracles and Kateri's Path of Sainthood

What has made Kateri famous, and has led her down the road to sainthood, is not as much anything she did in life as her entry into the realm of the miraculous after she died. What should be remarked on, at least in passing, is that at the same time that Kateri Tegakwitha's fame and religious glory were growing, her Christian Mohawk community was fulfilling its hoped-for role as a buffer between the French and the Iroquois in New York. In a letter written by Father Thierry Beschefer, Jesuit Superior in Canada, to the "Provincial of the province of france" on October 21, 1683, we read that:

> Those Barbarians [the Iroquois] have often Resolved to wage war against The french; but They have always been checked by those who kindred were at the sault [i.e., Caughnawaga]. This has been done above all, by The Agnies [i.e., Mohawk], who declared that they'd not Consent to such a war; that their nephews and children, who were in the country of the french, must first be withdrawn thence—and this the other have Never been able to do although they have spared nothing to effect their object. Our Iroquois have done still more; For, when Monsieur de la Barre, The King's Lieutenant-general in this country, went to see Them last summer, They offered him one hundred and fifty men to go to war, even Against their own nation, if the latter undertook to break the peace with The french. (*JR* 62:255-7)

In 1693, the Caughnawaga Mohawk were involved with an expedition against the Mohawk in New York. In 1696, the same year that the Jesuits were compiling the first list of miracles attributed to Kateri Tegakwitha, her compatriots were with Frontenac raiding the Onondaga. Certainly it was a time when the people of New France would have good reason to be sympathetic to the idea of a Mohawk Christian fighting in the spiritual realm on their behalf.

Soon after Kateri received last rites, invoking her aid brought about two reported healings, one Native and one French. In the fall of 1681, a great comet appeared in the sky. It was believed by many to be a deadly portent of events to follow. Rumours of war drifted through French and Native communities like a cold mist creeping up from the St. Lawrence. Then, a miracle was reported. According to Father Chauchetière:

> Five days after the apparition of the comet, God blessed the mission, for it was then that a sick man who had been given up was cured for the next day, after he had invoked the name of Catherine of the Sault. (*JR* 63:223)

For many such a miracle would demonstrate that, in spite of all else, God was not against them. Kateri Tegakwitha had interceded for the good of New France. Increasingly people would turn to her for such intercession.

The first novena, nine days of prayer, dedicated to Kateri came from Anastasie's daughter-in-law, Catherine, in 1682. She had a crippling disorder, possibly some form of arthritis, which had troubled her since she was eight, particularly in the spring. She also had a gambling problem. Her novena, held in March, was directed to help her with her physical affliction, but, according to reports, the novena successfully dealt with both of her difficulties. In Father Cholenec's words, Kateri, "usually cured the souls of those whose bodies she healed, if they were in need of this double assistance, even though they did not pray for it" (Béchard 1976:72).

Catherine's husband, Anastasie's eldest son, was next. In April he asked for Kateri's aid concerning a physical problem similar to the one his wife had been suffering. He, too, became well. But Kateri wasn't finished with him yet. He had a bad temper. Furious at something that his mother had said to him, he reputedly bolted from their longhouse and headed towards the St. Lawrence to literally drown his sorrows and his rage. His route to oblivion took him past Kateri's grave. As he approached this revered spot, according to Cholenec, "his feet halted and remained immobile, so that he could not move from the place" (Béchard 1976:72). He saw this as a sign, asked God's pardon for what he had intended to commit and then revealed this newest miracle in confession.

That summer Kateri was credited with paying back the favour she owed to Louis Garonhiague. **Garhio** ('Large or Beautiful Forest'), Louis's wife, had developed complications after giving birth in a field. A friend of hers had been keeping Kateri's blanket as a sacred relic. She gave the precious object to Garhio and went with the others to pray in the church for the afflicted woman. Left alone, Garhio covered herself with the blanket, begged Kateri to intervene for her and placed her hands where she felt the pain. She claimed a complete and instantaneous cure.

A number of people had relics of Kateri. Louis Garonhiague, sent as an envoy to Iroquois country, took a small pouch of earth from Kateri's grave site and tied it around his neck. In a manner virtually identical to a more traditional Iroquois carrying a medicine bundle, Louis employed the pouch as a spiritual medium through which he asked Kateri for a safe trip. He travelled to his former homeland and back without incident.

Not only Native Christians attributed miracles to Kateri Tegakwitha. On August 19, 1683, three Jesuit priests went to the chapel of the Caughnawaga mission: Fathers Claude Chauchetière, Nicholas Potier and Jean Morain. This chapel was the pride of the mission, some 60 feet long. According to Father Thierry Beschefer, it was "one of [the] handsomest buildings around Montreal" (*JR* 62:253).

Earlier that evening, two of the three priests had gone separately to pray at Tegakwitha's grave. The third had said the mass of the Holy Trinity, thanking God for the favours granted through Tegakwitha's intercession. There arose that night a ferocious gale, the worst in living memory to hit that area. When the gale struck, two of the Jesuit Fathers were in the second story of the chapel, while the third, Father Chauchetière, was ringing the heavy mission bell.

The wind collapsed the building. Despite the fact that two large bells came crashing down in his direction, Chauchetière:

> ... was saved and carried away from the place where he was, where a great hold was made by the beams, which broke in their fall the joists on which he was kneeling. He found himself in a place of safety, without fear, without wound, praying and kissing the relics which he wore around his neck. (*JR* 63:229)

Potier was only slightly less fortunate. He "leaped into the air with the rafters, which formed a sort of cage for him" (ibid.). Apparently, he escaped with only a slight wound on his face for all his acrobatic manoeuvres. Father Morain was the only one to suffer real injury. He fell amidst the ruins of the chapel and dislocated his shoulder. Still, he survived.

Father Chauchetière had no doubts as to the spiritual nature of what had happened and the role that Kateri had played in their survival. He later wrote:

I have always believed that it was she who... saved
me, when our chapel was blown down by the storm.
Then, in the opinion of all, I was miraculously saved;
and I believed that that virtuous savage repaid me
on that occasion for the services that I rendered her
during her illness. (*JR* 64:155)

Kateri's coffin was moved from the mission cemetery so it could
be placed in the sacred soil upon which the new church was built.
This was an honour usually reserved for revered priests, nuns and
benefactors of the church. The community moved in 1690, 1696 and
1720. Each time Kateri's bones would move with them. Yet there
continued a kind of mystique associating the old village site, where
she died and was first buried, with the young woman. According to
Jesuit Father E. J. Devine, writing in 1927:

All traces of the fortified village at the foot of the
Lachine rapid, where she lived and died, had long
since been obliterated, but there has always remained
with the Indians [i.e., Mohawks] a mysterious
attraction for the spot; even after two hundred years
it is still known to them as Kateri tsi tkaiatat—the
place where Kateri is buried. (Devine 1927:418)

Reports of the miraculous cures continued throughout the rest
of the seventeenth century, extending to include some leading figures
in New France. The following are two such testimonials, recorded in
1696, when a list of miracles was being compiled. De la Colombière,
Canon of the Cathedral of Quebec, presented this as his testimony:

Having been ill at Quebec during the past year, from
the month of January even to the month of June, of
a slow fever, against which all remedies had been
tried in vain, and of a diarrhoea... it was thought well
that I should record a vow, in case it should please
God to relieve me of these two maladies, to make a
pilgrimage to the Mission of St. François Xavier, to
pray at the tomb of Catherine Tegahkouita. On the
very same day the fever ceased, and the diarrhoea
having become better, I embarked some days

> afterwards to fulfil my vow. Scarcely had I
> accomplished one third of my journey, when I found
> myself perfectly cured.... [I]t is impossible reasonably
> to withhold the belief, that God in according to me
> this grace, had no other view than to make known
> the credit which this excellent maiden had with Him.
> For myself I should fear that I was unjustly
> withholding the truth, and refusing to the Missions
> of Canada the glory which is due to them, if I did not
> testify as I have now done, that I am a debtor for my
> cure to this Iroquois virgin. It for this reason that I
> have given the present attestation with every
> sentiment of gratitude of which I am capable, to
> increase, as far as is in my power, the confidence
> which is felt in my benefactress, but still more to
> excite the desire to imitate her virtues. (Kip 1873:115)

Daniel Greysolon Du Luth (after whom the Minnesota city by Lake Superior is named), when he was a captain in the French Marine Corps and Commander of Fort Frontenac (later Kingston), claimed the following in August of the same year:

> I... certify to all whom it may concern, that having
> been tormented by the gout for the space of twenty-
> three years, and with such severe pains that it gave
> me no rest for the space of three months at a time, I
> addressed myself to Catherine Tegahkouita, an
> Iroquois virgin, deceased at the Sault Saint Louis in
> the reputation of sanctity, and I promised her to visit
> her tomb, if God should give me health through her
> intercession. I have been so perfectly cured, at the
> end of one novena which I made in her honor, that
> after five months I have not perceived the slightest
> touch of my gout. (Kip 1873:116)

Similarly, during another such novena, Champigny, as Intendant one of the highest ranking officials in New France, was said to have regained full use of his voice after a year of vocal troubles.

Not just the rich and famous sought cures at the grave of the Mohawk maiden. The common people of New France resorted to Kateri

Tegakwitha in times of medical problems. When ordinary medicines would not work, people would, according to Father Lamberville, "swallow in water or in broth a little dust from her tomb" (*JR* 65:31). Cholenec reported in his 1696 collection of Tegakwitha's miracles that in 1693, a man named Andre Merlot had his "inflammation of the eyes" healed after combining holding a novena in her name with rubbing his eyes with a solution made up of water, earth from the area surrounding her grave and ashes from her presumably burnt clothing (Shoemaker 1995:49-50).

Prayers, masses, novenas and pilgrimages were dedicated by individuals and by whole parishes, Native and French alike, to Kateri Tegakwitha. Even taking off the religiously tinted glasses worn by the priests writing these accounts, a picture still emerges that Kateri became a guardian angel of hope for the Christian Native and French communities along the St. Lawrence during the late seventeenth and early eighteenth centuries. The Jesuit historian Charlevoix probably expressed the views of many contemporary believers in New France when he likened Kateri to Joan of Arc:

> Thus as the Capital of Old France saw a Shepherdess, so New France saw a poor Indian girl outshine in glory Apostles, Martyrs and Saints of all conditions. God no doubt willed, for our instruction and for the comfort of the humble, to glorify His Saints in proportion to their lowliness and obscurity on earth. (Lecompte 1927:27-28)

Although the reports of miracles diminished after the early eighteenth century, her significance continued. In 1754, her skull and some other of her bones, treated in the same manner as the sacred relics of saints, were brought to the new Mohawk mission of St. Regis, usually referred to now by its Mohawk name, Akwesasne ('Where the Partridge Drums'). Unfortunately, these were later burned in a fire.

Her fame and influence grew during the nineteenth century. In 1843, a few of her bone fragments were deposited at the base of a large cross raised about her tomb at Caughnawaga. In 1880, a large sarcophagus was erected over Kateri's original grave in that community. On this structure were inscribed the Mohawk words "Onkwe Onwe-ke Katsitsiio Teiotsitsianekaron." The phrase can be

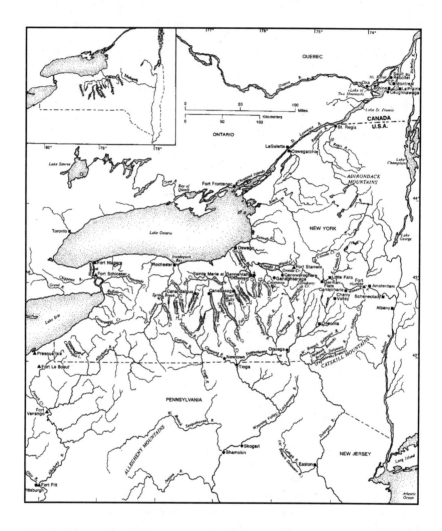

Iroquois territory in the seventeenth and eighteenth centuries. Core areas for each tribe in the seventeenth century are indicated by the placement of the tribal names in inset. Where river names have changed, earlier names are in parentheses.

From Tooker, Elisabeth. "The League of the Iroquois: Its History, Politics, and Rituals." *Handbook of North American Indians*, vol. 15, *The Northeast*, p. 418. Washington, D.C.: The Smithsonian Institution.

translated as 'of the real people[15] the beautiful flower that opens up, blossoms out,' and is associated with the epithet 'Lily of the Mohawks,' which is often applied to Kateri. In 1884, an Albany priest took her cause to the Vatican, proposing that she become canonized (i.e., made a saint). In 1890, near her New York birthplace, a massive granite memorial was erected, dominated by an impressive cross containing another one of Kateri's bone relics. The ceremony was just as large. Two thousand people came from Caughnawaga, Montreal and neighbouring parishes to attend. Three bishops conducted the proceedings, ably assisted by some sixty priests.

The cause of leading Kateri up the laborious stairs to sainthood was taken up in the twentieth century by the Jesuits in Canada and the United States and by the bishops associated with Albany and Montreal. Miracles were again being reported. In Cohen's *Beautiful Losers*, he uses a story that was published in April, 1906, in the Jesuit-run journal, *Le Messenger Canadien du Sacre Coeur*. It told of an Ojibwa woman from Manitoulin Island, reportedly suffering from syphilis ulcers in her mouth and throat, who was cured when, following the advice of a Jesuit priest (formerly a doctor), she dedicated a novena to Kateri (Cohen 1991:233).

In 1932, her cause was presented to the Vatican's Congregation of Rites (now termed the Congregation for the Causes of Saints). A great deal of effort was put into promoting her sainthood during the 1930s. This included the production of at least three written biographies, several plays, operas and a film. In 1939, the Tekakwitha Conference, an association for Native Catholics, was formed.

The twentieth century is a difficult time in which to become a saint. Miracles have to be proven by the postulator against the more-worldly arguments of the devil's advocate. Advances in medicine and in science generally have made it hard to prove that a cure was effected by miracle rather than by more natural causes. However, according to a statement made by a Vatican official in an article published in *Time* upon the occasion of Kateri's beatification:

> The conviction is growing... that other 'signs' should be accepted, such as a great number of extraordinary 'favors' or 'graces' that can be proved and attested by serious investigation. (*Time* 1980:33)

Kateri was declared venerable in 1943 and was beatified in 1980. She is just one step away now from sainthood. I hope she is able to reach that last step. That will make her story better known. It might even lead to a more accurate and sympathetic retelling of the history of her people in the seventeenth century.

Kateri Tegakwitha as a Symbol

Many people have heard of Kateri through the words of the well-known Canadian writer Leonard Cohen. Born in Montreal, not far from where Tegakwitha died, he probably early learned of her story, despite his being raised in the Jewish faith. In 1966, he published a book, *Beautiful Losers*, in which the main character, an aging scholar, has a passionate interest in Tegakwitha's life and death. To this fictional figure, and to the real-life Cohen too, Tegakwitha embodied the image of the beautiful loser; one who voluntarily surrenders the limited personal goals and gains of the self and the material world for a higher purpose.

This image helps me phrase some problems I have had in struggling to understand and appreciate Tegakwitha's story. Can she be said to be more beautiful for what she gained or more a loser for what she gave up and the way in which she sacrificed herself? Was she more a saint for New France and the world beyond it in time and place, or is she better portrayed as a hapless victim, without the redeeming sense of martyrdom, of the colonial forces which confronted her people? Or is all of this seeing too much into the life of one young woman trying to survive in a harsh environment.

As a symbol to Native people, Tegakwitha has received mixed reviews. In an insightful article entitled "The Making of the First Iroquois Virgin: Early Jesuit Biographies of the Blessed Kateri Tekakwitha," K.I. Koppedrayer wrote of how, for a contemporary Mohawk and an Algonquin both living at Caughnawaga, she was seen in opposing ways:[16]

> To the first individual, Kateri represents an alliance with Roman Catholicism and French institutions, both of which for him are unconscionable in light of present-tense relations between some of the more traditional and sovereignist Mohawk factions and the Quebec provincial government; to the second, Kateri offers an assertion of Indianness, the very nature of

which has been refigured as a result of assimilating attitudes. The symbol of Kateri is shared by these two individuals, and indeed by others, but as participants in an ongoing intercultural encounter, they accommodate themselves to it and to what it represents in quite different ways: Kateri is betrayal; Kateri is destruction; Kateri is synthesis; Kateri is hope and reconstruction; Kateri is past and present. (Koppedrayer 1993:279)

In recent years Kateri has been the focus of Native Catholics in their attempt to reconcile their Catholicism with their Native identity, not an easy task when that church has been associated with outsider control and with the effects of emotional, physical and sexual abuse in the residential schools of the twentieth century. Perhaps it is here where Kateri will do the greatest good for her people over 300 years after her death. In the words of Marie Therese Archambault, a Hunkpapa Lakota woman and a leading figure of the National Tekakwitha Conference in the United States:

> Her life appeals to contemporary native Catholics because of its elements of heroic survival in situations of human suffering and its evidence of spiritual transformation and personal spiritual power. After all, their own history has been one of suffering through removal and separation, and the communal and personal tragedies that attended these enormous losses. (Archambault 1996:624)

Appendix A: Buehrle's Naming

In Buehrle's influential work, she gives names to people not otherwise named in the literature on Kateri Tegakwitha. Some of them seem clearly false, more the product of an uninformed outsider's imagination than of the Mohawk language and culture. Four such names, given by Buehrle as proposed suitors for Kateri are Silver Arrow, Tiger Eye, White Lightning and Red Eagle. None of these appellations could be expressed in one word in Mohawk, as almost all names in the language are. Names she gives in Mohawk are plausible sounding. These include Kenhoronkwa for Kateri's father, which appears to be derived from a verb root meaning 'to be difficult, expensive or valuable' (Michelson 1973:82), which could possibly refer to his being difficult to kill. Her mother's name was presented as being Kahenta, possibly meaning 'Meadow, Field' (Michelson 1973:50). Buehrle has her younger brother named Otsikehta ('Sugar'), her two aunts as Karitha (possibly 'She Cooks') and Arosen ('Red Squirrel'), and her adopted sister as Ennita ('Moon'). The one name I cannot translate is Iowerano, the appellation for her adoptive father. As these names are not presented elsewhere, and as she did not cite her sources for obtaining them, the most likely scenario is that she created them in an effort to make the story more personalized and more real.

Appendix B: The Image of the Mohawk

Kateri Tegakwitha was a Mohawk of whom contemporary French writers and officials did not hesitate to speak of proudly as their own. This is rare. For the traditional historical portrayal of seventeenth century New France is of the Iroquois (especially the Mohawk) and the French as deadly enemies locked in a struggle in which the survival of the fledgling French nation was at stake. French Canadian historians especially tended in the past to paint this particular picture with a Mohawk-blackening brush.

More is lost in this conventional portrayal than just historical accuracy. As the Quebec licence plate proudly points out, French Canadian identity is linked with remembering the past: "*Je me souviens.*"[17] This gives them a source of strength and connectedness that many English Canadians, including myself, have good cause to envy. However, the link between history and identity has a negative side. If a narrow nationalism informs the historians who write the textbooks that teach both students and instructors, if larger-than-life heroes are created through constructing more-rabid-than-wolves villains of other peoples, then reconstructing and remembering the past can be aggressive, destructive acts. This is unfortunately true of most French Canadian historians up until the last edition of François-Xavier Garneau's influential and anti-Iroquois *Histoire du Canada*, first printed in 1845, was published in 1969-71. To Garneau, the Iroquois were "*des loups alteres du sang* [bloodthirsty wolves]" (Smith 1974:28), not merely people different from his own.

The presence of such historical teachings as those of Garneau helps to explain the overreaction of the SQ (Sûreté du Quebec) and much of the French media during the Oka crisis of 1990. It gives some kind of reason to the unreasonable, as when the writer Hélène Sevigny was asked in 1993, "Do you know that Quebecers see you as a traitor to your race?" when she was being interviewed for the launching of the book, *Lasagne: L'homme derrier la masque*, which she co-wrote with Ronald Cross (aka *Lasagna*).

This is not to say that, during the same period that Garneau was being printed and reprinted, historians writing in English were more accurate or less subject to bias. They were just less likely to single out the Mohawk as the enemy,[18] more willing to distribute more broadly the recipients of the stereotyping. Two examples of popular historical works on subjects close to the study of Tegakwitha's life will suffice to illustrate both the presence of bias plus the capacity to condemn other groups as well as the Mohawk. In Jesuit Father Francis X. Talbot's critically acclaimed *Saint Among the Hurons: The Life of Jean de Brébeuf*, published in 1949 and reprinted in 1956, we read many deeply prejudiced comments such as the following about the seventeenth-century Montagnais:

> Truly, they were a degraded and barbaric race. They were wanderers on the face of the earth, living between the hazardous extremes of starvation and plenty, with little forethought for the future, wild and untamed as animals, ferocious at times as beasts, without law or authority or any restraint. Could these men and women, truly as savage as any on earth, be brought to any level of culture or civilization?

> Their whole mode of life was that of a human animal following its most depraved instincts. Even the best were inconstant and treacherous, arrogant and defiant, ruthless and vengeful. (Talbot 1956:52 and 54-5 respectively)

In Isabel Thompson Kelsay's detailed biography of the Mohawk leader Joseph Brant, winner of several prestigious awards and published in 1984, the reader is faced with a good number of judgmental, inaccurate and mean-spirited comments (see endnote

14 below) such as the following statement concerning Handsome Lake, the Seneca prophet:

> No one thought any the less of a head man of the Senecas who bore the name of The Drunkard and, indeed, *it appears that almost any Indian anywhere could have borne that name.* (Kelsay 1984:29; emphasis mine)

Endnotes

[1] I have chosen to use the -g- here, rather than the more currently usual -k-, as Kateri's name was first recorded in that way and it is closer to the actual pronunciation. Generally speaking, when you see a -k- written in Mohawk with a vowel before and after, that -k- is pronounced as a -g-.

[2] In Michelson's translation, the word is composed of four morphemes or word parts:

> **te**: a prefix that refers concretely to 'twoness,' but also, abstractly to 'change;'
> **ka**: a pronominal prefix meaning 'she;'
> **kwit**: a verb root meaning 'to move;'
> **ha**: a suffix indicating that something is 'customary, usual, repeated.'

[3] In *The Handbook of Indians of Canada*, we have the following analysis:

> **Wampum** (the contracted form of New England Algonquian **wampumpeak**... the component lexical elements of which are **wamp**... a derivative of **wab**, '(being) white'.**.. umpe** or **ompe**... 'a string (of shell-beads);' **ak** or **ag**, the grammatic sign of the animate plural. (Hodge 1971:503)

[4] It literally means 'the great good.'

[5] Fenton and Tooker present the following discussion of the word:

> The name Mohawk, in general use in this spelling since Colden (1747), continues that originally used by the seventeenth-century English settlers in southern New England.... The most etymologically correct early spelling is Mohowawogs, 1638 (Roger Williams), which has the English plural -s added to a Narragansett or Massachusett word for 'man-eaters'.... (Fenton and Tooker 1978:478)

The word **Iroquois** may have a similar meaning. One plausible derivation for this word has it originating from a trade language established between the Micmac and Basque whalers. Peter Bakker has suggested that Iroquois is derived from the Basque word -hilo- (the -l- changing to -r- in early Micmac), with a locative suffix -koa-

(Bakker, 1990 "A Basque etymology for the word *Iroquois*" in *Man in the Northeast* 40:89-93).

[6] In Baraga's thorough nineteenth-century dictionary of the Ojibwe language, we have the following entries:

Nadowe. A kind of big serpent; pl.-g

Nadowe. Iroquois Indian; pl.-g

Nadowem, (nin). I speak the Iroquois language....

Nadowemowin. Iroquois language.

Nadowessi. Ot[tawa dialect] Sioux Indian; pl.-wag.... (Baraga 1878: Ojibwe-English, p264)

In Rhodes' modern *Eastern Ojibwa-Chippewa-Ottawa Dictionary*, he presented the following:

Naadwe na Iroquois; pl **naadweg**.

Naadwenaang ni Six Nations reserve...

Naadwesi na Iroquois, M[anitoulin Island dialect]; pl **Naadweswag**

naadwesi na species of snake, M; pl **naadweswag**." (Rhodes 1985:265-6)

[7] There is even some question as to whether it was Champlain who made that decision or the trader François Grave Du Pont (Trigger 1984:25)

[8] For use of the term for the last named relationship see Kip 1873:94. The term itself has respect built into it. In Northern Iroquoian languages, kinship terms expressing relationships in which one party is a generation older than the other have the older party expressed with the agent or subject prefix (see Steckley 1993:53). In Huron we have the following examples:

chiesk8ak: *you* have her as daughter in law

sarahak: *she* is father's sister to you

When the relationship is that of equals, both parties are part of the subject (e.g., the Huron **tiarase**, 'we two are cousins.'

[9] According to Morgan, only the Seneca, Tuscarora and Wyandot used this term in the nineteenth century, the other speakers of Northern Iroquoian languages employed their terms for 'mother' at that time (see Steckley 1993:40). Mother's sisters were called 'mother,' part of the kinship terminological system known as 'Iroquois' in the anthropological literature.

[10] Like a number of other early Jesuit recordings of Mohawk, this is a 'Huronized' version of a Mohawk word, the -d- here being a Huron not a Mohawk feature.

[11] Sometime late in the seventeenth century, Father Jacques Bruyas wrote a dictionary of Mohawk based primarily on his work with the people at Caughnawaga. The following is an entry in this dictionary:

"**Ganna^ck8a**, *marriage, coitus*...

Ja^cten ranna^ck8io *il n'est pas bon mary.* [he is not a good spouse]

Ganna^ck8are... *faire mal* [a reference to having sex]...

Ganna^ck8ax8an... *enlever la femme d'autruy.* [to take the wife of another]

> Ganna^ck8enha8i... *mener sa femme avec soy* [to take one's wife with one] (Bruyas 1970:67)

[12] This same conversation was presented in another 1715 publication of Cholenec's as the following: "It is settled..., it is not a question for deliberation; my part has long since been taken. No, my father, I can have no other spouse but Jesus Christ" (Kip 1873:104-5).

[13] The Huron term used for the Jesuits was 'hatitsihenstaatsi,' 'they are called charcoal,' because of the black robes typically worn by the missionaries. Contrary to the usual translation of the word, they did not literally call them black robes.

[14] Contrast this with Kelsay's misleading and thinly veiled critical remark concerning the chastity of Iroquois women:

> ... Young Indian girls and unmarried women were free; they might do as they pleased in sexual matters with no resultant stain on their character. Any wandering trader or blacksmith or soldier or, for that matter, any passing Indian could find a complaisant mate for an hour or a year. (Kelsay 1984:30)

[15] The literal translation of "Onkwe Onwe" is 'human beings who are human beings.' The term is used in Mohawk and other Northern Iroquois languages to refer to either the Iroquois or Natives as opposed to non-Natives. In Huron it has the latter meaning as well.

[16] The Mohawk individual accused Tegakwitha of being a prostitute, in having sexual relations and in betraying her heritage, as well as being a 'leaking pot' in delivering information concerning Iroquois military strategies and the nature of their military contacts with the Dutch and English. Both accusations are false, the second at least on the principle that such a shy, withdrawn girl wouldn't have known much about military matters. The Algonquin saw Tegakwitha as the source of his own gift of healing. According to Koppedrayer, he "portrayed Kateri not simply as an historical figure, but as a very powerful, and very present, force working towards a physical and spiritual reconstruction of the Indian people" (Koppedrayer 1993:278).

[17] While this phrase is generally associated with Québeçois nationalism today, it appears to have been taken from Eugene Tache's statement paying tribute to French and English Canada working together: "*Je me souviens que ne sous le lys, je crois sous la rose,*" meaning "I remember that born under the lily (i.e., the fleur de lys), I grow under the (English) rose."

[18] One exception to this is Stephen Leacock, famed English Canadian humourist and indifferent historian teaching at McGill University in Montreal. While he was generally negative in his writing about Natives, he saved his most virulent attacks for the Iroquois. In one of his works, for example, not only did he refer to them as the "hostile tribes of the Five Nations" and the "ravaging Iroquois," but concerning their

sound defeat of the French at Lachine he claimed: "There followed the massacre which ranks high in the history of horror" (Leacock 1941:26, 56 and 69). Concerning their falling on hard times during the dying years of the eighteenth century, he said: "Only those who have read too little of American history can shed tears for the Iroquois." (Leacock 1941:57). There is a great temptation to say, and perhaps it is true, that Leacock acquired his anti-Iroquois bias from having lived and taught in Montreal.

Bibliography

Archambault, Marie Therese. 1996. "Tekakwitha, Kateri," in *Encyclopedia of North American Indians*, ed. by Frederick E. Hoxie. New York, Houghton Mifflin, pp. 623-625.

Baraga, F. 1878. *A Dictionary of the Otchipwe Language*. Montreal: Beauchemin & Valois.

Béchard, Henri. s.j. 1967. "Tekakwitha (Tagaskouita, Tegakwitha) Kateri (Catherine)." *Dictionary of Canadian Biography* vol. 1, 1000-1700, pp. 635-6.

Béchard, Henri. s.j. 1976. *The Original Caughnawaga Indians*. Montreal: International Publishers.

Bruyas, Jacques. 1970. *Radical Words of the Mohawk Language with their Derivatives* (orig. written c1700, orig. pub. 1862). New York: AMS Press.

Buehrle, Marie Cecilia. 1954. *Kateri of the Mohawks*. Milwaukee: The Bruce Pub.

Chauchetière, Claude s.j. 1887. *La Vie de la B. Catherine Tegakouita dite a present La Saincte Sauuagesse par le R.P. Claude Chauchetière pretre missionaire de la Compagne de Iesvs*. New York: Cramoisy.

Cohen, Leonard. 1991. *Beautiful Losers*, orig. 1966. Toronto: McClelland & Stewart.

Cross, Ronald and Sevigny, Helene. 1994. *Lasagna: The Man Behind the Mask*. Vancouver: Talonbooks.

Day, Gordon and Trigger, Bruce. 1978. "Algonquin," in *Handbook of North American Indians*, vol. 15, *The Northeast*. Washington: Smithsonian Institution, pp. 792-7.

Devine, E.J. 1927. *Historic Caughnawaga*. Montreal: The Messenger Press.

Fenton, William N. and Tooker, Elisabeth. 1978. "Mohawk," in *Handbook of North American Indians*, vol. 15, *The Northeast*. Washington: Smithsonian Institution, pp. 466-79.

Hodge, F.W. 1971. *Handbook of Indians of Canada* (adapted by J. White in 1913 from a Bureau of American Ethnology Publication). Toronto: Coles Pub. Ltd.

Jury, Elsie M. 1967. "Skanudharoua. " *Dictionary of Canadian Biography*, vol.1, pp. 610-611.

Kelsay, Isabel Thompson. 1984. *Joseph Brant 1743-1807:Man of Two Worlds*. Syracuse: Syracuse University Press.

Kip, William Ingraham. 1873. *The Early Jesuit Missions in North America*. Albany: Joel Munsell.

Koppedrayer, K.I. 1993. "The Making of the First Iroquois Virgin: Early Jesuit Biographies of the Blessed Kateri Tekakwitha," *Ethnohistory* 40:2, pp. 277-306.

Leacock, Stephen. 1941. *Canada:The Foundation of Its Future*. Montreal: The House of Seagram.

Lecompte Ed s.j. 1927. *Kateri Tekakwitha: The Lily of the Mohawks 1656 - 1680*. Montreal: The Messenger Press.

Marshall, Joyce trans. and ed. 1967. *Word from New France:The Selected Letters of Marie de L'Incarnation*. Toronto: Oxford Univ. Press.

Michelson, Gunther. 1973. *A Thousand Words of Mohawk*. Ottawa: Nat. Museum of Man, Mercury Series, Ethnology.Div., Paper #5.

Rhodes, Richard. 1985. *Eastern Ojibwa-Chippewa-Ottawa Dictionary*. Amsterdam: Mouton.

Richter, Daniel K. 1985. "Iroquois Versus Iroquois: Jesuit Missions and Christianity in Village Politics, 1642-1686," in *Ethnohistory* 32(1):1-16.

Richter, Daniel K. 1992. *The Ordeal of the Longhouse: The Peoples of the Iroquois League in the Era of European Colonization*. Chapel Hill: Univ. of North Carolina Press.

Shoemaker, Nancy. 1995. "Kateri Tekakwitha's Tortuous Path to Sainthood," in *Negotiators of Change: Historical Perspectives on Native American Women*, ed. by N. Shoemaker. New York: Routledge, pp. 49-71.

Smith, Donald B. 1974. *Le Sauvage. The Native People in Quebec: Historical Writing on the Heroic Period (1534-1663) of New France*. Ottawa: National Museums of Canada.

Spittal, William G. ed. 1990. *Iroquois Women: An Anthology*. Ohsweken: Irocrafts.

Steckley, John L. 1986. "Catherine Gandeacteua-lay apostle." *Indian Record* 49 (2):15-6.

Steckley, John L. 1987. "Our saintly maid among the Mohawks." *The Canadian Messenger*, pp. 8-9.

Steckley, John L. 1988. "Enditenhwaen." *Arch Notes* 88-2:9-10.

Steckley, John L. 1992. "The Warrior and the Lineage: Jesuit Use of Iroquoian Images to Communicate Christianity," in *Ethnohistory* 19, (4):478-509.

Steckley, John L. 1993. "Huron Kinship Terminology." *Ontario Archaeology* 55:35- 59.

Talbot, Francis X. s.j. 1956. *Saint Among the Hurons: The Life of Jean de Brébeuf*. New York: Image Books.

Thwaites, Reuben G. (JR). 1959. *The Jesuit Relations and Allied Documents.* New York: Pageant Book Company.

Time. 1980. "The Long Road to Sainthood." *Time* 116, July 7, pp. 32-33.

Tooker, Elisabeth. 1978. "The League of the Iroquois: Its History, Politics, and Rituals," in *Handbook of North American Indians*, vol. 15, *The Northeast*. Washington: Smithsonian Institution, pp. 418-441.

Trigger, Bruce G. 1984. "Indian and White History: Two Worlds or One?" in *Extending the Rafters: Interdisciplinary Approaches to Iroquoian Studies*, ed. by M. K. Foster, J. Campisi, and M. Mithun. Albany: State Univ. of New York Press.

Trigger, Bruce G. 1985. *Natives and Newcomers: Canada's "Heroic Age" Reconsidered*. Kingston and Montreal: McGill-Queen's Univ. Press.

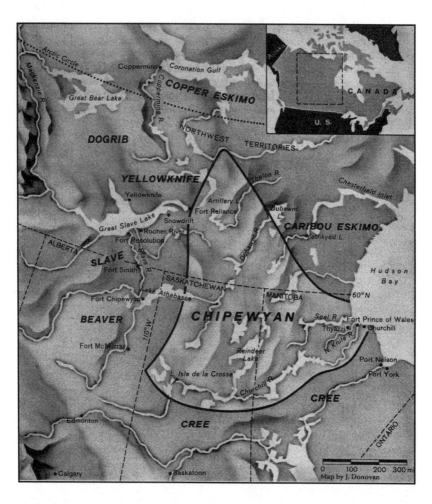

Map of Chipewyan territory. Oswalt, Wendell H. 1966. *This Land was Theirs*, p. 18. New York: John Wiley and Sons.

2

Thanadelthur

Indeed she has a Divellish Spirit and I believe that if
there were but 50 of her Country Men of the Same
Carriage and Resolution they would drive all the
Northern Indians in America out of there Country.
(James Knight, journal entry, May 9, 1716, cited in
Emberley 1993:105)

It is 1714, late in the year. A young woman, possibly a teenager,
appears at a fur trade post by the western shores of Hudson Bay. She
is hundreds of kilometres and more than a year away from family,
friends and her home country, probably somewhere in northern
Saskatchewan or the Northwest Territories (see map). The people
she is walking towards are of two nations: one, a traditional enemy
(the Cree)[1] she has been fleeing from; the other, a new nation whose
appearance, possessions and customs are rumoured to be like those
of no other group. It is a cold, November day, and she is described as
being "Allmost Starving." What followed is a series of events in which
she altered the destiny of her people, perhaps even ensuring their
survival. In his popular historical work *The Company of Adventurers*,
Peter Newman referred to her as "one of the most remarkable
personalities of the early Canadian fur trade" (Newman 1985:218).

In Hudson's Bay Company journals she was typically called "the
Slave Woman." This reflects English borrowing of a Cree term for
Northern Athapaskan speakers that usually referred to domestic
animals (see Appendix A). The English usage possibly echoes the
negative attitude that went along with the word as well. But she was

not of the Native nation (the **Dene Tha**) that was later to be known as Slave(y), she was Chipewyan. Although her name is not to be found in the written record during her lifetime, it is known to us through Chipewyan oral tradition recorded during the late nineteenth and early twentieth centuries.[2] She became a folk hero to her people. Her name was Thanadelthur. Thanadelthur means something like 'Marten Jumping' or 'Marten Shake.' The initial -**tha**- signifies 'marten,' a graceful, fast-moving animal whose beautiful fur rivals that of its cousin, the mink. Many Chipewyan women's names began with -tha- in those days, for as the explorer Samuel Hearne noted in his journal recording his Chipewyan-guided trips across the Canadian northwest from 1769 to 1772:

> ... the names of the girls are chiefly taken from some part or property of a Martin; such as, the White Martin, the Black Martin, the Summer Martin, the Martin's Head, the Martin's Foot, the Martin's Tail, &c. (Hearne 1958:59)

Chipewyan women's work included catching small game in snare traps and then preparing the pelts. It also involved sewing, which was sometimes done with the penis bone of a marten. Perhaps one reason why women were named after the marten was that they were wise in the ways of that animal.[3] They might have learned to think like a marten and to anticipate its moves.

Thanadelthur's people were then, as they are now, the largest and most widespread of the Northern Athapaskan-speaking nations. This branch of a broadly extended family of languages includes both their linguistic and cultural cousins to the immediate west—the Yellowknife, Dogrib, Slavey and Beaver—as well as more distant peoples living in Alaska, Alberta, British Columbia and the Yukon. The Chipewyan population at that time would have been at least 3500 to 4000 (as compared with around 5000 today; Wilson and Urion 1995:29). Their small communities could be found stretching across the north from the eastern shores of Great Slave Lake to the Kazan River in the Northwest Territories down to their traditional southern limit from the coastline of Lake Athabasca in northern Alberta and northern Saskatchewan across to the Seal River in the northern extreme of Manitoba (see map).

Over the centuries, Thanadelthur's people have been known by a number of outsider-imposed names. In the seventeenth century,

French Jesuits called them (and probably their neighbours) **Ikovirinioucks**, an insulting Cree term meaning 'louse people.' French traders at Hudson Bay from 1697 to 1714 used "*Platscotes de Chiens*" or variations of the Cree word **Atimospikay**, both meaning Dogrib. This refers to a Northern Athapaskan story of how their people originated from the rib of a dog.[4] During the eighteenth century, Samuel Hearne and other English writers usually called them 'Northern Indians,' while in the nineteenth century, they often used 'Caribou Eaters,' a translation of **Ethen-eldeli**, the name for the eastern-most bands. Finally, in the twentieth century, we find them most frequently named 'Chipewyan' (more familiarly 'Chips'), derived from **Chipwayanewok**, a Cree word meaning 'Pointed Skins' first recorded in 1776. This is generally said to refer to the way the fronts and backs of their traditional poncho-like robes would dangle down in points. However, the people themselves, in company with speakers of related languages[5] used and use **Dene** (pronounced 'din-eh'), which can be translated as meaning 'people' (see Appendix A).

The Chipewyan had names for their non-Dene neighbours as well: **Hotel?ena**, meaning 'Flatland Enemy,' and **?Ena**, simply signifying 'Enemy.' The Hotel?ena were the Inuit who lived in the virtually treeless wastelands to the north and east of the Chipewyan. Like the Chipewyan, the Inuit of the area depended on caribou for their food, clothing and many other vital supplies. In a bad year, when people had to travel farther than usual to find caribou (whose annual migration path could exceed 2200 kilometres), conflict between the two groups was both possible and likely. At least twice during the eighteenth century, the Chipewyan were recorded as killing off a whole camp of Inuit: in 1756 of 40, and in 1771 of 20 people (Newman 1985:253 and 264).

The Chipewyan can aptly be termed 'edge-of-the-forest' people, living primarily in the transitional area between the Barrens and the boreal forest. In the woods were their main threat, the Ena, known to English speakers as the Cree. This nation hunted, fished and built their homes both east and south of the Chipewyan. Their early eighteenth century battles made such an impact on Thanadelthur's people that 200 years later stories were still told not just of Thanadelthur but of other heroes such as **Dza-ghal-iaze** (Lower Leg Trembles Little) that led to victories against the Cree (Abel 1993:47).

What was particularly worrying to the Chipewyan early in the eighteenth century was that more than ever before they had been losing in conflicts with the ?Ena. The Cree from the Hudson and James Bay area had been very successful in the fur trade with the English of the Hudson's Bay Company. This enabled them to expand west, as major trade items included guns, powder and shot. Primarily used to aid hunting, these lethal weapons could provide a distinct advantage in warfare as well, for the Chipewyan and other Dene did not have access to these European goods. Thanadelthur's people were becoming more and more concerned. They had recently lost battles to the Cree both close to and inside Chipewyan home country.

Thanadelthur's Capture and Her Escape

Stories of stolen women are a significant theme in Dene oral tradition. Tales have long been told of their determination, vengeance on their captors and of valued goods brought back to their people (Kehoe 1992:524).[6] Copper was said to have originally come to the Dene people from such a woman.[7]

It is difficult to pinpoint precisely when Thanadelthur became such a stolen woman kidnapped by the Cree. In a version of her story told in 1879 by countryman **Alexis Enna-azè**, published in French by Petitot in 1886, it was stated that she had been with the Cree for "*plusieurs années*" (Petitot 1886:425) before she escaped. When Edward Curtis later recorded Chipewyan oral tradition, publishing it in English in 1928, that story has her with the Cree for something close to two years.

We likewise do not know exactly how old she was. According to Alexis Enna-azè, she had been a "*jeune fille*" ('young girl') when she was captured (Petitot 1886:426), so it is quite likely that she was a teenager when she got away.

In the fall of 1714, while camped on the north shore of the Nelson River, deep in Cree territory, Thanadelthur and a countrywoman escaped. Hopes of travelling home west before winter set in soon faded as the nights grew longer and the days became colder. So she came up with a plan both desperate and brave. She decided to head east towards the people she had recently learned were supplying the weapons that had tipped the balance of power away from the Chipewyan in favour of the Cree.

Think for a moment what that meant for her. Thanadelthur spoke no English. She knew of Europeans only by rumour. Evidence of their power came from the guns they traded with the Cree and from the bits of that strange hard substance, iron, that had been finding its way to Chipewyan camps through one means or another since the first half of the seventeenth century. What other bizarre and potentially dangerous features might European culture possess?

The situation was becoming desperate. At some point, Thanadelthur's companion died, leaving her alone. Her supply of food would probably have been perpetually low. For she could not stay too long at any one spot waiting for an animal to step unsuspectingly into her snare traps. If not constantly on the move, she herself could fall prey to the people from whom she was fleeing. Had she, like a Dogrib woman in similar circumstances later that century, made a fishing net by twisting the inner bark of willows (Hearne 1958:169), she would have to be careful not to cast her net too much in the open, or she could be enmeshed in a human net cast by her pursuers.

Then, several days after her countrywomen died, she saw tracks and followed them cautiously to a goose hunting camp on Ten Shilling Creek, not very far from Hudson Bay. Who discovered whom first is hard to determine. Either way, you can imagine what Thanadelthur must have felt when she saw that most (maybe all) of the goose hunters were Cree.

Thanadelthur Meets James Knight

She was taken to James Knight, a man who in his 70s was an aging but still fairly active veteran of the fur trade. He was the governor of the Hudson's Bay Company post (HBC) at York Factory, situated near where the Nelson and Hayes rivers flow into Hudson Bay. Knight was a man of ambition and drive. He had begun his work with the company as a carpenter during his mid-thirties. According to a biographer, Ernest S. Dodge, "Knight emerges as an able, gruff, rather illiterate man whose practical ability, energy, tenacity, and endurance assured his rapid advancement" (Dodge:1969:318).

Knight steadily moved up in the ranks. Despite a five-year separation from the HBC, instigated by allegations of the grave sin of private trading, he returned to the company in fine style, heading a fleet of four ships to recapture posts by the shores of James Bay and Hudson Bay from the French. While he worked for his company's profits in the fur trade, he wished to serve his company and satisfy his private dreams in more dramatic enterprises. He desired to unearth riches of gold and other precious metals. When he had last sailed across the Atlantic, he had brought with him "Cruseables, melting potts, borax, &c" (Newman 1985:219), the equipment and chemicals necessary for processing such metals. He also longed to discover the elusive Northwest Passage, through which a ship could sail across North America north of Hudson Bay. Less than ten years later, these ambitions led to his lonely death somewhere on or near desolate Marble Island on the extreme northwest part of Hudson Bay.

Knight had arrived at York Factory on September 5, 1714, reclaiming the post for the English after it had been held by the French since 1697. He had heard of the Chipewyan before meeting Thanadelthur. He had even encountered a Dene woman, one who had been taken prisoner by the Cree before coming to York Factory. She had set fire to his imagination of the possibilities of a Dene trade. Through gestures and the efforts of a translator, she was able to communicate to him that near where she lived there was an abundance of the metal[8] from which were made the shiny buttons on his formal tunic. Disease is always a factor in first contact. Soon, to use Knight's words, "it pleasd God shee Sickned & Dyed" (Geiger and Beattie 1993:37). This was on November 22, just two days before Thanadelthur's arrival.

Thanadelthur was not content merely to have come through her harrowing experiences alive. She was soon to conjure up dreams of her own to match those of James Knight: dreams to ensure the future survival and strength of her people. She knew firm ties must be made between the Chipewyan and the people who manufactured and distributed the weapons used by the Cree. She wanted the Chipewyan to have their own trading post farther north than York Factory, away from where the Cree came to trade.

At first, communication between Thanadelthur and Knight must have been difficult. She had to speak in her recently acquired second language, Cree, which was not even related to her native tongue. Knight claimed in his journal entry for that first day that "she speaks but this Country Indian [i.e., Cree] indifferently..." (as cited in Emberley 1993:103). It is hard to know whether he had sufficient competence in the language to be a good judge of her capacity, for he at least initially needed a Cree interpreter to translate what she said into English. Despite these linguistic limitations, Knight soon began to appreciate both Thanadelthur, whom he described as having "an

Extraordinary Vivacity of Apprehension" (Abel 1993:49), and what she had to say. He listened with especial interest when she spoke of a nation near hers that obtained copper as easily as other nations did beaver pelts. He would hear further of this ease of acquiring copper a year later when a Chipewyan boy would tell him:

> They go into the River the water is up there Knees
> they put down there hands and take up handfulls of
> Land and amongst that Land bitts of copper some
> bigg some Small... they hammer it with 2 Stones and
> Rubb it on Stones & to make it bright and in the
> Shape [required]... (Abel 1993:31)

There is probably some exaggeration here, mixed with a measure of truth. The boy had possibly learned early the benefits of feeding Knight's fantasy with what the old fur trader wanted to hear. However, as European explorers would discover in later years, the people and their extensive use of copper were real. The people referred to were the Yellowknife, who not only made yellow (i.e., copper) knives but also awls, lance tips, axe heads, arrowheads, ice chisels, beads, bracelets, needles, necklaces and even dishes.

The Expedition

As communication between Thanadelthur and Knight improved over the next few days and weeks, they came to realize that their dreams and interests had a great deal in common. They both wished for strong ties and profitable trade between their peoples and knew that meant that the Cree and Chipewyan had to be at peace. Between them they devised a plan. An expedition to contact the Chipewyan was arranged. Although a Hudson's Bay Company man, William Stuart, was officially designated in the company records as the leader, Thanadelthur would be both the expedition's driving force and its guiding light. With her she took gifts to smooth the path of peace for her people, plus a promise from Knight that a trading post would be built. The post would be constructed north of York Factory, by the mouth of the Churchill River. It was to be completed by the fall of 1716. This new fur trade centre was to be exclusively for the Chipewyan and other Dene.

Despite the lofty hopes that Thanadelthur and Knight had for its success, the potential for failure of this expedition was equally high. Of the 150 people involved, all but Thanadelthur and Stuart were Cree. How much would they wish for trade to be established between their gun-supplying partners and the Chipewyan? Such trade could very well end their military dominance over their traditional Dene enemies. Knight must have had some worries on this subject himself. On June 11, 1715, he promised the Cree "Large presents of Powder, Shott & tobacco with other Necessarys" to go on the expedition (Johnson 1952:42). His mind was still not at ease, for concern for what could happen to Thanadelthur was expressed on June 27, 1715, when he said to Stuart, "I order you to take care that none of the Indians abuse or misuse the Slave Woman that goes with you or to take she has from her that is to be given amongst her countrys people" (in Emberley 1993:103).

A similarly tall order was Thanadelthur's responsibility. How could she manage to convince the Chipewyan to respond positively to a large party of Cree moving towards and through their often Cree-threatened home territory?

The expedition left on June 30. It seemed ill-fated from the beginning. Sickness and a shortage of food soon became problems. They were forced to eat their dogs. Once they entered the Barrens, they had to split up into widely dispersed small groups so that their hunters could kill enough game to feed everyone. No single locality could support all the members of the expedition for very long. Some of the Cree died. In a letter penned sometime in the fall, that didn't reach Knight until the following April, Stuart wrote that he hadn't eaten for eight days. He suspected the worst, saying to his superior, "I do not think as as I shall see you any more but I have a good heart" (Geiger and Beattie 1993:49).

The Cree, more familiar with the boreal forest than the Barrens, and uncomfortable in the territory of their enemy, understandably wanted to turn back. All but one group did. Belonging to that stalwart band were Thanadelthur, Stuart, a Cree leader called 'Captain' (an appellation for Native leaders commonly used by Europeans) and 12 of Captain's men.

As they trudged through the cold, flat lands of the Barrens, this lone remnant of the ambitious expedition encountered more than its fair share of difficulties. Captain became sick. Stuart worried that Captain would die, causing the other Cree to lose heart and return to the tree-covered security of their own country. Fortunately, the Cree leader survived, especially fortunate in that he would have a vital part to play in what came later. Other problems, however, would soon plague the travellers. Two of their best hunters were sent out to find game for food; they became permanently separated from the others and had to head back to York Factory. The worst was yet to come.

They came across what looked like a Chipewyan camp, but they could detect no signs of life. As they walked into the camp, they saw evidence of a recent battle. Worse, nine corpses were soon discovered, the bodies of Chipewyan brutally slain by attackers who could only be Cree.

You can well imagine how the Cree felt when the all too easily connected pieces of this puzzle were put together. There were some, and Captain seems to have been one of these, who wished for peace with the Chipewyan. They knew this tragedy had dealt the prospects of such peace a vicious blow. Others, while not as concerned about peace between the two nations, knew that their own lives now would be in peril. All realized that once the young warriors of the Chipewyan discovered what had happened, they might not be too careful to distinguish between guilty and innocent Cree. Just to be Cree would be a crime fit for lethal punishment. Understandably, the Cree wanted to leave. Stuart, the nominal leader of the party, felt discouraged and was not fully prepared to try to convince the Cree to stay. That left only Thanadelthur.

Concerns of personal safety would have given her ample reason to accept, reluctantly, the general will to turn back. Yet Thanadelthur was determined that the expedition would succeed, no matter what obstacles might impede their progress. She argued with the others that they should continue on. She won the kind of compromise from the less enthusiastic members of her party that demonstrates that she was both persuasive and brave. The others were to stay where they were. She would proceed on by herself. If she did not return within ten days, hopefully bringing with her Chipewyan ambassadors of peace, then Stuart and the Cree could go back home.[9]

While the men in her group fortified their position, preparing for the worst to happen, Thanadelthur pressed on alone. She would not remain alone long. Within a few days, she encountered a large camp of at least some 400 of her people. The Chipewyan were living and moving in higher than usual numbers in those days.[10] Their recent losses to the Cree were one major reason why. This could very well have been a war party.

The Chipewyan were more than happy to greet with warm affection one who had been lost to her people for so long, someone who was not expected to return. She was another stolen woman who had come back to her people. However, they would receive with less warmth her words, when she told them of the expedition and of the plans she had. They were reluctant to go with her. But she was a woman with a cause.

In traditional Native culture, discussions of important matters usually took a long time to complete. Everyone with an opinion must be heard, for consensus agreement was the norm. Thanadelthur was like a marten jumping from tree to tree in pursuit of a red squirrel, its main prey. She spoke so long, day and night, that according to Knight's journal entry of May 7, 1716, she, "had made her self so hoarse with her perpetual talking to her Country Men in perswading them to come with her that she could hardly Speak" (Emberley 1993:104). She didn't have a long time to capture the minds of her people and drag them over to her way of thinking. Time was running out on Thanadelthur's compromise deadline. Finally, and with some reticence, they agreed. Thanadelthur took around 160 men (perhaps it is no coincidence that this number roughly equals that of the original expedition) with her back to the camp she had left over a week before. They came within sight of the camp on the tenth day.

Initially she appeared to the members of the camp with only two of her Chipewyan peace party. She did not want to to spark a defensive reaction on the part of the justifiably nervous and gun-carrying Cree. When Stuart went out to greet her, Thanadelthur signalled for the others to show themselves. In Curtis's early-twentieth-century recording of Chipewyan oral tradition concerning this event we hear this version of what happened next: "The white men had raised a platform on which they place the woman, so that her people could see her and have confidence. When she beheld her people coming, she sang with joy" (Curtis in Emberley 1993:114).

However, it would be a while before anything like such joy would be felt by the others. The Chipewyan and the Cree were now face to face, old and recent prejudice and offences confronting each other. Words of peace would constitute a new language for them. Thanadelthur's third job of convincing them would be just as difficult as the previous two, maybe more.

Thanadelthur was forceful with her people. According to Stuart, when some Chipewyan showed hesitance to make concrete moves in the direction of peace, "She made them all Stand in fear of her she Scolded at Some and pushing of others... and forced them to ye peace" (Van Kirk 1980:69).

The work to make the peace initiative succeed, however, was not just a one woman effort. Nor should the Cree be portrayed as the 'bad guys' in this story. Often in the writing of North American history and especially in historical fiction, when Native heroes and heroines have been created, it has been at the expense of the reputation of the nations that opposed them. Movies enlarge this distortion, as they project old-time written bias onto the big screen. In *Dances with Wolves*, the nasty Pawnee make the Lakota look especially noble. In *Last of the Mohicans*, the brutal Huron (played by the same actor that played the nastiest Pawnee) served as a foil for the romanticized last two of the Mohicans. It would be wrong to vilify the Cree here. They could see that warfare cost them as well (see Ray 1974:19-20), that there was a practicality to peace with the Chipewyan.

Captain had with him a sacred pipe. The Cree leader seems to have had the spiritual qualities essential in what in contemporary Native culture is referred to as a pipe carrier. According to the report Stuart presented to Knight, Captain:

> pulled out his pipe and Stemm and made a Long harrangue of the Sacredness of that thing & that it was not to be touched without they ware resolved to be true and perform what it was brought there fore and Smoked in then he lighted it and handed it about and after everyone had taken so many whiffs as was agreed on and all had takeing it none refuseing it he told them they were now to be perpetuall friends with that they all give thanks and a Shoot and Rised up and stroked them all on the head. (Abel 1993:50)

Peace, at least temporarily, was declared between the Cree and the Chipewyan. For two days this peace was formalized through an exchange of goods and a mutual adoption of young men into each other's families, a traditional practice among allies.

The party that Thanadelthur travelled back with to York Factory was a mixed one. Along with Thanadelthur and Stuart, it was comprised of ten Cree, including Captain, and what seems to have been a carefully balanced number of ten Chipewyan, including

Thanadelthur's brother. They made their way back safely to York Factory by May 7, 1716, almost 11 months after they had first embarked on their ambitious mission. While Stuart could well have tried to improve his position with his superior by taking credit for the expedition's success, instead he lay praise where it truly belonged. He declared that Thanadelthur was "the chief instrument in finishing of it what has been done" (Abel 1993:50).

Knight must have greeted Thanadelthur and the others with all the enthusiasm his heart could muster. And this wouldn't have just been because the Chipewyan were wearing ornaments of copper and came bearing promises of much more. The month before, from Cree members of the expedition who had returned to York Factory prior to the successful meeting with the Chipewyan, Knight had received the depressing letter from Stuart. Four days later, three more Cree had arrived, telling a story of having encountered some Chipewyan and killing them in self-defence. This convinced the old Hudson's Bay Company man of the failure of the expedition. His mood shifted dramatically when he saw Thanadelthur and the others appear. Jubilantly, Knight wrote in his journal, "By this success I believe our Company may begin to be thought a rich Company in a few years and if it please God to preserve me with Life and health to go through with what I Design" (Geiger and Beattie 1993:50).

Thanadelthur appears to have continued her role as outspoken promoter of the cause of peace and the trade, criticizing those who opposed it. According to Knight's journal of May 9, 1716:

> [N]ow she is her she doth Awe her Country Men they dare hardly speak to her and spares none our Indians [i.e., the Cree] in telling how basely they killd 9 of there people when they had Smok[d] the friendly pipe to make a peace.... (Emberley 1993:105)

Stuart reported that, upon learning that a Chipewyan man was found with a Cree woman, possibly one he had captured, she immediately, "took up a Stick and beat the Man twill She made him Roar out" (Geiger and Beattie 1993:51). Maybe, as well as fearing the negative effects of such a relationship upon the peace that had been established, Thanadelthur could sympathize with the Cree woman's situation. When an older Chipewyan man dared to suggest that they try to trade pelts that were substandard, she "... ketcht him by the nose Push'd him backwards & call'd him fool and told him if they brought any but Such as they were directed they would not bee traded" (Van Kirk 1974:44).

Thanadelthur was taking on the role of what Kidwell (Kidwell 1992) refers to as a cultural meditator in the fur trade, a role that a number of Native women assumed in Canadian history. Her performance as cultural meditator was not just confined to her criticism of opponents but included instruction as well. She made sure that her fellow Chipewyan knew which furs were considered the most valuable by the English and how to prepare them so they would get the best return in the trade.

Thanadelthur and Knight soon were eagerly discussing plans for the future Chipewyan/Hudson's Bay Company trade. There seems to have been a free flow in this discussion, not just Knight telling Thanadelthur what to do. In Knight's words, when he presented an idea, the Chipewyan woman would "Presently Give her Opinion whether it would doo or not" (Van Kirk 1974:44). Knight's primary interest seems to have been in gaining access to copper, while Thanadelthur wanted most to ensure that her people received the weapons and other useful goods then being traded to the Cree. They both felt that her role should continue to be an active one. Eventually, the two of them came to a mutually beneficial agreement. She was to talk with her people, telling them what they had to do on their side and what they would receive in return. She would contact her people and their allies who dealt with copper and arrange for them to have the metal brought to Hudson Bay. Early in the spring of 1717, she would commence a journey that she reckoned would last two years, taking with her a sixteen-year-old English apprentice, Richard Norton, who was to learn the Chipewyan language. Thanadelthur was so dedicated to the proposed venture that, although she appears to have taken a Chipewyan husband during this period, she told Knight that she would leave that man if he would not go with her to set up trade. Thanadelthur should not be considered as being completely altruistic in all of this; she did see to it that her brother was made a trade captain by Knight.

Events appeared to be proceeding in a positive direction. But it was a harsh winter, the winter of 1716-1717. With the severe cold came first-contact sickness among the Chipewyan at the post. In Knight's journal of December 8, 1716, he recorded the painful fact that Thanadelthur had fallen ill. On January 11, 1717, he wrote, "ye

Northern Slave Woman has been dangerously ill and I expected her Death every Day, but I hope she is now A Recovering" (Van Kirk 1974:45). Knight was very concerned.

The individuals who ran Hudson's Bay Company posts during the eighteenth and nineteenth centuries are typically presented as cold, hard businessmen, practical to a fault. James Knight undoubtedly had that side to him. His concern for Thanadelthur would at least in part reflect that aspect of his nature. If she died, her death could certainly hit him hard financially and darken his dreams substantially. She was his Chipewyan interpreter and his main contact in a new trade connection. If her people heard that she had died while at York Factory, they might suspect foul play on the part of the English or the Cree. Thanadelthur's illness, however, seems to have touched Knight on a spot softer than his money belt.

The two had an unusual relationship for a white man and a Native woman of the time. First of all, their interaction did not involve any physical intimacy. He was at least 50 years her senior. Knight's lust in life, even as a young man, seems to have been more for wealth than for sex. He had a wife back in England, but didn't seem to have spent much time with her. Further, theirs was not a relationship in which the white man was aggressive and in command while the Native woman was passive and obedient. The two fought at least once, understandably with such a strong-minded pair. On that one known occasion, Knight accused Thanadelthur of giving away a kettle that he had presented to her in June for her return journey. This shows that Knight, while he understood the economic and political value of gift-giving, probably did not fully comprehend the importance of generosity in Native culture.[11] People sometimes had to give away treasured objects when these would be asked for or merely known to be desired by another. Certainly, Thanadelthur would not have readily let the kettle, a prized item in the trade, leave her possession. Whatever the circumstances surrounding her giving away the kettle, Thanadelthur did not take his accusation lightly. His lack of understanding seems to have hurt her. They had crossed the cultural chasm in other matters, so this accusation might have come as a shock and surprise to the young woman.

At first, when Knight gave her a hard time for his lack of regard for his gift to her, she denied that she had ever given it away. When Knight then produced the kettle as evidence to the contrary, she claimed that it must have been stolen. Then she even threatened that she would direct her people to kill him if he went to Churchill River. According to Knight, she "did rise in such a passion as I never did see the Like before..." (Geiger and Beattie 1993:51). In return, the old man said that he "cuff'd her Ears for her" (ibid.). The next day, she either repented of her action or relied upon softer means to resolve the issue. She tearfully confessed that she had been "a fool & Madd" (Van Kirk 1974:44) and withdrew the threat, saying that her people loved him like a father. Perhaps that describes something of how she perceived her relationship with the older man.

Despite this incident, and beyond the narrow bounds of mere financial concern, Knight seems to have genuinely cared for the Chipewyan woman who shared his vision and earned his respect. He took the ailing Thanadelthur into his own private residence and did what he could to try to nurse her back to health.

Thanadelthur, too, demonstrated that she was thinking beyond personal, material gain. Her main concern at that dire time would appear to have been for her people and the opportunities that the trade offered, not the least of which was their continued survival. At the beginning of February, as she lay in what she must have known would soon become her death bed, Thanadelthur asked that Richard Norton come to her bedside. She intended to encourage the young man to continue the endeavour she felt was crucial to the future of the Chipewyan. When he arrived, she exhorted him, "not to be Afraid to go Amongst their Indians for her Brother & Country People would Love him and not Lett him want for anything" (Geiger and Beattie 1993:57).

Her condition worsened, and on February 5, 1717, Thanadelthur died. Knight's reaction speaks both of his admiration for her and of his deep sense of loss at her death. Concerning the former, he said, "She was one of a Very high Spirit and of the Firmest Resolution that ever I see any Body in my Days and of great Courage & forecast" (Van Kirk 1980:70).

Knight felt the loss deeply, largely because he was concerned that without her the project would fail. On the day of her death he wrote:

> The Misfortune in loosing her will be very Prejudiciall
> to the Companys Interests.... I am sure the Death of
> her was a very considerable loss to the company for
> the wintering her allmost 2 years with us & going the

> year to make the peace & being chief promoter and
> acter in it wch has caused respect to her & Carry^d
> Also a Great Sway Among the Indians.... I am so
> concernd for her Deathe... that I am almost ready to
> break my heart to think now I be Disappointed in
> this undertaking wherein I had such a fair Prospect
> of ye busineas would prove so Advantagious to the
> Company's Flourishing. (Emberley 1993:105)

What did Thanadelthur's work mean to the trade the Chipewyan
were to have with the English? The effects were not felt right away,
particularly as Thanadelthur was not the only one of her people that
failed to survive that winter. All the other Chipewyan at the post died
as well. Knight was left without a translator and intermediary.
Gradually, however, the plans he and Thanadelthur had set in motion
started to achieve results. And that spring, a Chipewyan woman,
reputedly purchased from the Cree for 60 skins, took Thanadelthur's
place, although not with her predecessor's dynamism and vision. First
Stuart, and then Knight, went to the Churchill River in 1717-1718 to
construct a post, Fort Prince of Wales, and to initiate trade with the
Chipewyan there. Knight followed Thanadelthur's advice that trade
at what is now Churchill, Manitoba should be restricted to the
Chipewyan and other Dene. He even refused to trade with a group of
Cree bearing furs who came up to the new post that year. He told
them to go back south to York Factory if they wanted to deal with the
Hudson's Bay Company.

The Chipewyan tentatively over the next few years travelled across
the Barrens to Fort Prince of Wales. Trust and tradition took a while
to get established. By the second half of the eighteenth century,
Chipewyan traders such as Keelshies and Matonabbee were able to
set themselves up as successful middlemen in the fur trade,
harvesting the benefits from the financial seeds that Thanadelthur
had sown.

What about the relationship between the Chipewyan and the
Cree? What became of the work Thanadelthur had done there? Again,
progress was initially slow. Not all groups of the Cree felt bound by
the temporary peace agreement of 1716, and some continued to raid
the Chipewyan. The Cree were not a centralized people with one
peacemaker speaking for all groups. Band by band, the peace process
slowly moved ahead. That June, a Cree leader known as Captain

Swan returned to Hudson Bay after establishing firm, peaceful ties with the Chipewyan. In the fall of 1718, Richard Norton, making good use of his growing knowledge of the Chipewyan language, helped to make peace between a group of Chipewyan by the Seal River, north of Fort Prince of Wales, and a Cree hunting party. Some skirmishes between the two nations took place later—conflicts more equal than before as the Chipewyan now had access to guns. However, by 1760 a lasting peace between the two peoples was established. Although conflict was to arise from time to time, the conditions that had brought about Thanadelthur's capture would never return. By the twentieth century, there were reserve communities in Northern Alberta where Cree and Chipewyan live together in harmony.

James Knight did not long survive Thanadelthur. In June of 1719, at almost 80 years of age, he set off to find the Northwest Passage, copper and gold. He was never heard from again (see Geiger and Beattie 1993 for an insightful modern investigation into what happened to him).

By the time he turned 30, Richard Norton was made chief factor and commander of Fort Prince of Wales, a position he held for about ten years. His son, Moses Norton, took over the position in 1762, more than ten years after his father's death.

In later years the fur trade connection that Thanadelthur helped establish was to prove to be a mixed blessing to her people. For much of the eighteenth and nineteenth centuries, the Chipewyan were able to establish and maintain a relatively independent position in the trade. Much to the disappointment of the English traders, Thanadelthur's people soon established a policy of trading only for necessities, not the fancy expensive frills. In the 1740s, James Isham characterized them as unusual in that they preferred:

> Dressing very plaine; using their former Custom's,
> Seldom trading [for] any finery for Such usses But
> what they traffick for is Chiefly necessary's for Life,
> such as powdr, shott Guns &c. (Abel 1993:61)

Sometimes over those years bands of the Chipewyan were even able to disregard the trade or to deal with it only at their convenience. This was particularly true of the eastern **Ethen-eldeli** or 'Caribou eaters' bands who could live off of the caribou hunt, having little need for much else. Chipewyan who became involved in the trade were more often middlemen than trappers, sometimes making profits that frustrated both their European and Native partners. In 1771, for example, they were recorded as charging their fellow Dene sixty marten skins for a two-pound brass kettle, roughly ten times what they had paid for it at the post at Churchill. When fur trade posts were established in Chipewyan country, Thanadelthur's people were not easily intimidated by white traders. One indication of this is the following quote from the trader Daniel Harmon in 1817, "Those Chipewyan are a savage people... and they have as I believe, killed more white men, than any other tribe in the North West country" (Abel 1993:82).

However, there were also considerable drawbacks. According to Hearne, smallpox killed up to about 90 percent of the Chipewyan in 1781. While he was probably speaking only about the eastern bands of the Chipewyan, the effects on the whole group would still have been devastating. As with other Native nations involved with the fur trade, the Chipewyan experienced some of the death and dependency brought on by the alcohol that the Hudson's Bay Company and its 40-year rival the North West Company would pour into the trade (see Abel 1993:77).

Thanadelthur's legacy to her people can still be called a positive one. The chapter on Shanawdithit, the last Beothuk woman, demonstrates how readily destruction can happen to Native people who get trapped by European disease and on the losing side of small-scale but constant conflict, without any other people being interested in their survival. The same could well have happened to the Chipewyan. The combination of long-term military losses to the Cree plus the inevitable deadly contact with the white man's diseases might well have caused the Chipewyan to cease to exist as a distinct people. However, Thanadelthur's legacy is not restricted to this speculation. The story of how she accomplished her goals, against odds and opposition, is a great gift to her people and is an inspiration to us all.

Epilogue

There is one aspect of Thanadelthur's story that has long puzzled me. How could a woman that dynamic come from a culture that all of my early reading told me assigned to women a lowly role earning no respect? The traditional historical and anthropological literature up until at least the 1960s presented Chipewyan women as submissive pack horses, dominated in all things by their husbands and fathers. They were the best Canadian example of the squaw/drudge (see Introduction). A classic statement of this type of representation comes from Diamond Jenness's *The Indians of Canada*, long considered by scholars to be the Bible of Canadian Native studies (or at least the Old Testament). Although first published in 1932, this book's influence is still strong. It appears in virtually all public libraries across Canada, and reprints are still sold in many bookstores. Thus many readers and students preparing school projects will continue to echo uncritically Jenness's unequivocal statement that Chipewyan women "ranked lower than in any other tribe" (Jenness 1932:386).

This view is reflected in many other works that have had an impact on our perception of Chipewyan women. In Douglas Leechman's popular *Native Tribes of Canada*, published in the 1960s, we read that Chipewyan women were "little better than slaves and beasts of burden" (Leechman 1962:204). Another significant work on Native culture, also published during the 1960s, is Wendell H. Oswalt's *This Land was Theirs*. In his long chapter on the Chipewyan, he writes, "Females were subordinated to men in every way, and the men were oppressive. Women were treated cruelly and held in gross contempt by the men" (Oswalt 1966:27).

To realize how ingrained this type of opinion is, all you need to do is read the entry on the Chipewyan in the most recent version of the prestigious *Encyclopaedia Britannica*. By doing so you will discover that: "Females were extremely abased, being married off in adolescence and living lives virtually as beasts of burden" (*Encyclopaedia Britannica* 1992, vol. 3, p. 243).

This image of Chipewyan women clearly does not fit well with the character and actions of Thanadelthur, nor with the way her people responded to her verbalized opinions. She appears to be more the type of person who comes from a culture in which women are listened to and respected and have a significant degree of freedom of action. How can the contradiction between the life of Thanadelthur and the typical depiction of Chipewyan women in the standard historical literature be explained? This portrayal also seems to differ significantly from what has been found in relationships between females and males in more recent Chipewyan culture. Henry S. Sharp, a long-term student of that culture, pondered the contradiction:

> [A]fter more than twenty-five years of fieldwork... I
> have never been able to reconcile the harshness of
> the images of Chipewyan gender relations presented
> in the historical record with the nature of gender
> relations that I have observed among contemporary
> Chipewyan. (Sharp 1995:61)

While Chipewyan women worked hard, carrying heavy packs on
their backs when they were travelling in summer and pulling loaded
toboggans in winter, the depiction of Chipewyan women as menial
drudges is inaccurate and misleading.

Why would such inaccuracy exist? This distorted picture owes its
origin mainly to a single primary source. That source is Simon Hearne's
well-known published account of his travels through the north from
1769 to 1772. Hearne was a good writer and a keen observer of life,
both human and animal. He does not fit neatly into the category of
European male writer looking to justify his compatriots' presence
and attempted domination of a people by harshly judging how they
treated their wives, daughters and sisters. It is probably more accurate
to state that what he was seeing, hearing and describing in his journeys
was not the traditional Chipewyan culture he thought it was. He was
a witness to a way of life severely affected by the fur trade.

Hearne's major source of information about Chipewyan women
was Matonabbee, a prominent Chipewyan trader. Matonabbee served
as the leader and main role model for a group (more accurately gang)
of like-spirited male Chipewyan traders whom Hearne was
accompanying. Hearne learned about Chipewyan male attitudes
towards their women from the often oppressive actions and words of
members of this group, particularly those of Matonabbee. Often quoted
is his pompous pronouncement on the role of females in his culture:

> Women... were made for labour; one of them can carry,
> or haul, as much as two men can do. They also pitch
> our tents, make and mend our clothing, keep us warm
> at night; and, in fact, there is no such thing as
> travelling any considerable distance, or for any length
> of time, in this country, without their assistance.
> Women... though they do every thing, are maintained
> at a trifling expence; for as they always stand cook,
> the very licking of their fingers in scarce times, is
> sufficient for this subsistence. (Hearne 1958:35)

Matonabbee, however, should not be considered a totally reliable source of information concerning traditional Chipewyan gender roles, relationships and attitudes. He was more a 'trading post Indian' (a relatively rare figure among his people) than he was a man who reflected the teachings of his people. He was born and spent his first years at the Churchill trading post that Thanadelthur had worked so hard to establish. After his parents died early in his life, the Hudson's Bay Company became as much his family as were his biological relatives. As he grew up working for the Hudson's Bay Company in a variety of jobs, he learned many value-developing lessons of life from his English mentors. Eventually he earned the outsider-determined status of what the company called the 'leading Indian' of the Chipewyan, as he brought in through various means more furs in trade than any of his compatriots.

A measure of Matonabbee's material success is the fact that he had seven wives at one time. It may also be a measure, however, of how far he had strayed from the ways of his people. Traditional Chipewyan culture included polygamy, with a man having two or three wives (probably often sisters) being the most commonly occurring pattern. However, to my knowledge, at no period, earlier or later, and with no other Dene nation did there ever occur a number as high as seven.[12]

To a certain extent Matonabbee treated his wives as the economic assets of the cutthroat entrepreneur he was. He acquired, through trade but also often through murder, theft and threat, an exceptionally large amount of pelts and European trade goods. To his way of thinking, he needed an abnormally high number of women to carry these goods and to process the pelts. Marriage was a way of hiring workers.

Matonabbee and the group of Chipewyan men that he and Hearne travelled with acted in an opportunistic and predatory fashion. They not only killed, maimed and stole goods from traditional enemies such as the Inuit but also from fellow Dene[13] and other Chipewyan. This was new, the product of changing times.

When the Hudson's Bay Company gave Matonabbee the title of 'leading Indian' of his people (Gillespie 1979:524), it seemed the fitting thing to do for their most productive Chipewyan contact. But he was not a chief with the support of his people. His standing, his authority, his power came primarily from the company, not from the Chipewyan. When the French captured Fort Prince of Wales in 1782, Matonabbee committed suicide by hanging himself—not the act of a man with his roots in traditional Chipewyan culture. The wives he had worked so hard to acquire were not to survive him by much. In the winter of 1683, all of his six remaining spouses starved to death.

Perhaps it is no coincidence that after Matonabbee died, Chipewyan women living in their own country were spoken of as having some influence on the trade. Alexander Mackenzie, who spent some time in that country from 1787 to 1793, commented that Chipewyan women "are always consulted, and possess a very considerable influence in the traffic with Europeans, and other important concerns" (Van Kirk 1974:43).

Appendix A: The Meaning of Key Names

a) Dene

The meaning and something of the traditional significance of the term Dene can be seen in the following quote from Clyde Kluckhohn's and Dorothea Leighton's classic work *The Navaho*:

> 'Navaho' is not their own word for themselves. In their own language they are dine, 'The People.' ... This term is a constant reminder that the Navahos still constitute a society in which each individual has a strong sense of belonging with the others who speak the same language and, by the same token, a strong sense of difference and isolation from the rest of humanity. (Kluckhohn and Leighton 1962:23)

In R. Wesley Heber's "Indians as Ethnics: Chipewyan Ethno-Adaptations" (Heber 1992:107-8), he demonstrates how the Chipewyan have used the term 'Dene' (represented as -dene-, -ttine- and -t'inne-) to refer to bands or ethnic divisions within their ranks. He presents both people and dwellers as translations in the following:

Kkpest'aylekke ottine	'dwellers among the quaking aspen'
Nunarna-dene	'people of the south'
Yodai-dene	'people of the west'
Ganikwe-dene	'people of the pine house'
Sayise-dene	'people of the rising sun'

The-ye-ottine   'dwellers at Stone Fort [or stone house]'
Keskye-hot'inne   'poplar house people'

Dene has direct parallels with other names from unrelated languages: the Inuktitut word **Inuit**, the Montagnais/Naskapi word **Innu**, the Ojibwe word **(A)nishnabe(k)** (see pp. 142, 185-7), and the Mohawk **Onkwe Onwe**.

b) *Slave or Slavey*

In *A History of the Original Peoples of Northern Canada*, Keith Crowe wrote: "The small and separate bands of Slavey people were not warlike, and the more aggressive Cree called them **Awokanak**, which means 'timid people,' or slaves" (Crowe 1974:49).

The cognate term in related languages, however, refers primarily to domestic animals, as can be seen in the following:

- a) East James Bay Cree - "auhkaan... domestic animal" (as opposed to "awesiis... wild animal" Cree School Board 1987:53); and
- b) Odawa - **"ookaan**... farm animal... pl. **ookaanag"** (Rhodes 1985:328)

This use of a term for a domestic animal extended to refer to a prisoner was a common practice in Native languages. Witness the following term in the Iroquoian languages of Huron and Mohawk:

- a) Huron - "gandask8a. Esclave, captif, animal domestique" (HF59:89); and
- b) Mohawk "burden animal, captive, slave, employee, kanaskwa" (Michelson 1973:76)

Endnotes

[1] It is hard to determine how often, prior to the arming of the Cree, the two groups fought and thus could be deemed enemies rather than peoples who avoided each other.

[2] Two early published records of Chipewyan oral tradition concerning Thanadelthur provide both her story and her name. The earliest, as spoken by Alexis Enna-azè in 1879, was published in French by Emile Petitot in 1886 (Petitot 1886:424-428). The second was recorded in English by Edward Curtis in 1928. The Slavey had a similar story about a woman called 'G'umbah' or 'Ptarmigan,' likewise captured by the Cree and also helping her people get involved with the fur trade (Crowe 1974:76).

[3] Thanadelthur referred to a friendly neighbour nation that "goes by the Name of Martin Indians by their abounding with such Great Quantity of Martins they have amongst themselves and are clothd with them" (Heber 1992:106). Perhaps there was a connection between this group's name and the naming of the Chipewyan women.

[4] That term eventually was to become the name associated with another Dene nation, the Thlingchadinne ('Dog-rib people'). See Hodge 1971:454 and Helm 1981:303-6.

[5] This includes the Apache and Navaho of the southwestern United States, termed Southern Athapaskans.

[6] In "A Discovery of Strangers", Rudy Wiebe incorporated the telling of such a story into his novel about 'Greenstockings,' a young Yellowknife woman taken by members of John Franklin's expedition in 1820 (see chapter eight, "The Stolen Woman").

[7] See Petitot 1886:412-22, Abel 1993:60 and "Tsanottine" in Hodge 1971:449.

[8] The buttons were probably gold-plated, copper or bronze.

[9] The difficulty of this task was reported in Knight's journal article for May 7, 1716:

> [I]t was as much as ever the Indian Woman and Wm Stewart could do to persuade them [i.e., the Cree] to the Contrary the Woman bid them Stay where they was and Shee would follow there tracks as had made there Escape [i.e., the surviving Chipewyan] and persuaded them [i.e., the Cree] to Stay in the Place for Ten days and if she did not find them in the time nor comeback they might return....
> (Emberley 1993:104)

Emberley misinterpreted this confusing passage, incorrectly stating that Chipewyan had killed Cree. It was later revealed that "Eight Lusty Young Fellows" among the Cree, a separate party within the expedition, had killed the Chipewyan. They claimed self-defence (see Johnson 1952:44).

[10] Thanadelthur informed Knight that there were 100 tents in the area, which Smith (1981:276) calculates as meaning there were 800 to 1000 people in the vicinity. While this seems plausible, Smith's implied view that this might be normal does not.

[11] This value of generosity in Native culture is articulated clearly in the following:

> Generosity is an important value in the Ojibwe ethos and seems to be rooted in two basic principles. The first is a recognition that all possessions, successes, and honours are from the Creator. Many times I observed people receiving such things respond in gratitude and thanksgiving by sharing with those near to that person. Secondly, generosity is rooted in the philosophy that giving to another furthers the development of relationships; by giving to another one is creating a kind of social security for oneself against possible future need. As one person told me, 'Sharing things and giving things away keeps our community going.' (Spielmann 1998:33)

[12] To my knowledge, the highest recorded number of wives for a Canadian Native was nine. The husband was Maquinna, a powerful Nootka chief of the early nineteenth century. A much richer resource base and more hierarchal society gave traditional Nootka leaders greater access to wealth and power than that permitted Dene leaders.

[13] This practice of plundering fellow Dene for furs was carried on by Awgeenah (English Chief), one of Matonabbee's followers. Eventually, he became a powerful middleman in the trade between English and Dene (Sloan 1987:20).

Bibliography

Abel, Kerry. 1993. *Drum Songs: Glimpse of Dene History*. Montreal & Kingston: McGill-Queen's University Press.

Cree School Board. 1987. *Cree Lexicon: Eastern James Bay Dialects*. Baie-de-la-Poste, Mitassini Lake, Cree School Board.

Crowe, Keith. 1974. *A History of the Original Peoples of Northern Canada*. Arctic Institute of North America. Montreal: McGill-Queen's Univ. Press.

Dodge, Ernest S. 1969. "Knight, James," in *Dictionary of Canadian Biography (DCB)* vol.2, pp. 318-320.

Emberley, Julia V. 1993. *Thresholds of Difference:Feminist Critique, Native Women's Writings, Postcolonial Theory*. Toronto, Univ. of Toronto Press.

Geiger, John & Beattie, Owen. 1993. *Dead Silence: The Greatest Mystery in Arctic Discovery*. Toronto: Viking.

Gillespie, Beryl C. 1979. "Matonabbee." *DCB* vol.4, pp. 523-4.

Hearne, Samuel. 1958. *A Journey to the Northern Ocean*, ed. by Richard Glover. Toronto: The Macmillan Company.

Heber, R. Wesley. 1992. "Indians as Ethnics: Chipewyan Ethno-Adaptations," in *The First Ones: Readings in Indian/Native Studies*, ed. by D.R. Miller, C. Beal, J. Dempsey and R. W. Heber, Craven. Sask.: Sask. Indian Federated College Press, pp. 104-113.

Helm, June. 1981. "Dogrib," in *The Handbook of North American Indians Volume 6—Subarctic*. Washington: The Smithsonian Institution, pp. 291-309.

Hodge, F.W. 1971. *Handbook of Indians of Canada* (adapted by J. White in 1913 from a Bureau of Amer. Ethnology publication). Toronto: Coles Pub. Ltd.

Huron French Dictionary. no date. Ms 59 (as cited in Victor Hanzeli, *Missionary Linguistics in New France*, 1969, The Hague, Mouton), Archive Seminaire de Quebec.

Jenness, Diamond. 1932. *The Indians of Canada*. Ottawa: King's Printer.

Johnson, Alice M. 1952. "Ambassadress of Peace." *The Beaver*. December, 1952, pp. 42-45.

Kehoe, Alice. 1992. *North American Indians: A Comprehensive Account*. Englewood Cliffs: Prentice Hall.

Kidwell, Clara Sue. 1992. "Indian Women as Cultural Mediators." *Ethnohistory* 39:97-107.

Kluckhohn, Clyde and Leighton, Dorothy. 1962. *The Navaho*. Garden City, New York: Doubleday & Co.

Leechman, Douglas. 1967. *Native Tribes of Canada*. Toronto: W.J. Gage & Co.

Michelson, Gunther. 1973. *A Thousand Words of Mohawk*. Ottawa: National Museum of Man, Mercury Series, Ethnology Div., paper #5.

Newman, Peter C. 1985. *Company of Adventurers*, vol. 1. New York: Viking Books.

Oswalt, Wendell H. 1966. *This Land was Theirs*. New York: John Wiley & Sons.

Petitot, Emile. 1886. *Traditions indiennes du Canada nord-ouest*. Paris: Maisonneuve Frères.

Ray, Arthur J. 1974. *Indians in the Fur Trade: their roles as hunters, trappers and middlemen in the lands southwest of Hudson Bay, 1660-1870*. Toronto: Univ. of Toronto Press.

Rhodes, Richard. 1985. *Eastern Ojibwa-Chippewa-Ottawa Dictionary*. Amsterdam: Mouton.

Sharp, Henry S. 1995. "Asymmetric Equals: Women and Men Among the Chipewyan," in *Women and Power in Native North America*, ed. by

L.F. Klein and L.A. Ackerman. Norman, Oklahoma: Univ. of Okla. Press, pp. 46-74.

Sloan, W.A. 1987. "Aw-gee-nah." *DCB* vol.6, 1821-1835, p. 20.

Smith, James G.E. 1981. "Chipewyan," in *The Handbook of North American Indians Volume 6 Subarctic.* Washington: Smithsonian Institution, pp. 271-284.

Spielmann, Roger. 1998. *'You're So Fat': Exploring Ojibwe Discourse.* Toronto: Univ. of Toronto Press.

Thorman, G.E. 1969. "Thanadelthur." *DCB* vol.2, 1701-1740, pp. 627-8.

Van Kirk, Sylvia. 1974. "Thanadelthur." *The Beaver,* Spring, pp. 40-45.

Van Kirk, Sylvia. 1980. *"Many Tender Ties": Women in Fur-Trade, 1670-1870.* Winnipeg: Watson & Dwyer Pub. Ltd.

Wiebe, Rudy. 1995. *A Discovery of Strangers.* New York: Quality Paperback Book Club.

Wilson, C. Roderick and Urion, Carl. 1995. "First Nations Prehistory and Canadian History," in *Native Peoples: The Canadian Experience,* 2nd ed., ed. by R.B. Morrison and C. R. Wilson. Toronto: McClelland and Stewart, pp. 22-66.

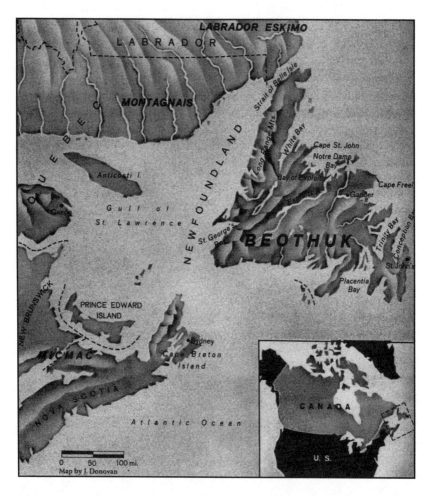

Map of Beothuk territory. Oswalt, Wendell H. 1966. *This Land was Theirs*, p. 66. New York: John Wiley and Sons.

3

Shanawdithit or Nancy April

When she fell into one of her melancholy moods and
ran off into the woods she would turn round saying,
'All gone widdun (asleep) Nance go widdun too, no
more come Nance, run away, no more come. (Howley
1974:182)

Shanawdithit was a Beothuk (usually pronounced Bey-aw-thick),
a people now no more. Although she may not have been the last of
the Beothuk (see page 102), the story of her tragic, untimely
terminated life is intertwined with those of how her people diminished
from independence to extinction in a few short generations. To tell
one tale is to go a long way in explaining the other; to not tell one is
to fail to do justice to the other. We will therefore begin this biography
by outlining who the Beothuk were. In this discussion we will be
initiating the investigation of the factors that led to their extinction
and to the increasing isolation and despair that Shanawdithit faced
throughout her young life.

Who Were the Beothuk?

a) Their Newfoundland Beginnings

The Beothuk were descendants of the third wave of people to
come to Newfoundland from Labrador. The first group, referred to by
archaeologists as the Maritime Archaic, crossed the Strait of Belle
Isle to the northern tip of the island around 3000 B.C.[1] They stayed

there about 2000 years, then either left or died off. The next people to make a similar crossing were the Palaeo-Eskimo, who began their stay around 850 B.C. and left about A.D. 950. The third such migration happened around 50 B.C. Included among the immigrants were the ancestors of the Beothuk. At the time of first significant contact with Europeans, around 1500, the Beothuk might have been the only permanent Native residents on the island (Marshall 1996:14), numbering from between at least 500 to over 1000. Archaeology and the early written reports of the area both tell us that the Beothuk had at some time access to all the major bays and much of the inland territory.

b) *Their Food*

What the Beothuk ate is important, as it suggests one reason why European settlement had such a tragic impact on their lives. Their food sources were of two kinds: inland and sea. Primary among the first were the caribou, a migratory species available to the Beothuk in October and November during the times of the large herds and again in smaller numbers in the spring. One of Shanawdithit's drawings (sketches 6 and 7) shows us how caribou meat was preserved by drying or smoking on racks that are part of a bark building. They would hunt the herds by channelling them through ever-narrowing passageways bordered by fences that were recorded in one instance as being 15 kilometres in length.

Caribou is a tremendous source of supplies for daily life: its flesh provides food, its sinew thread, its bones and antlers the raw material for weapons and utensils. Caribou hair is hollow, trapping air, thus making it ideal for insulation, softness and lightness; it is ideal for clothing, footwear, tents, bedding, blankets and bags.

During the summer, the Beothuk went down to the sea. The sea provided the people with an abundance of seals: harbour, harp and bearded. In another one of Shanawdithit's drawings (Figure 1), entitled "Different kinds of animal food," we see ample evidence of how extensively the Beothuk used this marine mammal. In the drawing we see tasty pieces of seal fat on skin, a 'boochmoot' or sled made out of an entire seal skin and a seal's bladder filled with oil for heating and lighting made by rendering down the fat of the animal.

Also in the picture is a "Birch rind [i.e., bark] vessel for boiling eggs in." The Beothuk prepared a peculiar concoction from the substantial eggs of the Great Auk, a bird now as extinct as the nation

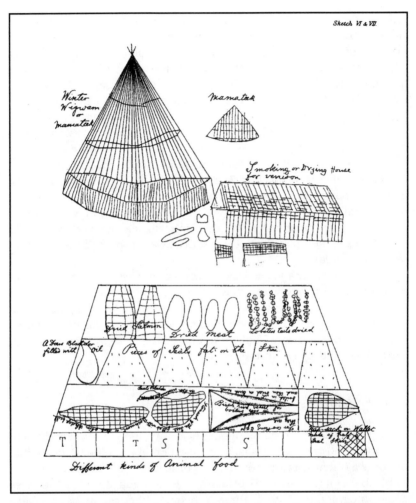

Figure 1. Shanawdithit's drawings. Howley, James P. 1974. *The Beothuk or Red Indians*. Toronto: Coles.

who once collected its eggs. They boiled the eggs, dried them in the sun and then ground them up to produce a powdered ingredient for their soups and stews. It was a clever adaptation to life in their home territory, possibly unique to the Beothuk.

The sea presented the Beothuk with other gifts as well. In the same picture we find depictions of lobster tails and dried salmon. The latter in particular were valuable to the Beothuk, especially in

July and August. Other fish important to the people were smelt and capelin, but not the expected cod, which are deep-water feeders. In another of Shanawdithit's drawings, one which could be depicting some of the sacred symbols of these people, we see what the Beothuk may have considered the most highly prized sea quarry. The second symbol from the left is a ceremonial pole with the image of a whale's tail on it, possibly that of the relatively small bottlenose whale.

The Beothuk were able to obtain these seafoods largely because of their unusual canoes, which were specially constructed for ocean-going travel. These 20- to 22-foot boats had to be made so that they would be difficult to tip over. The Beothuk gave them a keel running along the bottom and gunwales that rose on the sides to peak at the broad centre part of the canoe. For ballast they would use heavy stones. In the imaginative, frightening stories the settlers would sometimes make up and tell, the Beothuk were reputed to use human skulls for ballast.

The Beothuk made good use of several sources of food in season. Prior to contact they would have had a bountiful life. However, the weakness of such a way of obtaining food would be that if a crucial source were to be cut off when it was needed, the Beothuk would be vulnerable to starvation. That vulnerability would begin once European settlers started to circle the coast.

c) *Their Language*

Our knowledge of their language is scanty, limited to a compilation of around 350 words.[2] This is only a fraction of the tens of thousands of words a fluent speaker would have possessed.[3] Still we know enough to be able to say that the Beothuk spoke a language that no one else could understand. Of their three Native neighbours, one would have understand nothing of the Beothuk language. The other two would have found most of the language incomprehensible, except for a few familiar sounding words. Linguists are divided concerning what this partial sharing of vocabulary means. Some say that Beothuk was an isolated language, not related to any other tongue (Oswalt 1966:67). Others suggest that any similarities between Beothuk and the languages of their Algonquian-speaking neighbours, the Micmac and the Innu, are just the result of borrowings after long periods of contact. Still others, and I belong to this group,[4] feel that Beothuk was at least a distant cousin of members of the Algonquian family of languages. People who argue for this linguistic kinship do so based on the presence of an admittedly small group of cognates,[5] words that are similar in meaning and sound (see Appendix A). What convinced me that there exists a family relationship between Beothuk and the Algonquian languages was the following. These languages typically use some form of -**name**- (pronounced as 'nah-meh') in words denoting fish[6] (see Appendix B). This root appears to be productive in Beothuk as well, taking the form -**me**-[7] in the following words: "A-eshe**me**et lumpfish," "Datto**me**ish ... trout" and "Wesho**me**sh... herring" (Howley 1974: 303, 304 and 307). Even as a relative, however, Beothuk was too dissimilar from its cousins for its speakers to be understood by other Algonquians. Linguistically, as well as socially, the Beothuk stood alone.

d) *Their Social Relationship to Other Native Nations*

i) The Micmac

It is difficult to know just when the Micmac first started crossing to Newfoundland from Cape Breton. By the seventeenth century, Micmac were regularly visiting the island to hunt, trap and fish, and some were starting to settle there. At various times during the period from the second half of that century to the 1720s, there seems to have been conflict between the two peoples in the southwestern part of the island, particularly around St. George's Bay.

What did the Beothuk think of the Micmac? They referred to them as **Shanung** or **Shonack**.[8] The term is translated in the word lists as 'bad Indians,' but that is probably more a statement of the nature of the Micmac's relationship with the Beothuk than it is a translation.[9] The word contains no apparent morpheme or word part signifying 'bad.'[10] We learn more about the Beothuk attitude from what Shanawdithit told William Cormack in 1828. According to Cormack, she said:

> ... from infancy all her nation were taught to cherish animosity and revenge against all other peoples; that this was enforced by narrating, during the winter evenings, the innumerable wrongs inflicted on the Boeothics by the white men and by the Mik-maks... and that if the Boeothics made peace and talked with... the Micmacks, who... belonged to the bad spirit, that

they would not, after they died, go to the happy island.
(Marshall 1996:158)

English writers of the nineteenth and twentieth centuries have often laid significant blame on the Micmac for the extinction of the Beothuk. This accusation is not justified by the evidence. The main strategy applied by both Native nations with regard to each other seems to have been mutual avoidance. The numbers of each group would have made this a relatively easy strategy to follow. The mid-eighteenth-century population of the Beothuk would have diminished to something like 350. Even by the early 1800s, the largest Newfoundland Micmac community of St. George's Bay only numbered between 60 and 150 people. In 1810, seasonal hunting and trapping parties reached between 200 and 300 in the Bay d'Espoir area on the south coast.

It is unfortunate that the two peoples did not have a more positive relationship. Had such been the case, the Micmac might have given refuge to the surviving Beothuk. As it is, the last 'full-blooded' Beothuk may have lived with the Micmac. In 1910, anthropologist Frank Speck spoke with a woman, Santu Toney (ca. 1837-1919), who said that her father 'Kop' had been a Beothuk captured as a small boy. She was born by the shores of Red Indian Lake, the location of the last known Beothuk band.

An odd twist to the notion of blaming the Micmac was the once popular theory known as the Micmac mercenary myth. The myth claimed that the French hired the Micmac as mercenaries to kill off the Beothuk. This was formally presented as the reason for the imminent extinction of the Beothuk in William Cormack's inaugural address as president of the Beothuck Institute in 1827 (Howley 1974:183) and accepted by many writers for years after that (Maclean 1971:121, 292, and 319), including the prominent anthropologists J.N.B. Hewitt of the Smithsonian's American Bureau of Ethnology and Albert Gatschet (Hodge 1971:61). It was given new life in 1978 when Barrie Reynolds, writing the article about the Beothuck in the influential *Handbook of North American Indians*, claimed: "Particularly lethal was the encouragement given the Micmac by the French to attack them" (Reynolds 1978:106).

There is no evidence that directly supports the contention of an antagonistic relationship between French and Beothuk. They made sporadic but failed attempts to trade with the Natives of Newfoundland (Marshall 1996:53 and possibly Howley 1974:20). Any conflict they might have had would have been of an even less significant order. The French, limited to the west coast and the extreme north of the island (west and east), simply did not have the same amount of contact with the Beothuk that the English did, and thus had no good reason to want them out of the way. Finally, the Micmac were more independent players on the historical stage than these English writers give them credit.

Another question needs to be asked. Why would people be so eager to believe the Micmac mercenary myth? One answer is that it would implicate two peoples whose presence in Newfoundland was opposed by English officials. The French had attacked and captured the capital city of St. John's twice during the eighteenth century (1708 and 1762) and maintained their rights to the French Shore until 1904. The Micmac were suspect because of their French connection and because they were becoming involved with the fur trade on the island. In 1765, Governor Hugh Palliser ordered the Micmac off the island, to no avail.

Another reason could be a growing sense of guilt. The Beothuck Institute had been formed in 1827 by leading members of Newfoundland society who felt some measure of concern for the disappearing Beothuk. Newfoundlanders generally at that time seem to have been anxious about the diminishing numbers and chances for survival of the Beothuk. Most had never seen a member of the ill-fated people that shared the same island and thus would have felt little animosity towards them. Feeling guilty about actions their fellow English Newfoundlanders committed, they could feel comforted by having someone else share the blame. The romanticism of the time was also a factor. A typically nineteenth-century literary form was the "Last of the...," with the writer telling the romantically tragic story of the extinction of some Native group that had lived in eastern North America. James Fenimore Cooper's *Last of the Mohicans* was the most famous of this genre. For the Beothuk there was *Ottawah: Last Chief of the Red Indians of Newfoundland*, originally published in London in 1848, then reprinted in Philadelphia and translated into German. The Micmacs were the villains of this piece, which went a long way to increase the popularity of the Micmac mercenary myth.

ii) The Innu: Montagnais and Naskapi

Other Algonquian-speaking neighbours were the Innu, also named the Montagnais and Naskapi, and known to the Beothuk as the **Sho-udamunk** or **Shaunamunk**.[11] We know the Beothuk came from

Labrador, where the Innu have long lived. Archaeology suggests to us that less than 1000 years ago, the ancestors of both peoples used the same variety of flint quarried in northern Labrador to make tools (Marshall 1996:259). Thus there was a pre-contact link of some sort between them. There are reports during the eighteenth century of a small Innu presence in Newfoundland, confined mostly to trapping expeditions in order to trade with the French. While it seems that the Innu knew better than anyone the whereabouts of the Beothuk, there is no clear evidence of a well-established contact between the two peoples. In 1842, J.B. Jukes, who indirectly learned about the Beothuk from Shanawdithit through John Peyton Jr., said that they

> were acquainted with another tribe of Indians whom they call Shaunamunc, and with whom they were very friendly. These come from Labradore.... The Red Indians traded with these Shaunamuncs; receiving stone hatchets and other implements from then and they mutually visited each other's countries. (Marshall 1996:60)

The Beothuk, then, seemed to have one friend or at least an occasional trading partner among their Native neighbours. But did that mean, as Jukes (Howley 1974:26) and a few others (Maclean 1971:319-20) have suggested, that the Innu provided a Labrador escape route for the Beothuk? Such is highly unlikely. The Innu have no oral tradition of such a group influx. Shanawdithit does not seem to have been aware of any bands left outside of her own. Further, the Beothuk's strategy when pressured seems to have been to retreat into the interior. Initially, that strategy seemed to work, but the long-term consequences would be disastrous.

iii) The Inuit

The ancestors of the Beothuk shared the island of Newfoundland with the Inuit, who arrived there around 850 B.C. and stayed as permanent residents until about 950 A.D. Little is known of the interaction of the two groups. The Beothuk named the Inuit **Ashwan** (Howley 1974:303), which may have been cognate with the Algonquian root meaning 'to eat something raw,' from which came the word 'Eskimo.'[12] There are eighteenth-century reports of hostility between the two peoples, but there is at least one reference to some trade (Marshall 1996:54-55). Jukes, indirectly informed by Shanawdithit, stated that the Inuit were "despised for their filthiness" by the Beothuk (Howley 1974:26). Clearly the Inuit were not allies the Beothuk could go in times of European troubles.

The Beothuk and the Europeans

During the 1500s, the interaction between the Beothuk and Europeans from a number of different nations followed a destructive pattern that would be repeated through subsequent centuries. There would be a few doomed attempts at trade, some kidnappings and the Beothuk would learn to stay out of sight whenever Europeans came into view. No positive relationship would be established, then or ever.

During the seventeenth century, the Beothuk felt the press of the newcomers only slightly; for even by 1684, there were still only 120 permanent English residents. During the eighteenth century, this trickle of immigration became a raging current, washing away Beothuk territory like so much silt in a spring flood. The Beothuk gradually retreated into a smaller amount of space until they were confined almost exclusively to one area. The heart of Beothuk territory became Red Indian Lake, situated about dead centre in Newfoundland. This large lake is connected to the sea through the dangling lifeline of the Exploits River, the longest river on the island. The river-lake combination almost completely bisects Newfoundland from northeast to southwest. The river flows into Exploits Bay, part of the broader expanse of water that is Notre Dame Bay. By 1754, there were some 400 settlers in the area of this bay, where the Beothuk still fished and collected seabird eggs, and 3000 more on the rest of the island. Within 20 years that figure jumped to at least 12,000, reaching 20,000 by 1804. During 1814-15 alone, 11,000 new immigrants came to Newfoundland from southern Ireland.

The toll on the island's resources was heavy. Seabirds were slaughtered in thousands, for their eggs, meat and valuable feathers. The Great Auk was gone from Newfoundland by 1800 and extinct worldwide by 1844. The English salmon fishery, averaging a take of some 100,000 kilograms per year between 1717-1735, rose to more than five times that amount during the last fifteen years of the century (Marshall 1996:63). This was a very competitive business, with people setting up nets and weirs farther and farther up the major salmon rivers. By 1786, these traps were 44 kilometres up the Exploits River. Seals were hunted to an average of 31,000 per year from 1786 to 1792, when the hunt began in earnest, to species-threatening numbers of 218,000 in 1819 and 687,000 in 1823 (Marshall 1996:78-79).

Similar statistics exist for English fur trapping. The trade was initially set up during the early 1720s. Average sales for trapped furs were about £615 from 1722 to 1754 (Marshall 1996:71), more than doubling for the remaining period of that century (op. cit., p. 75). L.F.S. Upton clearly depicts the devastating effects that these trappers, known as "furriers," had on the Beothuk:

> They laid their trap-lines across the Beothuck' deer runs, thus disrupting the caribou hunt. They destroyed campsites and stores of food, and stole the Red Indians' stocks of fur.... Travelling through and living off the land, the furriers became wise in its ways: they learned how to identify Indian trails and campsites, to calculate the age of the track or length of time a fire had been abandoned. This knowledge made them dangerous enemies, as much at home in the interior as the Beothuck themselves. (Upton 1988:50)

Furriers committed the first official killings of Beothuk in 1732; the Beothuk weren't recorded as killing any European until 30 years later. This tells us much concerning the pattern that was to develop. The furriers and salmon fishermen were clearly the aggressors, using as justification that the Beothuk stole sails, nets and metal objects that could be fashioned into spears, arrows and knives. They often killed Beothuk on sight, sometimes attacking families and murdering women and children. Some would hunt Beothuk as if they were animals. Lieutenant John Cartwright, a sympathetic observer who led a expedition up the Exploits River in 1768 to explore and investigate the 'Indian problem,' reported: "He that has shot an Indian values himself more upon the fact than had he overcome a bear or wolf and fails not to speak of it with a brutal triumph, especially in the mad hours of drunkenness" (Howley 1974:36).

Beothuk retaliation was minimal. They killed a few Englishmen along the coasts, but they did not seek vengeance upon isolated furriers inland, although they easily could have. They did not harm any women or children. Instead they seemed to have preferred to play a deadly game of hide and seek (see Appendix C).

It should be pointed out that the northeast was the wild frontier of the island, beyond the regular control of the law.[13] Most Anglo-Irish Newfoundlanders of the time quietly fished for cod in peaceful settlements. They rarely if ever saw any Beothuk and never harmed their fellow islanders.

Shanawdithit

When Shanawdithit was born, probably in 1801, Beothuk deaths usually outnumbered births each year. Her people had dwindled to perhaps one-fifth of their number at first European contact. Approximately 200 lived in four small, seasonally temporary locations. It was not just violence at the hands of the salmon fishers and furriers that killed them; people were starving because they could not always gain access to much-needed marine resources. European immigrants brought diseases to which the Beothuk had no immunities. As was the pattern with other Native nations, probably at least half of the Beothuk succumbed—tuberculosis was the main reported culprit, but there were others.

Bounties

In 1803, a dangerous precedent was set that would have a dramatic effect on Shanawdithit's life. William Cull, a furrier from Fogo Island, had captured a Beothuk woman and had brought her to the capital city of St. John's. He was paid £50 for his troubles, as the authorities believed that she could be used to establish positive contact between the English and the Beothuk. The next year, William Cull took her back along with presents the officials hoped would facilitate friendly interaction.

This incident seems to have been the first step in setting into motion a new governmental policy. While well-intentioned, this policy was to be ultimately destructive. A £50 reward was put up for anyone who could successfully bring in a Beothuk to talk with the authorities. This figure was increased to £100 in 1810. You can see how out of touch some of the officials promoting this policy were in the fancy and formal phrasing of Governor Richard G. Keats' proclamation of August, 1813:

Such as may hereafter meet with any of the said Indians inhabitants are especially called upon by a kind and amicable demeanour to invite and encourage communication, and otherwise to cultivate and improve a friendly and familiar intercourse with this interesting people.-If any person shall succeed in establishing on a firm and settled footing an intercourse so much to be desired, he shall receive one hundred pounds as a reward for his meritorious services. But if any of His Majesty's subjects, contrary to the expression of these, His Royal Highness's commands, shall so far forget themselves, and be so lost to the sacred duties of Religion and Hospitality, as to exercise any cruelty, or be guilty of any ill treatment toward this inoffensive people, they may expect to be punished with the utmost rigour of the Law. (Howley 1974:91)

This policy, tried just as fruitlessly in Tasmania at about the same time, amounted to a bounty for 'bringing them back alive.' The policy created no peace between the two peoples. We will never know how many people died resisting their 'peaceful capture' or fleeing from warm, food-stocked homes into unfamiliar territories where food was scarce and protection from the elements difficult to establish. How would the Beothuk know the benign intent of someone who could not speak their language and who, at an earlier time, may have been trying to drive them away or kill them? Certainly they knew about kidnappings. In June of 1758, furriers had, upon coming across a Beothuk home, shot and killed a woman and child and took a boy of about nine years with them. The boy, who was named Tom June after the month of his capture, was raised by a settler family, became involved with the local fishery and died sometime in 1788. In August of 1768, furriers killed a Beothuk woman and captured her son, who was about four years old. He was called John August. The next winter he was exhibited in Britain—for two pence a peek. He also became a fisherman and died in 1788. In 1791, three men attacked a family, shot and killed a man, wounded a boy and took a young girl named Oubee. She was adopted into an English family and died in Britain on or before 1795.

The Ill-fated Expedition of 1811

One important source of what we know about the Beothuk and about what took place during Shanawdithit's lifetime is somewhat unusual—her drawings. According to William Cormack, who encouraged her to depict aspects of her culture as well as key events in her life: "She had a natural talent for drawing, and being at all times supplied with paper and pencils of various colours, she was enabled to communicate what would otherwise have been lost" (Howley 1974:225).

From one of Shanawdithit's drawings and the accompanying notes added by Cormack, we get a census of the Beothuk population in 1811. There were three encampments, all located beside the body of water named after them, Red Indian Lake. Only 72 Beothuk lived in those three encampments. The inevitability of their decline can be seen in the fact that there were more adults, 22 women and 20 men, than there were children, a mere 30. Was this because of the diminishing food supply? Were the Beothuk forced into the leaner, meaner economy of giving food first to the adults because the people needed the providers to be strong in order to get more food? Such a practice was not unknown among other peoples under similar circumstances. Did the women go hungry so often that they were less fertile? Were fewer children surviving from conception to birth and through the precarious first year of life because their mothers were undernourished and were forced to move quickly, often and far to obtain food and to escape encroaching furriers and salmon fishers? Or was it generally that the toughness of life preyed first on the little ones?

Shawnadithit's memory across the 18 years from 1829 back to 1811 was good, even though the process of remembering would have been a hurtful one—picturing 71 faces she would never see again, except with her mind's tearful eye. She knew how many people were in each settlement, even in each **mamateek**—the Beothuk version of the birchbark wigwam. From one of Shanawdithit's drawings (Figure 1) we see that there were two basic sizes of those houses, the larger of the two being a winter dwelling. We can determine that Shanawdithit's mentally reconstructed census of 1811 is of the winter, for the number of people living in each mamateek was relatively high. In her encampment, the largest of the three, there were three mamateeks: one with nine adults and six children, the second with six of each, and the third with eight adults and seven children.

Perhaps Shanawdithit remembered 1811 well as one morning, early in that year, began with fear and violence. Imagine being wakened before dawn, about 6:30 a.m., on a cold January 24 morning, with the sights and sounds of intruders invading your village, breaking into your home. Twenty-three men and one boy stood before Shanawdithit, the other startled children and the men and women of her tiny community. Three of those men were probably no strangers: the dreaded furriers William Cull, Thomas Taylor and Matthew Hughster. They stood out from the other outsiders as they wore no uniforms and they carried rifles rather than the more innocuous-looking pistols worn by the people they had led to the encampment. Their presence would have heightened the tension severely.[14]

There followed three-and-one-half tense hours of negotiation, with few words spoken and fewer understood.[15] Even the gift-giving gestures of the uninvited guests would be open to suspicion, as that was an unusual way for white people to act. Four Beothuk men left with the intruders. At least two were uncles of Shanawdithit. One, Nonosabasut, was probably the leader of the community. The largest mamateek was his. He suspected a trap. Two men in blue were left behind. Shanawdithit and others standing around her might have wondered out loud: "Are they here to ensure that we cannot escape?" The men in blue couldn't have said anything to calm the people's fears, the Beothuk words had no meaning for them.

Time passed in uncertainty. Tension grew as first Nonosabasut then, not long afterwards, another one of the four returned, having fled from the strangers. When a third came back, the people must have believed that the time for action had arrived. The Beothuk killed the two British navy marines so that the whole community might be able to get away without the white men being able to pick up their trail quickly. This decision must have been hard to reach as it entailed risking retaliation and having to abandon a warm home in the January cold.

One grim footnote to this story must be mentioned, and it requires explanation and a balanced discussion. In the lower left-hand corner of one of Shanawdithit's drawings, written by Cormack, are the following words:

> *Marine Head* stuck on a pole around which the Indians danced and sang two hours in the woods at A, they having carried the head with them. The other marines head they left at B and on their return there in the

spring they danced and sang round it in like manner.
(Howley 1974, sketch 1, between pages 238 and 239)

The points A and B that Cormack referred to show a circle with a head on a pole. Cormack seems not to have been above the typical morbid white fascination and fear of the custom sometimes inaccurately referred to as skull worship (see Fardy 1988:14, 95-6). It is well to point out that the skulls were trophies of war, not objects of worship. The dancing and singing most likely were statements of thanksgiving to the spirits, celebrating that the Beothuk had not been defeated in the surprise attack by the English. Survival itself was a victory worthy of a ceremony in those harsh days.

Non-Native writers during the nineteenth century and most of the twentieth century were silent concerning the European practice of taking skulls as 'trophies of science.' No negative comments were recorded when the skulls of Shanawdithit's uncle and aunt were removed from their burial hut, eventually to be taken by Cormack to Britain, where they remain today in the Royal Scottish Museum in Edinburgh. Photographs of their skulls appear in a biography of Demasduit (Fardy 1988:91-2). Nor do we read any disparaging remarks concerning the fact that Dr. William Carson, under whose medical care Shanawdithit was placed, took her skull and presented it for study to the Royal College of Physicians in London. It was destroyed by a bomb during World War II.

What happened to the fourth member of the group of Beothuk who went with the Englishmen? He appears to have remained with them until they discovered the headless marines. Then, understandably, he fled. Shanawdithit records the story of this man, her uncle, with a small figure in the sketch depicting the events surrounding the 1811 invasion. He is shown walking a dotted line that represents the path he took to try to escape the English and to attempt to find his people again. Cormack added written comments from information he received from Shanawdithit. First, there is the somewhat comic "Trousers thrown away during his flight." This apparently refers to swan-skin pants her uncle had been given by the English. The next written comment is "Nancy's uncle running from Captain b. after returning to the Lake and witnessing what had happened." Shanawdithit was often termed Nancy April by Cormack and others, the last name reflecting the month of her eventual capture. Finally, we read the good news that after the Beothuk refugees had travelled through the cold, dark night, they had reached a spot where they remained for a day and a half until they saw Shanawdithit's uncle, who had "escaped and joined them" there.

It was all a sad mistake, typical of the time. The mission of the early morning intruders had been one of peace. Lieutenant David Buchan (i.e., Capt b) of the British Royal Army, the leader of the expedition, was travelling under orders to try to establish a positive relationship with the Beothuk. His superiors hoped that this would put an end to the killings. Fortunately for the Beothuk, there would be no retaliation. Buchan understood why they had killed the marines and fled. In words that reflect the man's compassion, he wrote, "My opinion of the natives is not the worse for the fatal circumstance that has occurred, for I do not think the deed to have been premeditated" (Howley 1974:89).

One other tragic aspect of this failed peace initiative should be mentioned. It brought the Beothuk into closer physical contact with Europeans, probably resulting in the spread of disease to the Native group, thus hastening their extinction.

Shots in the Forest

It was probably within only a few years of this incident when Shanawdithit had another great scare. She was washing caribou meat by the shores of the Exploits River. After she had finished her task, and was turning around to walk up the river bank, a shot rang out from across the river. In less time than it takes to take a deep breath, she was hit in the back and legs, probably with buckshot. She dropped the meat and limped away into the protecting woods as fast as her bleeding legs could carry her. She would be shot on at least one other occasion in her lifetime.

The man who shot her in this case was the Micmac furrier, Noel Boss. He bragged some time later that he had killed 99 Beothuk before that day. By his reckoning, Shanawdithit would have made the even century. While his kill score was probably exaggerated, his furrier attitude was certainly authentic.

She would lose close family members to shooting deaths in 1818. Her mother, a brother and a sister were shot to death "... when attempting to reach an island, in a canoe, to collect the eggs of wild fowl" (1836 report, in Marshall 1996:207). That was an especially sad year for Shanawdithit; her father died that same year, as did someone referred to mysteriously as her "lover" who:

... at a time when they were perishing for want of food, followed a deer [caribou] for some days over the country, which was covered with snow, and lying down to rest, he fell asleep and was frozen to death. (ibid.)

The Peytons

No story of Shanawdithit could be told without some discussion of the Peytons, father and son. Broadly speaking, they were neighbours of the Beothuk, they lived by the mouth of the Exploits River. John Peyton Sr. was born in 1747 and had become over the years a very successful fish and fur merchant. Typical of the well-to-do members of the Newfoundland merchant class of the time, he divided his time between earning money in Newfoundland and spending it in Britain. Magistrate John Bland identified Peyton as the greatest enemy the Beothuk had. In a letter dated September 1, 1790, he described a situation in which a Beothuk couple had been killed, their daughter kidnapped and taken to Britain:

> I am not certain that the men charged with this murder were not in the employ of one Peyton, who for many years has possessed a Salmon Fishery in the Bay of Exploits, and at this time resides at some place near Poole in England. Peyton had rendered himself infamous for his persecution of the Indians. The stories told of this man would shock humanity to relate, and for the sake of humanity, it is to be wished are not true.... (Howley 1974:56)

The following year, Peyton led a summer raid on the Beothuk. After travelling for three days, Peyton and his gang struck a small Beothuk encampment. They attacked quickly, firing their guns so as to kill as many as they could before any Beothuk could run away. When the raiders stepped inside one of the mamateeks they saw

> a man so much wounded as not to be able to stand.- One of Peyton's traps was lying by him, the bed of which he had been beating into arrows on a flat stone which served as an anvil. When they entered the wigwam, the wounded man sat on his bench &

> defended himself with the remaining part of the trap:
> but being soon overpowered, Peyton wrested it from
> him, & beat out his brains with it. (Such 1978:65)

Clearly John Peyton Sr. was a man who wanted to do away with the Beothuk. Not so easy to interpret is John Peyton Jr. He was born in Britain the same year as the raid (1791), his parents' only child when John Sr. was in his mid-forties. The son inherited his father's business and did well in his own right. By 1818 he was appointed as a Justice of the Peace for the Twillingate-New World Island area of Notre Dame Bay.

Shanawdithit would soon learn that the Peytons were to be feared. In 1816, as a girl in her teens, Shanawdithit witnessed the killing of one of her people at the hands of John Peyton Sr. and two accomplices. No trial resulted, despite the fact there was then a law against killing Beothuk. The incident must have made quite an impact on Shanawdithit. In 1829, she was able to represent what happened in one of her drawings, including what went on both before and after the murder.

On the night of September 18, 1818, seventeen-year-old Shanawdithit was part of a small band of Beothuk that committed a theft from John Peyton Jr. that would have deadly consequences in the near future. Usually in the past they had taken a few small items: knives, axes, marten traps, hooks, lines or canvas from sails. This served more to annoy the wealthy fish merchant than to spur him to retaliatory action. In the last few years, however, the Beothuk had been more bold; desperate times and dwindling numbers required more drastic measures. Unfortunately, this would also increase the severity of the reaction.

Peyton's substantial house and well-stocked storage buildings were located at Lower Sandy Point in the Bay of Exploits by the mouth of the Exploits River. 'Wild Indians' had been seen in the area recently, so Peyton placed guards to watch over a large open boat that was loaded with the season's haul of salmon and furs, as well as two muskets, two silver watches, some marten traps, assorted kitchen utensils and a small amount of money. Peyton stood watch himself until about midnight. In part satisfied that nothing was going to happen, in part too cold and tired to stand on the exposed wharf much longer, Peyton took a break for a short nap, lying on a couch in his house, his clothes still on.

Let's shift now to the Beothuk perspective. It was mid September, which can be a cold, desolate time along the northeast shores of Newfoundland. Before they went back up the Exploits River to their wintering site on Red Indian Lake, the Beothuk group would try to raid the Peytons. This Beothuk party was undoubtedly in need of food and of any useful items that would make winter survival more possible and starvation less of a threat.

For several days they had been hiding in the woods covering a high ridge overlooking Peyton's place. On top of the ridge was Canoe Hill, so-named because it resembled a canoe turned over. On that hill was a tall birch tree, from whose branches a Beothuk scout looked out and relayed to the others what was going on below. They knew that Peyton's boat contained enough salmon to feed the whole Beothuk population, then doubtless under 50. It would be more dangerous a raid than they were accustomed to; that was evident by the fact that there was someone constantly on guard beside the boat. Maybe they would be returning home empty-handed to the children and the elderly. They did not intend to give up easily, however. The prize to be won was too important, the price of failure too high. They had managed to creep down to the water and to their canoe, which they silently paddled to a place of safety underneath the pier to which the boat was tied. As Peyton watched over his boat, he was standing over the very people he was trying to keep away from his possessions.

Then their opportunity came. They heard Peyton's steps walking towards the land and perhaps saw him go into his house—for how long no one knew. Quickly, they seized their chance. Shanawdithit, young enough to still see this as an adventure, must have heard her heart pounding so loudly it would have seemed to have been audible to others. Quietly, they slipped the boat from its moorings. They were unfamiliar with handling a vessel such as this, so with their canoe they towed and drifted it across the bay to a spot some 15 kilometres away. They would not reach the other side before their night's work was discovered by the boat's owner. Restless and suspicious, he had slept for only about an hour and a half. Fortunately, he had no idea where his boat had been taken to, once he discovered that it was missing, and it was too dark to go chasing after them. The Beothuk, then, had time enough to beach the boat on the shore beside the mouth of Charles Brook. Such equipment and supplies as they could use and carry with them they took. Significantly, they did not take the two muskets, instruments of the death of friends and family alike. Instead, they broke the two weapons so they would kill no more Beothuk.

Peyton was incensed, but he proceeded in a more legalistic manner than his father would have. Perhaps that was his nature. Perhaps the times were more civilized than in his father's day. Perhaps as a newly minted justice of the peace he had to at least be seen to operate within the law. After he retrieved his boat, Peyton calculated that his net loss, including both theft and damages to his property, was between £149 and £150. He then applied to the governor to be permitted to go inland and fetch his stolen goods. Naturally, permission was granted.

Getting back his property was one reason for him to want to travel into Beothuk country. There could very well have been others. Visions of £100 bounties may have danced before his eyes. Bring back one Beothuk and he would almost break even, especially if he were to find some of his stolen goods. Bring back more than one and he could turn a profit. Further, it is not unlikely that dark thoughts of retribution lurked in the back of his mind. Certainly, the least imaginable reason would be the one he presented to the court later that year: "… the rescuing of that tribe of our fellow-creatures from the misery and persecution they are exposed to in the interior from Micmacs, and on the exterior by the Whites" (Howley 1974:108).

The stage was set for confrontation on March 5, 1819. The Peyton gang was made up of old John Sr., then in his early 70s, young John Jr. and seven or eight furriers working for them. They took by surprise the Beothuk encampment of 31 (all the remaining Beothuk): 7 couples and 17 others living in 3 winter mamateeks. There are two fundamentally different types of accounts of what happened. The first is the one that was presented in court and accepted by the presiding judge. The second, more truthful, was what came to light years after the case was over and innocence had been declared. The differences will be pointed out section by section.

First, both versions agree that the Peyton party flushed out a group of Beothuk that included a woman carrying an infant. Not as capable of escaping as the others, she passed the infant on to a nearby man. Stories of the capture of this woman, Shanawdithit's aunt Demasduit, differ distinctly depending on the source. According to the defendant, John Peyton Jr.:

> I could not tell at this time whether the Indian I saw
> was a male or female. I showed myself on the point
> openly, when the Indian discovered me she for a

moment was motionless. She screamed out as soon as she appeared to make me out and run off. I immediately pursued her, but did not gain on her until I had taken off my rackets [snowshoes] and jacket, when I came up with her fast, she kept looking back at me over her shoulder, I then dropped my gun on the snow and held up my hands to show her I had no gun, and on my pointing to my gun which was then some distance behind me; she stopped. I did the same and endeavoured to convince her I would not hurt her. I then advanced and gave her my hand, she gave hers to me and to all my party as they came up. (Howley 1974:107)

The events seem even more innocuous and innocent when Governor Hamilton reports of the affair to the Earl of Bathurst:

Mr Peyton however, by throwing away his arms, and making signs of an amicable nature, induced one to stop, who upon his coming up proved to be a woman, and who interchanged with himself and his men, such expressions of a friendly disposition as appeared to be perfectly understood by her. (Howley 1974:119)

In 1829, another member of the Peyton party, E. Slade, admitted the following, putting the capture in a slightly more sinister light:

[T]he woman... did not run so fast. Mr [Peyton] loosened his provision bag from his back and let it fall, threw away his gun and hatchet and set off at a speed that soon overtook the woman. One man and myself did the same, except our guns. The rest, picking up our things followed. On overtaking the woman, she instantly fell on her knees, and tearing open the c[a]ss[o]ck, (a dress composed of deer-skin bound with fur), showing her breasts to prove she was a woman, and begged for mercy. (Howley 1974:99)

Another member of the party, John Day, included in his version of what happened a reason why Peyton and the others were able to catch up with her. It had nothing to do with her being convinced of his dubious peaceful intentions. Reported, albeit second-hand, by a good friend a short time after Day's death, his story went as follows:

> ... [S]he was very ill at the time of her capture, yet she took her baby in her arms and ran after the other Indians as they retreated, but was not able to keep up with them. Her husband seeing she was likely to be captured, turned back and took the child from her, but in her weak state she could not run fast enough and was soon overtaken. (Howley 1974:281)

The next part of the story where the versions differ markedly is in the reaction of Demasduit's husband, Nonosabasut. Along with several other Beothuk, he approached the men who were attempting to kidnap his wife. They put their bows down when menaced by the guns of the white intruders. Missing from Peyton's account and from the governor's whitewashing report was Nonosabasut's first gesture. Slade refers to it at some length:

> [T]he ill fated husband of... our captive, advanced with a branch of a fir tree (spruce) in his hand. When about ten yards off he stopped and made a long oration. He spoke at least ten minutes; towards the last his gesture became very animated and his eye "shot fire." He concluded very mildly, and advancing, shook hands with many of the party.... (Howley 1974:99)

Day identified the role of the spruce bough: "Breaking off a fir bough he placed it on his forehead, as a flag of truce and boldly came towards the white men" (Howley 1974:281).

Nonosabasut drew out a hatchet, but the weapon was taken from him at gunpoint. The English raiders then proceeded to leave with his wife in tow, despite all he had tried to do to peacefully persuade them not to take her away. You can well imagine what was going on in his mind—"I can't let them they take away my wife, the nursing mother of my infant child!" This was too much for the Beothuk husband and father. Nonosabasut then staged, with no weapons but his hands, a one-man attack on the group of armed men. He made a good account of himself and seemed to have managed to grasp John Peyton Sr. by the throat or collar. Ultimately, however, his fate was predictable. He was shot dead. The Peytons and their accomplices would then spin a tale of self-defence against a crazed 'wild Indian.'

Shanawdithit was an eyewitness. In a portrayal both sad and simple, she later depicted (Figure 6) on paper the scenes surrounding the event: her uncle speaking to the furriers, his dead body lying on the ice. The probable impact of the man's death is succinctly stated in the words of the great Newfoundland historian George Storey:

> It is a plausible conjecture that his death removed the most experienced and decisive leader of the surviving Beothuck, sealed the enmity between the two competing peoples, and hastened the disintegration of the remnants of the tribe. (Storey 1983:243)

Demasduit tried unsuccessfully three times to escape. Eventually, she was taken to St. John's where she was named Mary March, named like others before her after the month of her capture. As it was then illegal to kill a Beothuk, a court case ensued. Not surprisingly, the plea was self-defence, the justification of Peyton's expedition the obtaining of stolen property (some of which was brought back from the Beothuk) and the unlikely altruism of the statement quoted above, i.e., that the Peytons wanted to save the Beothuk from their Micmac enemies. Their right to kidnap Demasduit does not seem to have been questioned. The witnesses all were white men, as were the lawyers, the judge, the jury and everyone else in court except for Demasduit, who did not speak or understand English well enough to know what was happening. The victim was 'just a savage.' The defendants included a prominent merchant and a justice of the peace. Innocence was the predictable verdict. The foreman of the jury stated that:

> The Grand Jury are of [the] opinion that no malice preceded the transaction, and that there was no intention on the part of Peyton's party to get possession of any of them by such violence as would occasion bloodshed. But it appears that the deceased came by his death in consequence of the attack on Peyton, Sr., and his subsequent obstinacy, and not desisting when repeatedly menaced by some of the party for that purpose, warrant their acting on the defensive. (Howley 1974:105)

How would they expect the man to react when someone was abducting his wife? Was it "obstinate" to persist in resisting such an abduction? Can kidnapping ever be a non-violent act with "no malice" preceding it?

In one of Shanawdithit's pictures (Figure 6), a spot "B" was drawn to show where the next tiny act in this tragic play took place. The words written underneath the spot are Cormack's, "Mary March's child died here at B 2 days after its mother was taken away" (Howley 1974: Sketch III).

Did the child, a little girl, die of exposure or of the disease that Demasduit might have been suffering from? Or did Demasduit expose her breasts to John Peyton Jr. not just to show that she was a woman but also a nursing mother with a child that might starve without her?

One more sad scene of this tragic story remains to be told. It was acted out sometime early in February, 1820, one month shy of a year since Shanawdithit had last seen her aunt. Her people, now numbering 27, were camped in 3 mamateeks by the shores of the Exploits River. Someone saw and then reported a party of some 50 Englishmen making their way slowly upriver on the sometimes treacherous ice. If the person or persons who spied them had a chance to get a good look at the Englishmen, at least two faces would have been familiar, John Peyton Jr. and Commander David Buchan. The Beothuk then hastily packed what they could carry and fled unseen by the invaders downriver to the unlikely hiding place of the river mouth; they stayed there for roughly a month.

Cautiously they returned, taking complicated, fox-like routes whenever they saw the campsites or the footprints of the Buchan and Peyton party on the river ice. When the Beothuk refugees returned to the winter encampment they had left so quickly, Shanawdithit and the others saw signs that the Englishmen had been there in their absence. Then they spotted it: a cloth tent pitched beside one of the mamateeks. Carefully, they opened the flap and saw, suspended six feet above the ground, a long box covered with brown cloth. All around the box on the ground were objects of English manufacture, some of them wrapped up in a familiar looking coat.

Inside the box they found, probably to no one's surprise but to everyone's horror, the recently deceased body of Demasduit. More goods were placed inside the coffin, as was also the custom of the Beothuk.

The original intent of the second Buchan expedition, as tragic as the first, was to bring Demasduit back to her people, one final effort to establish peace. She had died of tuberculosis on the way home on

January 8. Some three months later, when spring was in the country but not in their hearts, the remaining Beothuk buried Demasduit beside her husband.

There is an ironic twist to all of this. Even had Demasduit been returned alive to her people, as was planned, she might have been rejected, even killed, by them. A writer indirectly informed by Shanawdithit claims that:

> [A] tradition of old times told that the first white men that came over the great lake were from the good spirit, and that those who came next were sent by the bad spirit; and that if the Boeothics made peace and talked with the white men which belonged to the bad spirit... that they would not, after they died, go to the happy island, nor hunt, nor fish, nor feast in the country of the good spirit, which was far away, where the sun went down behind the mountains. (Jukes 1836, in Marshall 1996:215)

Those who were kidnapped were supposedly thought contaminated by the contact with whites. According to the same source:

> [I]t was an invariable religious principle laid down by her people to sacrifice to the m[a]nes [i.e., spirits] of the victims slain by the whites and the Mik-maks any Boeothic who had been in contact with them. (ibid.)

There could be some truth to this. The woman that William Cull returned to the Beothuk in 1803 was rumoured to have later turned up in Anglo-Irish settlements; perhaps she had little choice. Demasduit may also have felt that she had passed a line of no return. Once she was in St. John's, she seemed more anxious to get her baby back and stay with the English than to return to her people.

Not much is known about what life entailed for the Beothuk over the next two years. According to Shanawdithit, in the winter of 1822-3 there were 27 Beothuk left alive. They lived in four mamateeks by a lake in the watershed of Badger Bay, two bays north of where the Exploits River flows into the ocean.

In one of those mamateeks lived Shanawadthit's father's brother, the same one who had been the last to escape Buchan's party in

1811. Along with him were his daughter and five others. No one living in that mamateek would survive the year. This household's tragic story began in March. Shanawdithit's uncle and her female cousin headed to Badger Bay, hunger driving them to search for mussels and other shellfish. The path they took, like the one the man had taken 12 years before, was depicted in one of the Shanawdithit's drawings (Figure 7). This time, the path ended not with a joyous reunion but with a pair of killings. Two furriers, Stephen Adams and James Carey, shot the uncle then the cousin. As we will see, no conviction ensued.

Six more deaths followed shortly thereafter in the Beothuk camp, starvation the most likely culprit. The remaining 19 then moved camp to the east, occupying now three mamateeks. There two died, maybe children who had lived with Shanawdithit's uncle. Then, sometime in April, a decision was made inside Shanawdithit's mamateek. They would follow the trail of desperation her father's brother and her cousin had taken to Badger Bay. They needed the mussels there to ease their pangs of hunger. In Shanawdithit's map (Figure 7) we see that the path they took was the same as the one followed by her uncle and cousin before.

Different accounts tell us varying versions of what happened next. There is also some question as to who is involved. We find people being referred to as Shanawdithit's father, mother and a sister that was their daughter; yet Shanawdithit's parents were reported as having died in 1818. There are two possible explanations. One is that Shanawdithit was adopted after her parents' death; the other relates to kinship terminology. It could be that the Beothuk called their mother's sister by the name of mother. This is not uncommon in the anthropological literature and is a feature of the Eastern Algonquian language Delaware (O'Meara 1996:393 and 534). Likewise, the Beothuk might have referred to father's brothers as 'father,' this also found among a good number of Native peoples (see Steckley 1993:37).

We do know that the family came into contact with a party of furriers led by an old family acquaintance, William Cull. **Mamjaesdoo**, the one referred to as Shanawdithit's father, seems to have been the first to die. He fell through the spring ice, either attempting to escape from the furriers or trying to stop them from taking his wife. They had become separated during the search for food. Another family member, whose identity was never revealed, disappeared at this time as well.

Most accounts agree that **Doodebewshet**, referred to as Shanawdithit's mother, was the first to come into the hands of the furriers. Through hunger and probable sickness she did not have the will, nor the capacity, to resist. Her two daughters were soon to join her in surrendering to the furriers, perhaps as much as two weeks later.

They all received new names, like prisoners being assigned numbers. As has been mentioned before, Shanawdithit was called Nancy (or Nance) April after the unhappy month of her capture. Her sister became Easter Eve, named after the day of her taking. Doodebewshet was called Beth Decker, as the party who captured her was engaged in decking a vessel.

At this point the spotlight usually focuses on Shanawdithit and leaves in darkness the others who remained in the encampment, whom Shanawdithit would never see again. They included another one of her father's brothers, her brother with his daughter and son, Demasduit's mother, that woman's sister and sister's son, two of Demasduit's brothers, one having with him his wife and son, and a female cousin. What happened to these people? In 1824, two Micmacs saw and reputedly exchanged "friendly gestures" (Howley 1974:224) with a party of Beothuk in two canoes across the Exploits River. In the spring of 1826, signs of a Beothuk presence in the area had been spotted by some Micmac not far from Badger Bay. There is nothing concrete after that.

Going against the likely expectations of the Beothuk mother and her two frightened daughters, William Cull did not kill the three Beothuk. He took his £300 worth of captives to Twillingate, then a bustling little town of 720. Shanawdithit had never seen that number of people in all her life, let alone all at once, coming out of their houses to stare. Once there, Cull handed them over to someone the three women knew well and feared—John Peyton Jr., the local magistrate. For a second time, their fate was abandoned to someone the Beothuk had learned not to trust. Again, there would be a pleasant, but somewhat suspicious surprise.

Peyton took them to St. John's, a 300-kilometre trip on the open sea by schooner. Also on board was one of the two men who had killed Shanawdithit's uncle and cousin in March and was being brought to trial.

We have several descriptions of Shanawdithit from people who saw and met her in St. John's. Probably the best physical description, albeit a somewhat romantic sounding one, is attributed to John McGregor, writing in 1836:

> Her person, in height above the middle stature,
> possessed classical regularity of form. Her face bore
> striking similarity to that of Napoleon, and the olive
> cast of her complexion added to this resemblance.
> Her hair was jet black; her finely pencilled brows—
> her long, darting lashes—her dark, vigilant, and
> piercing eyes, were all remarkable striking and
> beautiful. Her teeth were white, even and perfectly
> sound. Her hands and feet, small and well formed.
> (Marshall 1996:204)

Shanawdithit was clearly a woman of some spirit. This was exhibited when, along with her mother and sister, she was dressed up in fancy European-style clothes and paraded through the main streets of St. John's. According to an eyewitness, James Wheeler, an old man telling stories of his youth:

> [T]he people stopped everywhere to look at them,
> especially the young folk, himself among the number,
> and when the children would crowd around them,
> Shanawdithit would make a pretence of trying to catch
> some of them. They would immediately scatter in all
> directions, child like, then she would give vent to
> unbridled laughter. Their fear appeared to be a matter
> which greatly pleased her, nor did she seem the least
> abashed at anything. (Howley 1974:174)

Both McGregor and Dr. William Carson agree that, despite her capture, she maintained a sense of pride that brooked no treatment that she thought lacked in respect (Marshall 1996:204). We also learn that she had considerable artistic talent. We are told, for example, of one instance in which:

> when a black lead pencil was put into her hand and a
> piece of white paper laid upon the table she was in
> raptures. She made a few marks on the paper
> apparently to try the pencil; then in one flourish she
> drew a deer perfectly, and what is most surprising,
> she began at the tip of the tail. (Howley 1974:175)

Later on, she would demonstrate that her talent had been developed on several traditional Beothuk media; she carved combs out of caribou antlers. Additionally, "She would take a piece of birch bark, double it up and bite with her teeth into a variety of figures of animals or other designs, i.e., to say when the bark was again unfolded, the impressions thereon would be such" (Howley 1974:175).

Shanawdithit and her mother and sister were only a few weeks in St. John's together. While they were there, the trial of the killers of her uncle and cousin was taking place. One can gain a sense of the one-sided bias of the evidence presented from the following account of the killing, written by Methodist minister Rev. William Wilson in June, 1823. Wilson is not the most reliable of reporters, clearly uncritical of anything the furriers said:

> In the month of March last a party of men from the neighbourhood of Twillingate were in the country hunting for fur. The party went two and two in different directions. After a while one of these small parties saw on a distant hill a man coming towards them. Supposing him while at a distance to be one of their own party, they fired a powder gun to let their friend know their where-about. The Red Indian generally runs at the report of the musket, not so in the present instance, the man quickened his pace towards them. They now, from his gait and dress, discerned that he was an Indian, but thought that he was a Micmac and still felt no anxiety. Soon they found their mistake and ascertained that the stranger was one of the Red Indians. He was approaching in a threatening manner with a large club in his hand. They now put themselves in a posture of defence and beckoned the Indian to surrender. This was of no use, he came on with double fury, and when nearly at the muzzle of their guns one of the men fired and the Indian fell dead at their feet. As they had killed the man without any design or intention, they felt deeply concerned, and resolved at once to leave the hunting ground and return home. (Howley 1974:171)

This story sounds suspiciously like the one that Peyton had concocted concerning the killing of Nonosabasut, the man's brother. How likely is it that a man armed only with a club would run a long way to attack two gunmen? Are we to suppose that the dead man's daughter attacked the self-defending furriers in the same way before she too was killed? The non-furrier, non-white witnesses were dead, so we cannot know the other side of the story. And what was the verdict? In Rev. Wilson's words, "as there was no evidence against them, they were acquitted" (ibid.).

Shanawdithit and the others were taken by Peyton back to the mouth of the Exploits River and were then left at Charles Brook, where in happier times five years before Shanawdithit and her raiding party had landed with Peyton's boat. Presents were left with the three women, yet another futile peace-making endeavour. Two of them carried another gift from the white men as well. From their first days in St. John's, it was remarked that Doodebewshet and her eldest daughter were not well; they were suffering from tuberculosis.

Doodebewshet seems to have had some ability as a healer. As they camped by the shore of the Exploits River, she built a sweat lodge, a small covered structure in which she put water and medicinal herbs on heated rocks. By this means Doodebewshet intended to heal her ailing daughter through sweating and by breathing in the medicine. This traditional method, often effective for ailments and disorders the Beothuk suffered from prior to contact with Europeans, did not work in this case; the young woman died.

Peyton's son Thomas, a friend of Howley's, reported much later what happened next:

> Nancy and her mother then paddled up to Lower Sandy Point, where she told the men in charge of the salmon station her sister had gone "winum," asleep, dead. The men then went down and buried the body. Her mother died a few days later at Sandy Point. Nance sewed the body up in a blanket and it was buried there, she was then sent down to Exploits Island to Mr Peyton's house. (Howley 1974:282)

After the death of her sister and mother, Shanawdithit lived as a kind of servant at the Peyton household for five years. According to the recollections of a man who lived in the vicinity:

> Whilst she lived with Peyton she acted, freely and without being obliged, the part of servant, and a very industrious and intelligent servant she was. She made the fire, prepared the tea, swept and scrubbed

the floor, washed the clothes, cooked &c. (Howley
1974:180)

She seems to have had responsibilities with the Peyton children
as well. Bishop Inglis reported that "She is fond of children, who
leave their mother to go to her..." (Howley 1974:296). Perhaps this
last remark presents us with a clue as to why an often antagonistic
relationship existed between Shanawdithit and Mrs. Peyton. Eleanor
Mahey from Carbonear was 17 when she married 30-year-old John
Peyton Jr. in February, 1823. The down-to-earth Beothuk woman was
likely more fun for the children to be with than their mother—raised
as the latter probably was in the aristocratic tradition of
Newfoundland's elite. It wouldn't be surprising if Mrs. Peyton resented
having her parental authority undermined by a 'savage.'

Several witnesses record Shanawdithit's jibes at the expense of
the apparently brittle Eleanor Peyton. An elderly Mrs. Jure reported
to Howley, long after the fact, that when she and Shanawdithit both
worked for the Peytons, the Beothuk woman was "very pert at times,
and when her mistress had occasion to scold her, she would answer
very sharply, 'what de matter now Missa Peyton, what you grumble
bout'" (Howley 1974:175).

A man whose mother had been a servant of the Peytons also said
that Shanawdithit "openly defied Mrs Peyton when the old lady
happened to be cross with the servants. Nance would laugh in her
face, and say, 'well done Misses. I like to hear you jaw, that right;' or
'jawing again Misses'" (Howley 1974:181).

The tension between the two women was also alluded to by John
Stark in a letter of September, 1828 telling William Cormack of
Shanawdithit's leaving the Peyton household. In that letter Stark
wrote: "I ought to say that Mrs. Peyton was quite willing for her to
come away..." (Howley 1974:202).

Could this antipathy be explained in part because there was
something sexual going on between Shanawdithit and John Peyton
Jr.? Both were probably more creatures of the frontier than was the
apparently proper Mrs. Peyton. It is unlikely, however, that there
was anything happening between John Peyton and Shanawdithit. All
accounts that report of her relationship with men speak of her refusing
their advances (see Howley 1974:175 and 181). The exception occurred
when she ran her fingers through the large red beard of an
embarrassed sailor, red being a revered colour to the Beothuk. They

were termed 'Red Indians' because of the red ochre that they used to colour their skin, hair, clothes and other possessions.

One writer, commenting on Shanawdithit's relationship with men, said the following:

> She was strictly modest and would allow no freedom on the part of the opposite sex. Once when an individual attempted some familiarity he was so rudely repulsed that he never afterwards dared to repeat the offence. She would not tolerate him near her. He was a Mudty man (bad man). (Howley 1974:181)

Curiously, this same source, a man named Gill whose mother worked for the Peytons when Shanawdithit lived there, claimed:

> Nance was a married woman, according to her own account and left two children in the interior, which she used to express great anxiety about. She said her tribe was very strict about the moral law, and visited severe penalties on any one who transgressed. Burning alive at the stake being the fate of the adulterer, which was witnessed by the whole tribe who danced in a circle around the victim. (Howley 1974:181)

These two stories, of her being a married woman and of her people having strict punishments for adultery, are probably linked and could well have been tools employed by Shanawdithit to keep English men away from her. Perhaps, with her mysterious unnamed lover dead, she wanted no part of any other man, especially one who was English.

The nature of Peyton's and Shanawdithit's relationship will probably never be known. Equally mysterious is why he even kept her at his home. He initially seems to have thought of Shanawdithit, her mother and sister as a burden. He charged the government £51, 15 shillings and 4 pence for lodging her from August 1 to October 16, 1823, and for other expenses incurred in taking care of the three women. Perhaps he had come to feel guilty concerning his family's role in the destruction of the Beothuk. As stated above, there was a romanticism concerning 'vanishing' nations of the east coast. That may even have influenced Peyton, now that the Beothuk no longer could raid his supplies.

One practice engaged in by Shanawdithit during her stay at the Peytons's should be mentioned. It tells of the loneliness and the fatalism that accompanied her being the last Beothuk. Uncharitably, the instances described were presented by some writers as exemplifying her melancholy nature. Referred to were times when Shanawdithit would go into the woods for days, taking a kind of vision quest. As she would go to enter the woods, "she would turn round saying, 'All gone widdun [asleep or dead] Nance go widdun too, no more come Nance, run away, no more come'" (Howley 1974:182). Going into the woods was a way of speaking to the spirits of her mother and sister. Doing this seems to have given her a measure of happiness:

> [S]he generally came back singing and laughing, or talking aloud to herself. She would also frequently indulge in the same practice at night, and when asked what was the matter would reply, Nance talking to her mother and sister. When told not to be foolish, that they were dead and she could not talk to them, she would say, 'a yes they here, me see them and talk to them.' (Howley 1974:181)

The next white male to influence Shanawdithit's life was William Epps Cormack. He was definitely a character of the nineteenth century: the well-educated, scientist-explorer-philanthropist, somewhat eccentric child of a well-to-do-merchant's family. Newfoundlander by birth, but raised mostly in the aristocratic circles of upper-class Scotland, he studied botany, biology and geology at the University of Edinburgh and University of Glasgow.

He returned to his native Newfoundland in 1822 to become the first white man to walk across the island, exploring its far reaches from late August to December. While he successfully recorded the flora, fauna and geology of the area, naming places along the way, he did not encounter that which he wanted most to see—Beothuk. On October 2, 1827, he set up a fund and founded the Boeothick Institution, "for the purpose of opening a communication with, and promoting the civilization of the Red Indians of Newfoundland" (Howley 1974:184). Included in the number of wealthy patrons of the institution was John Peyton Jr., who was unanimously thanked for his good work and was "requested to continue to use his best endeavours to promote the humane objects of this institution" (Howley 1947:186).

In September, 1828, two men from the institution arrived at the Peytons to take Shanawdithit away to St. John's; John Peyton Jr. was not there. Mrs. Peyton, not wanting to make such a decision hastily on her own, initially asked them to wait until her husband got back. Eventually, however, she agreed. Her husband was later to object strongly to this move.

Shanawdithit arrived at St. John's on September 20, 1828, to great fanfare. What happened next is curious. While Cormack declared that obtaining information from Shanawdithit about her people was of vital importance, he had a strange way of showing his supposed great interest. He was more often away than at home during her stay in the city. His absence may have something to do with the social impropriety of a single woman, 27 years of age, living with a single man in his early thirties. A friend wrote a letter to Cormack, warning him of the potential danger to his reputation.

Perhaps Cormack stayed away because he simply preferred the more exciting work of founding organizations, setting off on expeditions and starting grand new projects to the more mundane labour of sitting down with Shanawdithit and getting her to answer his questions. In late October, with an Innu, a Micmac and an Abenaki as his guides, Cormack tried to uncover signs of Beothuk still alive and outside of 'captivity.' They went to Badger Bay and found indirect evidence that some people had been in a Beothuk encampment that spring and summer. However, they were disappointed in finding nothing and no one on the Exploits River or at Red Indian Lake. He returned after a month-long journey in the interior, but he did not stay home long.

After six weeks, he was off again in January 1829, new dreams to chase, his old ones causing him to declare financial insolvency. Much of what we know of the Beothuk comes from those six weeks. Before he left, Shanawdithit gave him three presents as tokens of their last farewell: a lock of her hair, a quartz crystal from the shore of Red Indian Lake and a rounded piece of granite.

After Cormack left, Shanawdithit lived with the family of James Simms, Attorney General of Newfoundland. We do not know what she was thinking or doing at that time. Her mind was probably travelling back in time. We do know that she was dying of tuberculosis. She was probably aware of what the symptoms meant; she had seen them often enough. On June 6, 1829, she died in a local hospital, and on June 8, she was buried in the Church of England cemetery on the south side of St. John's. She didn't stay there. Just as English-speaking Newfoundlanders could not leave her people alone, so they could not let her bones rest. Her body was exhumed, her skull taken for 'scientific purposes.' Her headless body was reburied. In 1903, the graveyard was dismantled to make way for the railway. Her bones became lost. Like her people, they disappeared.

The last words in this biography come from the perceptive comments of Newfoundlander John Bland, magistrate and a soul sympathetic to Shawnadithit's people. In 1790 he wrote:

> It ought to be remembered that these savages have a natural right to this island and every invasion of a natural right is a violation of the principle of justice. They have been progressively driven from South to North, and though their removal has been produced by a slow and silent operation, it has nevertheless had all the effect of violent compulsion. In proportion as their means of procuring subsistence became narrowed, their population must necessarily have decreased, and before the lapse of another century, the English nation, like the Spanish, may have affixed to its character the indelible reproach of having extirpated a whole race of people. (Howley 1974:58)

Appendix A: Beothuk Cognates with Other Algonquian Languages

The following are examples relating Beothuk words to those in some Algonquian languages spoken in eastern Canada: Micmac, Abenaki and East James Bay Cree (which is very similar to Innu):

Beothuk	Micmac	Abenaki	East James Bay Cree	English
manus[16]	**minichk**	**mins**	**miinish**	blueberry or berry
shiibin	**siibu**	**zibo**	**siipii**	river (as in Mississippi)
moosin	**mkisin**	**makezen**	**maschisin**	shoe (i.e., moccasin)

Appendix B: Fish Terms Using -N(a)m(e)- in Selected Algonquian Languages

1) Ojibwe

In Rhodes's Ojibwa dictionary, the root appears as -**nme**- c.f., "nme" for "sturgeon," "nmebin" for "carp, sucker," "nmegos" for "brown trout," and "nmegshens" for "rainbow trout" (Rhodes 1985:313; see Baraga 1878, Ojibwa-English 269-70 for 'name').

2) East James Bay Cree

In this language we have -**name**-: "nameu... sturgeon," "namepii ... white sucker [or] red sucker," "namekush... lake trout" and "names... fish" (Cree School Board 1987:412).

3) Western Abenaki

In this language we have -**nama**- in the following entries: "namagw... lake trout," "namas... a fish," "namasi... be a fish," "namasika... there are many fish," "namasiya... fish meat" and "namasiz... a small fish, minnow, shiner..." (Day 1994:347-8).

Appendix C:Cartwright's 1768 Account of the 'Wild Northeast'

From Lieutenant Cartwright's 1768 account we have the following:

> The Indians from their secret haunts in the woods, let not a motion of all these people escape them; and in order to be on their guard, are careful to post themselves where they can command a view of all approaches, and secure an easy retreat. Their wigwams are frequently erected on a narrow isthmus; so that their canoes may be launched into the water on the safe side, whenever an enemy's boat appears.

Both day and night they keep an unremitting and wary lookout; so that to surprise them requires in general uncommon address and subtlety. Even to gain a sight of them is no small difficulty; for they enjoy in so much perfection the senses of sight and hearing, that they seldom fail to discover the advance of the fishermen early enough to make their retreat, without so much as being perceived. This is known to every one who has traversed these islands, as the traces of Indians are found by such persons wherever they land, and sometimes such fresh signs of them, as a proof they have not quitted the spot many moments, and these appearances are observable every day yet whole seasons sometimes pass without an Indian being seen by them. They cannot be too watchful for surprises in their wigwams have generally proved fatal to them, and upon sudden accidental meetings it has been the usual practice of the fishermen to destroy them unprovoked, while the terrified Indians have attempted nothing but to make their escape.... (Howley 1974:36)

Endnotes

[1] For these dates (Marshall 1996;13), and for much more, I am indebted to Ingeborg Marshall for her excellent magnum opus *A History and Ethnography of the Beothuk.*

[2] This knowledge comes entirely from Shanawdithit, her aunt Demasduit and a young girl named Oubee who was captured in 1791.

[3] There is a common misconception that Native languages have relatively few words in their vocabulary. To give evidence to the contrary, the Ojibwe and East James Bay Cree dictionaries used in this unit contain 9100 and 15,000 Native/English entries respectively. Both dictionaries, although excellent works, do not completely represent the total number of possible words. As Gordon Day wrote in the introduction to his 538-page listing of Abenaki roots: "a dictionary of an Algonquian language must inevitably fail to exhaust its seemingly unlimited potential for word-making" (Day 1994:IV).

[4] I first learned about this when I was a student of John Hewson at the Department of Linguistics at Memorial University of Newfoundland. I am much indebted to him for much of my knowledge about Micmac and Beothuk.

[5] Generally speaking, a short list of cognates is shaky ground upon which to build connections of language relatedness. Borrowings across languages often complicate the picture. Ojibwe 'mkizin' and English 'moccasin' look alike and have a similar meaning. But that is because English speakers appropriated the word from an Algonquian language. In addition, mere coincidence can help create what looks to be a handful of cognates shared by two unrelated languages. The human mouth can only produce a limited variety of speech sounds. During the late eighteenth and early nineteenth centuries there were scholars who, from short lists of such coincidental similarities (called 'false cognates') between Native languages and Hebrew, felt that they had proven that Native people were the lost tribes of Israel.

[6] Aubin 1975:97-8 and Hewson 1993:128-9.

[7] This is to be expected in an Algonquian language, as -me- appears in construction for words concerning fish in other Algonquian languages (Aubin 1975:10 and Hewson 1993:111 and 143).

[8] Howley 1974:306. Differing entries such as this suggest that more than one dialect of Beothuk may be represented.

[9] What seems just as likely is that Shanung could mean 'southerners.' There are two reasons to suggest this. First, Shanung looks something like the Algonquian noun root for 'south' that gave the Shawnee their name (See Mary McKee chapter and Hewson 1993:180). The East James Bay Cree terms for 'south' have -**shaawan**- in them (Cree School Board 1987:460). Second, the Micmac came from the south.

[10] The one recorded word or morpheme that does seem to signify 'bad' in the Beothuk language is the one presented in the following entry: "Muddy, mandee... mud'ti... **bad, dirty**, mudeet **bad man**..." (Howley 1974:306). This would appear to be cognate with the Algonquian root 'machi-,' which means 'bad' or 'evil' (Hewson 1993:91).

[11] The entry for their name in the word list published by Howley gives "good Indians" as a 'translation' for this term (Howley 1974:306). As with the term for Micmac, this is not so much a translation of the word as it is a statement of the relatively positive relationship that the Beothuk had with the Innu as compared to the avoidance relationship they had with the Micmac.

[12] Algonquian cognates signifying raw, at least begin with the -ash- with which this word begins (Hewson 1993:21-2).

[13] The contrast between the 'wild and woolly northeast' of Exploits Bay, and the rest of the island was made in 1793 by John Reeves, Chief Justice of Newfoundland:

> This is a lawless part of the island, where there are no
> magistrates resident for many miles, nor any control, as
> in other parts, from the short visit of a man-of-war during
> a few days in the summer; so that people do as they like,

and there is hardly any time of account for their actions. (Howley 1974:55)

[14] James P. Howley, whose vast compilation of data on the Beothuk stands as a key reference work despite its being first published in 1916, had an insightful comment concerning how Buchan might have avoided tragedy in this expedition:

> ... Buchan made a great mistake in taking along with him so many of the furriers, those inveterate enemies of the poor Red man, whose very presence was alone sufficient to cause their distrust. I believe were he to have taken instead some of those Canadians that he mentions, Micmac's, Abanakie's, or [Montagnais] but especially the latter, they would have probably succeeded in making themselves understood by the natives, and thus his interview, which at first promised so well, might have resulted very differently.... (Howley 1974:91)

[15] The leader of the expedition, Lieutenant Buchan, commented after the fact, "I had to regret their language not being known" (Marshall 1996:141).

[16] Some Beothuk berry terms appear to have the Algonquian root -min- for 'berry' in them. "Menome **dogberries**" (Howley 1974:320), "Shamye **currants**" (ibid.) and "Shau-da-me **partridge berries**" (ibid.) are all good candidates. One term for gooseberry, "Jiggamint" (Howley 1974:305) appears to be quite similar to the Algonquian root "*ka:wimina" (Aubin 1975:40).

Bibliography

Aubin, George F. 1975. *A Proto-Algonquian Dictionary.* Ottawa: National Museums of Canada.

Baraga, Frederick. 1878. *A Dictionary of Otchipwe Language.* Montreal: Beauchemin Valois.

Bock, Philip. 1978. "Micmac." *Handbook of North American Indians*, vol.15, *The Northeast.* Washington: Smithsonian Institution, pp. 109-22.

Cree School Board. 1987. *Cree Lexicon: Eastern James Bay Dialects.* Baie-de-la-Poste, Mistassini Lake: Cree School Board.

Day, Gordon M. 1994. *Western Abenaki Dictionary: Volume 1: Abenaki-English.* Hull: Canadian Museum of Civilization.

Fardy, Bernard D. 1988. *Demasduit: Native Newfoundlander.* St. John's: Creative Publishers.

Hewson, John. 1981. "Beothuck Language," in the *Encyclopedia of Newfoundland and Labrador*, vol. 1, ed. by J.R. Smallwood and R.D.W. Pitt. St. John's: Newfoundland Book Publishers (1967), pp. 181-2.

Hewson, John. 1993. *A Computer-Generated Dictionary of Proto-Algonquian.* Hull: Canadian Museum of Civilization.

Hodge, F.W. 1971. *Handbook of Indians of Canada.* Toronto: Coles Pub.

Howley, James P. 1974. *The Beothuck or Red Indians.* Toronto: Coles (reprint from 1915).

Maclean, John. 1971. *Canadian Savage Folk: The Native Tribes of Canada* (orig. 1896). Toronto: Coles Pub.

Marshall, Ingeborg. 1996. *A History and Ethnography of the Beothuk.* Montreal & Kingston: McGill-Queen's University Press.

O'Meara, John. 1996. *Delaware-English, English-Delaware Dictionary.* Toronto: University of Toronto Press.

Oswalt, Wendell H. 1966. *This Land Was Theirs:A Study of the North American Indian.* New York: John Wiley & Sons.

Pastore, Ralph and Story, G.M. 1987. "Shawnadithit." *Dictionary of Canadian Biography,* vol.6, 1821-1835. Toronto: Univ. of Toronto Press, pp. 706-09.

Reynolds, Barrie. 1978. "Beothuck." *Handbook of North American Indians,* vol.15, *The Northeast.* Washington: Smithsonian Institution, pp. 101-8.

Rhodes, Richard. 1985. *Eastern Ojibwa-Chippewa-Ottawa Dictionary.* New York: Mouton.

Rowe, Frederick W. 1977. *Extinction: The Beothucks of Newfoundland.* Toronto: McGraw-Hill Ryerson.

Steckley, John L. 1993. "Huron Kinship Terminology." *Ontario Archaeology* 50:35- 59.

Storey, G.M. 1983. "Demasduit." *Dictionary of Canadian Biography,* vol. 5, 1801-1820, pp. 243-4.

Such, Peter. 1978. *Vanished Peoples: The Archaic Dorset & Beothuk People of Newfoundland.* Toronto: NC Press.

Upton, L.F.S. 1979. *Micmacs and Colonists: Indian-White Relations in the Maritimes, 1713-1867.* Vancouver: Univ. of British Columbia Press.

Upton, L.F.S. 1988. "The Extermination of the Beothuck of Newfoundland" (orig. pub. in the Canadian Historical Review in 1977), in *Out of the Background: Readings on Canadian Native History,* ed. by R. Fisher and Kenneth Coates. Toronto: Copp Clark Pitman, pp. 45-65.

Winter, Keith. 1975. *Shananditti: The Last of the Beothuck.* Vancouver: J.J. Douglas Ltd.

Wright, James V. 1995. *A History of the Native People of Canada, Volume 1 (10,000-1,000 B.C.).* Ottawa: Canadian Museum of Civilization.

*Nah-ne-bah-wee-quay [deceased]
Wife of Wm Sutton,
Sarawak Tp. Ont.*

Copy of the posthumous printed illustration of Mrs. William Sutton that was printed alongside her husband's in the 1880 *Illustrated Atlas of the Dominion of Canada*, p. 109. Reprinted by permission of the County of Grey-Owen Sound Museum.

Copy of the tintype image of Mrs. Catharine B. Sutton (Mrs. William Sutton), showing her holding a book. Reprinted by permission of the County of Grey-Owen Sound Museum.

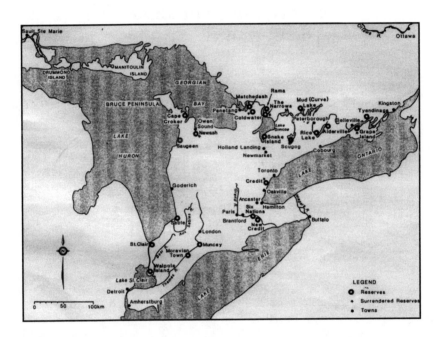

Canadian Indian mission stations visited by Peter Jones in the mid-nineteenth century.

From Smith, Donald. 1987. *Sacred Feathers: The Reverend Peter Jones (Kahkewaquonaby) & the Mississauga Indians*, p. 236. Toronto: University of Toronto Press.

4

Nahnebahwequay ('Standing Woman') or Catharine Sutton

> Bearing with her the vellum of her pedigree, a tawny skin, of pleasing aspect, and most gentle manners, refined by Christianity, and gifted with the simple eloquence of nature, she was chosen at a general Indian council, held last summer, to make known to the Government and to the Queen the hard case of the poor Indian. (*The Colonial Intelligencer and Aborigines' Friend*, 1859-1866, p. 148)

> She is a giant; there are few women in the 19th century who were more courageous. (Donald Smith as quoted in Smyth 1998)

Nahnebahwequay's story, like the stories of so many other Native people, is a story of fighting for land. This one is different, however, in that she won; not the war nor even a decisive battle, but at least a small, significant skirmish. Descendant of the first peoples of the land, she fought for a basic right that the newest immigrants to Canada at that time, the 1860s, could more or less take for granted: the right to buy her own land. She went to great lengths, more accurately great distances, to win her victory, to earn her plot of earth. One could say that Nahnebahwequay was following some kind of tradition of her people, the Mississauga. For it seems that from the time of initial contact with Europeans, the Mississauga were almost always fighting someone for land: first in battle with the Iroquois, then on paper with the government.

In order to understand any issue of Native rights, we must first look deep into the history of the matter. Accordingly, we will begin the story of Nahnebahwequay's life with a look at how her people arrived at the situation into which she was born.

The Mississauga

People usually associate the word '**Mississauga**' with the city of that name, located just west of Toronto. However, that is not where the Mississauga called home when they first encountered the French in the seventeenth century. Where did they live then? To find that out we have to do a little linguistic detective work.

There is an old deerskin map written in Huron that is a guide to a treasure of history. It is the oldest surviving map (ca. 1641) that includes all the Great Lakes. Along most of the north shore of Lake Huron is written "**Aovechissaeton**," a Huron version of 'Mississauga.' The -**m**- (nonexistent in Huron) is replaced by the -**w**- sound represented by -ov-. The -**ton**- is a miscopy of -**ronnon**-, meaning 'people' in Huron.

The name 'Mississauga' can be interpreted with -**missi**- meaning 'large' (but see Appendix A) and -**ssauga**- meaning 'river mouth.' The large river mouth can be seen on the map, roughly midway across Aovechissaeton country. Now it is called Mississagi Bay, and the river flowing into it, not surprisingly, the Mississagi River.

The Mississauga were not alone; their surrounding neighbours spoke languages and had beliefs and practices almost identical to their own. Collectively, these peoples are usually known as the '**Ojibwa(y)**'. This word, like the similar 'Chippewa,' is said to be derived from an Ojibwa term referring to their 'puckered up' moccasins. French writers first used the word to designate a group closely connected with the Saulteaux, who lived to the west of the Mississauga. Gradually, application spread to related peoples now living in Ontario, Manitoba and Saskatchewan in Canada, and Michigan, Minnesota, and Wisconsin in the United States.

However, as with many names associated with Native nations, this is not what the Mississauga called themselves. When they spoke of who they were beyond being Mississauga, they used '**(A)nishnabe**' (plural adding -k). Prior to contact with Europeans this word, hereafter written as Nishnabe (see Appendix A), was probably used primarily to refer to 'human beings.' After contact it came to refer to 'Natives,' particularly those of a shared linguistic and cultural heritage. The name is so used today by the Ojibwa, Algonquin, Odawa, Potawatomi and Saulteaux.

The first written record of the Mississauga fighting to defend their land occurred in 1653. In that year, along with their Nishnabe neighbours to the west and east, the Saulteaux and the Amikwa (Beaver), they successfully repulsed the attack of some 120 Iroquois warriors—no mean feat. The Iroquois had for the previous ten years or so put together an unprecedented, almost unbroken string of victories in the land south of Lake Huron. This enabled them to drive the Huron-Wendat, the Petun and Neutral out of their Ontario homelands.

According to nineteenth-century Nishnabe writer George Copway, in 1650, a council of peace was held between Nishnabe and the Iroquois at "**Massessauga**" (Copway 1972:79). When that was violated, the war began. Nishnabe tradition records that they sent 700 canoes of warriors into southern Ontario (Copway 1972:87). Throughout the rest of the seventeenth century, these two sides would square off in a running series of confrontations. In Nishnabe communities in Ontario, and even among the Cree living as far north as James Bay,[1] stories have long been told of the many battles that were fought during those days. Sometimes still, locations of the dead are pointed at when elders walk or sit outside telling tales to children.

Even place names bear witness to what took place then. Take, for example, '**Nottawasaga**,' a name for a river, a bay and in shortened form (i.e., Wasaga) a beach and town in southern Ontario. When Nishnabe elder Fred Wheatley taught the Ojibwa language to a group (including Canadian historian Donald Smith and myself) of eager young students, nurses and scholars in 1971-1972 at the Indian Friendship Centre in Toronto, he taught us that Nottawasaga meant 'the river mouth of the Naadawe.' Naadawe can refer to a kind of snake, but it typically signifies the Iroquois. When asked why the river and bay bore that name, Fred replied, "because that was where the Naadawe were waiting to ambush the Ojibwa."[2]

By the 1680s, the Nishnabe were starting to take the fight to the Naadawe. Slowly they moved into the Ontario territories of the Iroquois. Most people living or spending sleepy summer days in peaceful, cottage-country sites such as Penetanguishene, Peterborough, Rice Lake, Madoc and the Bay of Quinte would be surprised to learn that major battles in the Nishnabe winning of southern Ontario were fought there. According to Peter Schmalz, a particularly significant battle, the Battle of Skull Mound, took place by the mouth of the Saugeen River. This is not far from the land that Nahnebahwequay would fight government bureaucracy for 170 years later. The mound was said to have been formed by the skulls of slain Iroquois.[3]

In 1701, a general peace was signed between the Iroquois Confederacy and the Great Lakes nations with whom they had been in conflict. By that time, the Nishnabe had deeply rooted themselves in the fertile soils of southern Ontario. The name 'Mississauga' remained attached to many of them. How many actually were Mississauga in origin, and how many had as their ancestors the former northern neighbours of the Mississauga such as the Amikwa and the Nikikoek, whose names have disappeared, is hard to tell. Throughout the first half of the eighteenth century, people referred to as Mississauga established themselves in the south as both traders and formidable warriors.[4]

The Mississauga were then primarily allied with the French. Yet they, like the French, looked after their own interests first. They cleared for themselves a trade route to the English in Albany, New York, and would let neither French nor Iroquois block that path. During the French against English war of the 1750s to 1760s, they worked hard to maintain as much independence as they could. They arranged with the Iroquois not to fight or kill each other in battles that had Nishnabe and French on one side, Iroquois and English on the other. Wabbicommicot, a Toronto area Mississauga leader, influenced many of his people not to join with Pontiac, an Odawa and therefore a fellow Nishnabe, in his battles with the English.

Later on, during the American Revolution and the War of 1812, the Mississauga were much courted by both British and Americans. But governments on both sides of the border would abruptly end the courtship once the heat of war had subsided and the fighting might of the Mississauga warriors was no longer desired. The contrast between wartime promises and peacetime practices is accurately summarized by Nahnebahwequay in her article published in the *Christian Guardian* of May 28, 1862:

> I cannot help thinking about those times, now past, when Governors and Generals used to meet our

fathers in the Great Councils, and made great
promises that were never, never to be broken while
grass grew and waters ran. All our fathers who did
not fall in the wars remained faithful to the British
throne, and their children have followed their steps
in loyalty. But the wars have passed away, and but
few of the old veterans... are now alive... and
advantage is taken of our weakness and ignorance,
so that our fisheries, hunting-grounds, lands and
homes are taken from us, whether we like it or not.
They are first coveted, and then some plan is
concocted to get them; and those pledges made to
our grandsires by British noblemen have been and
are still every day shamefully violated, so that the
poor Indians have ceased to have any confidence in
the Government.... Little did those bold Indian
warriors think when they were listening to the fine
promises made by British noblemen that the
successors of those crown officials would, in a few
years, rob their children of their birth-right. (Sutton
1862)

Times were changing in the land of the Mississauga. Flooding
their territory like springtime rivers were the Loyalists, those living
in the United States who had sided with the British crown in the
American Revolution. They were offered land on the British side of
the border. Large numbers flowed north. From 1783 to 1785 alone,
roughly 10,000 settlers from the US poured into Ontario. According to
Schmalz, in Upper Canada at that time Europeans probably equalled
the Nishnabe in population (Schmalz 1991:105). And they were just
beginning to move into the area.

With the settlers came four fellow travellers that changed forever
Mississauga life. One was contagious, killing disease. Smallpox, but
also measles and tuberculosis, wiped out perhaps one third of the
Credit River Mississauga from 1787 to 1798, their population dropping
from over 500 to roughly 330.

Then there was **shkodewaaboo** ('fire water;' Rhodes 1985:617) or
whisky that white traders used in their dealings with the Mississauga.
It inflicted horrific damage on the independence, pride, supportive
family structure and sheer numbers of the Mississauga. One telling

statement of this damage comes from Pahtahsegua (Rev. Peter Jacobs), a Mississauga teacher, preacher and writer, in a letter published in the *New York Christian Advocate* of June 17, 1836. After speaking generally of the devastating effect alcohol had on the Mississauga, he spoke in more personal terms:

> [M]y father and mother died when I was very young, in drinking the fire water to excess.... My sister and brother-in-law then took me to bring me up. But in a short time they died also in drinking the fire water to excess. My sister was frozen to death on a drinking spree, on new year's day.... And in about one year from this time one of my sisters, in a drunken spree, was struck with a club on her head by her husband, which caused her death. And in the same year my brother was tomahawked in a drinking spree, at Montreal. Thus the fire waters have left me without father or mother, and without brother or sister in the world. (Schmalz 1991:133)

Although Pahtahsegua went on to publish a small volume describing his travels, and to preach to the Saulteaux out west, he eventually became "constantly bedevilled by heavy drinking and sank into poverty and oblivion" (ibid.).

What else did the settlers bring? There is an old Native joke that goes something like this: "When the white man first came here, we had the land and he had Christianity. Now the white man has the land; all we have left is Christianity." As we saw in chapter one, the relationship between Natives and Christianity has certainly been bittersweet. There are horror stories, particularly concerning the Christian-run residential schools operated through slightly more than half the twentieth century;[5] however, it would be wrong to say that Christianity's impact was as reliably negative as were the aforementioned elements of the white plague—crowding settlers, disease and alcohol. There is a positive side to the ledger as well, particularly when Natives were given the opportunity to run their own show when they had a chance to obtain positions of religious authority.[6] During the nineteenth century, the Methodist church provided a number of bright young Mississauga with the benefits of Western education when many settlers were illiterate. As a relatively democratic religious organization in its early years, the Methodist church gave them a path of opportunity as preachers and teachers. Unfortunately, nineteenth-century Ontario was not ready to extend that path to lead to positions of significance outside the church. And when the Methodists became part of the Ontario establishment, they would begin to restrict and even close off the opportunities that Nahnebahwequay and her peers had followed.

Nahnebahwequay's Adoptive Father

A good example of both the opportunities provided by the Methodist church to the Mississauga and of the frustrating restrictions that cast a shadow on those lights can be found in the story of Kahkewaquonaby ('Sacred Feathers') or Peter Jones. He and his English wife, Eliza, were major influences on Nahnebahwequay. He is often referred to as her uncle, although there is no genealogical evidence to support that assertion. Perhaps, as a male member of her clan and being of the preceding generation, 'uncle' might be how she would address him. He would become her unofficially adopted father.

Sacred Feathers was born in 1802. His mother, Tuhbenahneequay, was Mississauga. His father, Augustus Jones, was Welsh and a surveyor who also had a Mohawk wife of more 'official' standing. At 14, Sacred Feathers was taken by his father from his almost exclusively Mississauga surroundings to live near Brantford with his Mohawk stepmother and her family and to learn European ways of living through formal education and farm work. In 1823, he experienced a profound religious conversion when exposed to a series of enthusiastic outdoor Methodist camp meetings held in a nearby Christian Mohawk community.

Once he joined the Methodist church, Sacred Feathers rose in influence like the eagle which was his clan totem and the source of his name. Preaching his three favourite European gospels of Methodism, literacy and farming, Sacred Feathers was instrumental in establishing a model Methodist Mississauga community by the banks of the Credit River, which was home to Nahnebahwequay. He successfully went to the United States and Britain to raise funds for Native education. An accomplished writer, he translated hymns and parts of the Bible and wrote the popular, posthumously published

History of the Ojebway Indians. Yet there were impediments to his flights of accomplishment. He was denied a mission of his own, even though he was more than qualified for the position. Likewise, Indian Affairs did not give him the job he very much wanted, despite the support of the influential Egerton Ryerson, his good friend. An ex-military man, scarcely experienced with Natives and not knowledgeable in Native matters, got the job.

The Treaties: Signing Away the Land

The fourth feature that came with the settlers was the treaties. After Britain beat France on the Plains of Abraham, a document was put forward that is often termed the Magna Carta of Native rights: the Royal Proclamation of 1763. It declared that the land that is now included in Ontario, as well as much of the rest of current Canada, was to be considered 'Indian land.'[7] The only way that this land could be taken away from Native people would be through 'public purchase,' that is, a treaty. But it wasn't like the normal purchasing of property: imagine a group of people forcing you to sell your home, then setting the price, then putting the money gained from the purchase into their bank account so that the funds could be administered 'for your own good.'

Piece by large piece, the Mississauga had their land 'publicly purchased.' Two of the early transfers provided a much-welcomed home for the Mohawk and other Iroquois who had been forced to abandon their ancestral territory after choosing to fight on the losing side of the American Revolution. On October 9, 1783, land stretching back off the northeastern shores of Lake Ontario, from the Gananoque River in the east to the Trent River in the west, was purchased from the Mississauga. John Deserontyon and his band of Mohawks settled in that winter. On May 22, 1784, the Mississauga announced at a council meeting at Niagara that they would permit a large tract around the Grand River to be transferred to the Crown for the purposes of giving it to the more than 2000 Iroquois led by the Mohawk Joseph Brant. While they were initially apprehensive about allowing their former enemy to live so close to them,[8] they decided it was better than having settlers as neighbours.[9] The Mississauga would later benefit from the good will this would engender.

The Mississauga signatories of this public purchase included the "Sachems [i.e., peace chiefs] and War Chiefs and *Principal Women* of the Messissauga Indian Nation."[10] While it is difficult to trust the awkwardly written English renditions of the free-flowing Native names on the treaties, "Wapeanojhqua" might have been one of those women. Her name appears to end with the -**qua**- of 'woman.'[11] We see "principal women" also represented in a treaty signed on October 24, 1795. Significantly, Mississauga women had a say in the political decisions made by their people, while other Canadian women would have to wait for more than 100 years before they would receive the right to vote.

Next, in a series of poorly recorded deals in 1784, 1787 and 1788, the northern shoreline from the Trent River west to what is now Scarborough changed hands. How far inland the transfer went is the subject of historical rumours: some sources claim it reached "as far back as a man could walk, or go on foot in a day."[12] Natives came to believe that it went the distance a gunshot could be heard.[13] Another treaty had to be signed in 1923 to try to clear up the resultant legal mess.

On September 23, 1787, Toronto and surrounding townships, some 250,880 acres, were negotiated for in a provisional land surrender. The deal, known as the Toronto Purchase, stayed in limbo until August 1, 1805, when eight Mississauga chiefs, headed by Quinepenon (Golden Eagle) of the Otter clan, met with government officials on the flatlands beside the Credit River. It was a significant spot in the dealings between the Mississauga and the whites. Trade important to both had regularly taken place there in earlier days, as the name for the river bears witness. The Mississauga called the river **Missinnihe**.[14] The word is based on -**missin**-, meaning 'image, mark.'[15] This refers to the marks made in the books of the white traders recording both items given out on credit and the pelts paid later to cancel the debt (Baraga 1878:224, Ojibwa-English). This sense of the word appears in the early translation 'Trusting Creek' (Smith 1987a:255), and in the current name 'Credit.'[16] But Mississauga trust did not extend to the Toronto Purchase; they already felt confined on the land left to them. This is noted by Quinepenon, as is the suspicion held by the Mississauga women that the deal would further impoverish their nation:

> [I]t is hard to give away more land; the young men
> and women have found fault with so much having
> been sold before. It is true we are poor, and the women

say we will be worse if we part with any more....
(Clarkson 1967:27)

Quinepenon[17] had good reason to distrust settlers and the government. He believed that the earlier treaties had promised that "the Farmers would help us" (Smith 1979:467) and that his people could "encamp and fish where we pleased" and felt that the promises that been violated. In 1797, the government had passed a "Proclamation to Protect the Fishing Places and Burying Grounds of the Mississauga," but neither type of valued location was protected effectively by this legislation.

The meeting of August 1, 1805, was not just to confirm the Toronto Purchase. The rest of the Lake Ontario shoreline was coveted by the incoming, mostly American immigrants and by the government that was eager to welcome them. On August 2, land extending west of Etobicoke Creek all the way to Burlington Bay was signed away. Fishing and corn-growing were vital to the survival of the Mississauga, so Quinepenon and other leaders fought hard to receive the concession of reserving to the "Missasague [*sic*] Nation:"

> the sole right of the fisheries in the Twelve Mile [Bronte] Creek, the Sixteen Mile Creek, the Etobicoke River, together with the flats or low grounds on said creeks and river, which we have heretofore cultivated and where we have our camps. And also the sole right of fishery in the River Credit with one mile on each side of said river. (Indian Treaties and Surrenders 1971, vol. 1. p. 36)

Quinepenon's fear were realized. By the time the August 2 treaty was confirmed the next year, a settler had destroyed the chief's cornfield as well as the field of a Mississauga widow who had to provide for four children. The same man, a squatter by the rules of the treaty, had built a fish weir on Bronte Creek which prevented the salmon from swimming upstream to spawn. According to Quinepenon, another white man had so polluted the Credit River "by washing with sope [i.e., soap] and other dirt, that the fish refuse coming into the River as usual, by which our families are in great distress for want of food" (Smith 1979:467).

The next time the government came to ask for more Mississauga land was 1818. Much had happened since 1806; immigrants, mostly

British, had swelled the ranks of white people in Upper Canada. By 1812, Natives made up barely more than 10 percent of that colony's population (Dickason 1992:224). The Credit River Mississauga continued to diminish in number: 330 had become 200. The toll on their chiefs was even heavier. Of the ten leaders who had signed the last treaty, only two would be around to put their mark on paper in 1818. Included in the dead was Quinepenon. The tragic manner of his death clearly marks the end of an era. The sense of the moment has been eloquently captured by Donald Smith:

> During the War of 1812 a group of Mississauga gathered by a river mouth at the western end of Lake Ontario. As the warriors squatted around him the old chief... slowly began to tell of the fast in which, through the grace of unseen spirit powers, he had obtained protection against arrows, tomahawks, and even bullets. And he would demonstrate this gift. He took a tin kettle and, with some difficulty on account of his age, walked a short distance away from the circle. As soon as he raised the kettle up before his face a warrior was to fire, and Kineubenae [Quinepenon] would collect the bullet in the kettle. The marksman, like the others, believed in Kineubenae's "medicine" and he fired. The chief instantly fell. The band, to their horror, found that "the lead went into his head and (had) killed him on the spot." That one bullet did more than kill a respected leader; it shook the faith of many Mississauga in their traditional way of life. (Smith 1979:467)

The land that the government wanted in 1818 was the 'Mississauga Tract,' a tract west of the Toronto Purchase and north of the land acquired during the other 1806 treaty. There was a new feature to this deal: annual payments or annuities. In return for obtaining possession of some 648,000 acres, the king, through his representative William Claus, promised to pay the Mississauga, "... yearly and every year *for ever* the said sum of five hundred and twenty two pounds ten shillings currency in goods at the Montreal price..." (Indian Treaties and Surrenders 1971 vol. 1:48; emphasis mine).

Forever lasted a short time; this promise was broken. Two years later, William Claus, the Deputy Superintendent General of Indian Affairs, came to speak with them again. The Mississauga were justifiably suspicious. What did he want now? So much had been taken. One leader summed up the feelings of many when he said:

> You came as a wind blowing across the great Lake. The wind wafted you to our shores. We... planted you— we nursed you. We protected you till you became a mighty tree that spread through our Hunting Land. With its branches you now lash us. (Schmalz 1991:105)

Claus wanted them to agree to give up their exclusive fishing rights and sell all of their remaining land:

> Saving and reserving, nevertheless, always to the said Acheton, Newoiquiquah, Woiqueshequome, Pausetawnouguetohe and Wabakagige and the people of the Mississagua Nation of Indians and their posterity for ever a certain parcel or tract of land containning two hundred acres.... (Indian Treaties and Surrenders 1971, vol. 1:52)

According to Claus, the proceeds from the sale of the land would:

> be applied towards educating your Children & instructing yourselves in the principles of the Christian religion—and that a certain part of the said Tract never surrendered will be set apart for your accommodation & that of your families, on which Huts will be erected as soon as possible. (Smith 1987a:39-40)

Two things are generally true about such Native land agreements. One is that the two parties, Native and government, have a different understanding about what took place. The second is that the government rarely delivers all that it has promised. Concerning the first, Claus felt that the Mississauga had given up their rights to all the land but the 200 acres. The Credit River people thought differently.

This can be seen in this quote from a letter sent by two of their leaders to the lieutenant-governor in 1829. They believed that Claus had said:

> The white people are getting thick around you and we are afraid they, or the yankees will cheat you out of your land, you had better put it into the hands of your very Great father the king to keep for you till you want to settle, and he will appropriate it for your good and he will take good care of it; and will take you under his wing, and keep you under his arm, & give you schools, and build houses for you when you want to settle. (Smith 1987a:40)

The land which was supposedly reserved for the Mississauga forever did not remain theirs for more than a few years. To my knowledge, the Mississauga still haven't received the promised two hundred acres or compensation for its loss.

Further, there seems to have been two different timetables for the two sides of this transaction. The government got its hands on the land surrendered fairly quickly, but six years passed (the "soon as possible") before the government began to fulfil even a part of its side of the bargain. Not until the fall of 1826 were 20 homes built for the Mississauga alongside the mouth of the Credit River.

Another part of the 1820 deal was that the Mississauga were to receive annuities from the monies accrued from the sale of their lands. The monies were held for the Mississauga 'in trust' by the government. But some of the government officials could not be trusted. Once they grasped the money in their hands, they treated much of it as if it were their own.

In 1826, Peter Jones confronted Colonel James Givins, the Indian agent responsible for the Mississauga, concerning the fact that they were being paid £50 less in annuities than was agreed upon in the treaty. The reply given by the man the Mississauga called 'the Wolf' smells of a cover-up. He claimed that he "was not at liberty to explain" (Smith 1987a:79) why they were not getting the sum of money owed to them. Doubtless, someone, perhaps the Wolf, was skimming the money off the top like so much thick cream.

The Mississauga of the Credit were growing concerned about what their rights actually were to the land. They were hearing nasty rumours.

Chief James Ajetance (spelled 'Acheton' above),[18] Peter Jones's adopted father, said to Givins, "Having heard some bad birds crying that we did not own any lands on the Credit, we wish to know from our great father how much land we really possess" (Smith 1987a:100).

Givins flatly stated that in his opinion the Mississauga had surrendered all their rights away. Despite its questionable legality, his opinion carried weight.

The Mississauga were feeling increasingly hemmed in. They had established a trade of salmon in exchange for flour, cattle and other goods, but this mutually beneficial commerce was being interfered with in nasty ways, as can be seen from the words of a petition signed by Peter Jones and 53 others on January 31, 1829, and sent to Sir John Colbourne, the lieutenant-governor of Upper Canada:

> We now want the fish in our river, that we may keep our children at home to go to school, and not go many miles back to hunt for provisions.... But now, Father, we will tell you how wicked white men have used us.—They come in the fall and spring, and encamp for many weeks close by our village. They burn and destroy our fences and boards in the night; they watch the salmon and take them as fast as they come up; they swear and get drunk and give a very bad example to our young people, and try to persuade them to be wicked like themselves, and particularly on the Sabbath.... Others go to the mouth of the river and catch all the salmon; they put the offals of salmon in the mouth of the river to keep the fish from passing up, that they may take them with a seine near the mouth of the river in the lake; and often in the dark they set gill nets in the river and stop all the fish. By those means we are much injured and our children are deprived of bread. (Mackenzie 1833 in Fairley 1960:47-8)

Nahnebahwequay

One of those children was Nahnebahwequay. She was born by the Credit River in 1824. Her parents were **Myawekeshigoqua** or Mary (often called Polly) Crane of the Otter clan and **Tyatiquob** or

Sunegoo of the Eagle clan. Her name has essentially two parts. The first part, -**nahnebahw**-, is a form of the verb 'to stand,' perhaps meaning either 'to stand up' or 'to stand here and there' (see Appendix A). The second part is -**equa**-, meaning 'female, woman' (see Introduction). The same element appears in the ending of her mother's name and in the concluding -**eequay**- of Sacred Feathers's mother's name, Tuhbenahneequay. The translation for her name that Nahnebahwequay liked to use was 'Upright Woman.' Sometimes, as well, she signed her letters and was referred to as 'Nah-nee.' We will follow that practice here by referring to her mainly as 'Nah-nee.'

What was to become her surname, **Sunegoo** (also spelled Sonego), refers to either black or a grey squirrel (see Appendix A). It seems to first appear in the ethnohistorical record in the treaty of 1805 as 'Osenego,' referring to a leading figure in the Eagle clan. This man was probably Nahne's grandfather, her father's father. Missionaries and government officials were then giving the Mississauga European-style surnames rather than the single names of traditional practice. Often they converted the single name of a father to the surname of his children. Nah-nee would pass a version of the name on to Wesley, one of her sons.

In 1826, when Nah-nee was two, she was one of 88 children in a community of 226 people. In 1830, she was 1 of about 50 children in the Methodist school by the Credit River. The girls that year were taught by a white woman, Miss Rolph, while the boys were taught by Edway Ryerson, a brother of the more famous Egerton Ryerson. The Mississauga children learned the three Rs of reading, writing and arithmetic, and the two Gs of geography and grammar. The school was described by William Lyon Mackenzie in a *Colonial Advocate* article of December 30, 1830, in the following way:

> The school room is a large and commodious apartment-with tiers of raised benches in the rear; on one division of which sit the girls, and the boys on the other. There are also desks and slates for ciphering and copy books and copper-plate lines for those who write. The Bibles and Testaments are chiefly those of the London Society for Promoting Christian Knowledge.... Among the school-furniture, are a handsome map of the world; the Arithmeticon; attractive alphabets on pasteboard; regular figures

> illustrative of geometry... figures of birds, fishes, and
> quadrupeds ... accompanied with the history of each
> animal; the figure of a clock... by which to explain
> the principles of the time-piece. The walls of the
> school are adorned with good moral maxims; and I
> perceived that one of the rules was rather novel,
> though doubtless in place here.—It was, **"No
> blankets to be worn in school."** (Mackenzie in
> Fairley 1960:46; emphasis mine)

Christianity made an early and deep impression on Nah-nee.
Unlike people of her parents' generation, she was baptized in her
first year, 1825. She was christened as Catharine Brown, being named
after an exemplary Cherokee Christian who had died at 23, not long
before Nah-nee was born. She would be a devout Christian all her
life. When Nah-nee was faced with the powerful and persistent
government opposition, her faith gave her the strength to carry on
her fight.

It is important to note that although she accepted the religion of
the Europeans, she never denied her Native heritage, rejecting it for
the culture that brought Christianity to her people. In a letter of
1861, she wrote:

> I am an Indian; the blood of my forefathers runs in
> my veins, and I am not ashamed to own it; for my
> people were a noble race before the pale-faces came
> to possess their lands and home. (*Friends'
> Intelligencer* 1861:119)

When Nah-nee was about ten years old, she came under the
influence of a devout Methodist woman, Eliza Jones, Sacred Feathers'
English wife. Shortly after arriving in the Credit River community,
near the end of 1833, Eliza began instructing young Mississauga girls
in practical skills and religion. In 1847, Nah-nee wrote a heartfelt
letter to Eliza concerning those days:

> Dear sister when I was a child you gave me clothes
> to were... you taught little Indian girls in that little
> house a cross the road and you taught them how to
> sew and many other things.... When I look back in

days that are past and gone how good you were to CB
Sunegoo who once lived at Credit what a naughty girl
she was not to now you kindness. (Smith 1987a:148)

Eliza kept that letter for the rest of her life.

In 1836, the strings that connected the two friends were drawn tighter, as Nah-nee seems to have been unofficially adopted by Peter and Eliza Jones. She needed family at that time. She had recently lost most of her siblings to disease, one to drowning. Her father would die on May 7, 1842. Only her sister Mary, and her mother would live on into her adulthood.

The next year, 1837, 13-year-old Nah-nee and her 'aunt' Eliza travelled together in what must have seemed at the time to be a once-in-a-lifetime trip. They sailed across the Atlantic to Britain. Nah-nee received two kinds of lessons there. First, she spent some time at a British school, furthering the formal education she had received at the mission school in the Credit River community. The second kind of lesson came from Sacred Feathers, who had joined them in Britain. He had come to meet with the 18-year-old Queen Victoria so as to present the powerful monarch with a petition from his people and a wampum belt. His purpose in so doing was:

to give her the meaning of the wampum, and [to tell]
her that the white wampum signified the loyal and
good feeling which prevails amongst the Indians
toward her Majesty and her government; but that the
black wampum was designed to tell Her Majesty that
their hearts were troubled on account of their having
no title-deeds to their lands; and that they had sent
their petition and wampum that Her Majesty might
be pleased to take all the black wampum, so that the
string might be all white. (McLean 1970:19)

Nah-nee would attempt such a venture later, on her own, her message essentially the same.

In spite of the insecurity of their situation, the Mississauga still worked hard to develop their community in such a way as to be equal to their Euro-Canadian neighbours in those newcomers' own terms. Some may have felt that such an accomplishment might lead to a governmental reckoning that the Mississauga deserved to keep their

land. This equality of accomplishment they achieved. As succinctly
stated by historian Donald Smith:

> In just ten years the Indians, with their own labor,
> had built a hospital, a mechanic's shop, and eight
> barns and had added over twenty houses to the
> original twenty. They had enclosed for pasture and
> farming nine hundred acres, or nearly one-third of
> their reserve. On their farms they raised wheat, oats,
> peas, Indian corn, potatoes, and other vegetables;
> several cut hay and had small orchards. The band
> ran two sawmills. Even at the mouth of the river they
> had made many improvements. The village of Port
> Credit had been laid out, and they had sold town
> lots. With £2,500 of annuity money the Mississaugas
> purchased two thirds of the shares of the Credit
> Harbour Company. Under their direction as its
> majority stockholders, the company had constructed
> a port that could accommodate any ship on Lake
> Ontario. (Smith 1987a:157)

The land rights of the Mississauga were highly dependent not so
much on the letter of the law as they were on the whims of whoever
might be the lieutenant-governor of Upper Canada at the time. In
Nah-nee's own words, as published in the Methodist paper, the
Christian Guardian on May 28, 1862, "One Governor comes and exhibits
an interest in the welfare of the Indians, but soon he is succeeded by
another who destroys all those well-arranged plans" (Sutton 1862).

Perhaps the worst such offender was Lieutenant-Governor Francis
Bond Head. He was completely ignorant of Native culture, blind to
Native rights and unaware of how some Mississauga communities,
such as the one on the Credit, had managed to adapt successfully to
European-style living. Thus Bond Head had all the qualifications
necessary to concoct a potentially genocidal scheme. He proposed to
scoop up all the Natives living in southern Ontario and dump them
on Manitoulin Island, a place he knew little about. He claimed that
the move would be 'for their own good,' as he could not otherwise
'protect' them from the encroachment of the white settlers. In reply,
Chief Joseph Sawyer of the Credit River band rightly pointed out the
devastating effect that such a plan would have on his community:

> Now we raise our own corn, potatoes, wheat... we
> have cattle, and many comforts and conveniences.
> But if we go to Maneetoulin, we could not live; soon
> we should be extinct as a people; we could raise no
> potatoes, corn, pork, or beef; nothing would grow by
> putting the seed on smooth rock. We could get very
> few of the birds the Governor speaks of, and there
> are no deer to be had. We have been bred among the
> white people, and our children accustomed. (Smith
> 1987a:162-163)

In a desperate effort to get their rights respected, the Credit
River band decided that Sacred Feathers should go to Britain to present
their case to the Queen. The land deals were signed, after all, in her
name. This was what had presented Nah-nee with her opportunity to
travel across the ocean with her adopted parents.

The strategy appeared to work. The Mississauga preacher got to
speak to Lord Glenelg, the Colonial Secretary, a move Bond Head had
tried to block. Sacred Feathers informed Glenelg:

> So long as they hold no written document from the
> British Government to show that the land is theirs
> they fear that the white man may at some future day
> take their lands away from them.... (Smith 1987a:165)

Already sympathetic, Glenelg was convinced. He recommended
to Queen Victoria that the Credit River Mississauga be granted title
deeds. She approved. Nah-nee must have shared with her adopted
parents the euphoria of the moment at this great victory. Surely now,
they could feel secure on their land and be able to get on with their
lives.

They would have even been happier if they had known that the
odious Bond Head had resigned. In part because he was no more
competent in dealing with Canadians of European heritage than he
was with Natives: Bond Head had faced a rebellion that had led to his
resignation.

Soon after their triumphant return to their homeland, the three
Mississauga had another joyful occasion to celebrate. Like her adopted
father before her, Nah-nee had fallen in love with someone from
Britain. His name was William Sutton. Born in 1811 in England, the

son of a mechanic, he had come to the Toronto area in 1830. As deeply religious as Nah-nee, he had conceived the idea of engaging in Methodist missionary work among the Natives of his new land. We do not know when the couple first met. We do know that on January 9, 1839, as a budding bride barely into her teens, Nah-nee was married, by her beloved 'father' Rev. Peter Jones, to a man roughly twice her own age.

Life looked promising for Catharine and William, and for the Mississauga of the Credit. Lieutenant-Governor George Arthur, the successor to the unpopular Bond Head, seemed to be an improvement on his predecessor. He did not appear to be actively pursuing a policy of taking the Credit River flatlands away from the Mississauga. He was even considering the proposal that the Mississauga receive deeds to their land. Catharine and William would then be able to raise children (they would eventually have seven) and crops in a secure, prosperous Mississauga community. Or so one might think, if one were unfamiliar with Native land rights issues.

Arthur, like other Canadian government leaders before and since, was killing the hopes of a Native people with ill-informed good-will. In January, 1840, he wrote that his opposition to the community receiving deeds "arose from the good-will he had towards them, as he feared if they had deeds many of them would soon dispose of their lands" (Smith 1987a:178).

Arthur was wrong. The Mississauga of the Credit had no intentions of selling their land off piece by piece. They had a sense, seemingly unknowable to government officials, that for more than a few individuals to prosper, the band had to be strong as an entity. The community was a well from which people drew the water of identity and strength. Cover up the well, and the people thirst for what has been lost.

It did not help that the Chief Superintendent of Indian Affairs at the time, the man who handled their annuity payments and their funds generally was S.P. Jarvis. Jarvis was, to put it mildly, less than honest, and did not feel that he was accountable to the band for what he did. This is clearly stated by Smith in the following:

> In his eight year term of office from 1837 to 1845,
> never once did the chief superintendent give the Credit
> Indians a report on their band funds. They had no
> idea whether they had received the full amount of

> their annuity, and they obtained no financial
> statement at all on the sale of their lands at Twelve
> Mile Creek and Sixteen Mile Creek and on the Credit
> River. (Smith 1987a:177)

Government officials involved with Indian Affairs have often
historically been given much leeway when it comes to personal empire
building and misappropriation of funds. Jarvis, however, was such an
extreme example, it seems, that he was investigated by the Bagot
Commission and was stripped of his power in 1844. He left in some
disgrace in 1845.

When Jarvis lost his power, a strange, almost miraculous, event
took place. In August of that year, Governor-General Charles Metcalfe
handed over financial control of the band's funds to the band itself.
Now that might not seem like much to the casual observer of Native
history; however, as Smith duly notes, this was "the first time in
Canadian history an Indian band had obtained financial control over
its trust funds" (Smith 1987a:195). Throughout much of the twentieth
century, Canadian Native bands would have longed for such control,
such influence over their own destiny. As good a measure as this
was, however, without title or deed to their land, this was too little,
too late for the Mississauga of the Credit River. By the mid-1840s, it
was clear to the whole community that they would have to find a new
place to live. But where could they go?

Obviously the government and the white settlers were not going
to help them answer this question in any positive way. The Credit
River Mississauga had to look to their own kind for assistance in
finding a new home. Such was soon to be forthcoming. At a general
Ojibwa council meeting held in July, 1845, the Saugeen and Owen
Sound bands invited all the other Nishnabe bands in the southern
part of Ontario to settle just to the north of them, in the Bruce
Peninsula.

Scouts from the Credit River community checked out the farming
prospects of the area. The reports they brought back were not very
encouraging. The community was used to farming prime land. Such
land was limited on the Bruce. Most thought that moving there would
not be a good idea.

Imagine being Nah-nee, then a wife and mother just 21 years
old. She and her husband William had worked hard to establish a
prosperous farm, second in value only to that of her adopted father.
In her own words later, she wrote, "Our first home was a very good

one, the whole farm being under good cultivation" (*Friends' Intelligencer* 1861:120). By the end of 1845, they had three children to take care of: Joseph or Sahgarsega (b. 1842), her namesake Catharine or Nahwekegeegoquay (b. 1844) and little Sophia or Nahkooquay (b. 1845) (see Appendix A for an interpretation of their names). Moving would be hard. Yet that is what they decided to do in the fall of 1845. Choosing to make the move was a painful decision for Nah-nee. This can be seen in a letter she wrote shortly after leaving the only home she had ever known:

> I often think of the day I left the Credit. It was a solemn hour and I trust it was a sweet season for our souls. We wept and prayed and sang together. (Wesleyan Methodist Missionary Report, 1845-46)

The feelings were mutual. According to the Wesleyan Methodist Missionary Report 1845-6, she had been the leader of a class of young women "who felt her loss severely."

Nah-nee must have felt some loneliness at first. Only three families from the Credit River band moved up north with them. Their new community, however, would make them feel welcome soon enough. All the newcomers were adopted into the band.

What happened to the other members of their community? They received an offer that seemed almost too good to be true. In April, 1847, the Six Nations Iroquis met in full council. They had heard through the 'moccasin telegraph' of the desperate position of the Mississauga of the Credit. They remembered how the Mississauga had made land available to them when they had needed to move north away from the resentful Americans after fighting on the side of the British during the American Revolution. Their choice was clear. Feeling, in their words, "a great pleasure in returning the compliments to their descendants [i.e., those whose ancestors gave the land to the Iroquois]" (as quoted in Smith 1987a:212), they invited the Mississauga to take possession of some of the land on their reserve, near what is now Hagersville, Ontario. The Credit people accepted. That community today is known as the Mississauga of the New Credit.

A point should be made here concerning the significance of this gesture. These people were traditional enemies; a good deal of mistrust and some prejudice existed between the two peoples (Smith 1981:80). And this wasn't all just traditional enmity. Peter Russell, the

Administrator of the Government, had instituted a policy of keeping the Iroquois and the Mississauga apart so that they would not find common cause against government and settlers. In a telling letter of 1798, Russell instructed the government agents William Claus and James Givins:

> to do everything in [their] power (without exposing the object of this Policy to Suspicion) to foment any existing Jealousy between the Chippewas [i.e., the Mississauga] & the Six Nations; and to prevent as far as possible any Junction or good understanding between those two Tribes. (Smith 1981:80)

What became of the land and the buildings that Nah-nee and her people so treasured? A prominent English businessman named Capreol bought the property in the 1860s. He had grandiose plans that never came to fruition. The Mississauga Golf and Country Club later bought the 200 acres originally promised to the Mississauga, part of the property that Capreol had purchased. This was in 1905; the cost was $12,000. Some of the log buildings survived well into the twentieth century. For a number of years the chief's house was used by members of the golf club. Now if you drive on the Queen Elizabeth Way west across the bridge that spans the Credit River, you can still see the flatlands on which the Mississauga once had their homes. Very few of the many thousands that motor past there every working day know anything of the Native history of this visual oasis easing their drive to and from work. It is as if the Mississauga never lived there, nor had any claims to the land.

When they moved in the fall of 1845, Catharine and William Sutton were given some 200 acres of land by what was then called the Nawash (also spelled 'Newash') band. The property was situated just a short distance north of Owen Sound. The industrious family was not there long before they had brought some 40 to 50 acres of that land under cultivation and had constructed a "commodious house, barn and stable." From 1845 to 1852 they prospered from their hard work there.

The Suttons, however, had more they wanted to do. Both Catharine and William were devout Methodists, and felt a strong sense of mission concerning bringing to her people what they believed were the twin European blessings of Christianity and agriculture. In 1852, they gathered together their family and their most portable possessions and ventured north to the Garden River Reserve near Sault Ste. Marie, a place west of the old country of the early Mississauga. Their work there was to run a farm that was intended to provide a model to teach the local Nishnabe. This would have been quite a challenge. The soil and weather conditions were different from what they were accustomed to in the south. Further, local Nishnabe had greater access than did the southern Mississauga to the riches of the hunt, the trapline, the net and the fishing spear.

Catharine and William lived there for only a couple of years, until 1854. Perhaps this was by plan. They had given up neither their land nor their buildings back at Nawash. From Garden River they moved on to what must have been similar work in a Methodist mission in the Nishnabe country of the Upper Peninsula, Michigan. Again, they remained in their mission community for only a relatively short period of time. They would stay there until 1857. During that period, one more child, their son Wesley or Sunegoonee was born in 1856 (see Appendix A).

The year 1857 was a signal one Native affairs in Canada. On June 10 of that year a bill entitled "An Act to Encourage the Gradual Civilization of the Indian Tribes in this Province, and to Amend the Laws Respecting Indians" (often called the Act of Enfranchisement or Civilization Act) was passed. The very name of this piece of legislation sounds both highly judgmental and deeply ominous. Clearly the government wanted Native people to change.

The Civilization Act was to provide a means through which Natives would acquire the rights and duties of white citizens by becoming politically 'enfranchised.' To many white people claiming sympathy with Natives, but not possessing much understanding, the Civilization Act must have sounded good. The problem with this kind of thinking, shared by very few Natives when this act and its similar successors have been passed or proposed over the years, is that it ignores some basic truths. Enfranchisement is a way for governments to avoid the responsibilities they had signed for in the treaties and other paper promises. It provides an honest-sounding golden opportunity for governments to have the money such as annuity payments they owed Native groups forgotten like bad debts in a bankruptcy case. Enfranchisement appears more fair than it really is.

Secondly, as discussed earlier, the Mississauga needed to work together and prosper as whole social entities before more than a few 'fortunate' individuals could succeed, skimmed off like so much cream.

Enfranchisement for those who had become 'civilized' meant they would have to separate themselves from their own people. Their lifestyle and loss of legal status as 'Indians' would virtually necessitate such a separation. This would be destructive for both those individuals and for the group as a whole.

Third, is the question of identity. Legal sameness is a step towards assimilation. Since first contact to the current day, the majority of Native people have consistently desired that Native identity persist in one form or another. They do not want it to disappear. This has always been difficult for many Canadians of different heritage to accept. Perhaps this relates to the fact that even though such Canadians have reconciled themselves to loss of the identity of their former homeland (and feel that others should do likewise), the homeland and the identity persist in others without them (e.g., England and English identity, Italy and Italian identity). Such would not be true if Native people would give up their distinct identity.

Very few Natives 'took advantage' of the Civilization Act to become legally 'civilized.' That should say something about the inadequacies of the act and the approach it represents.

The same year, 1857, was also a big year for the Nishnabe living on the 10,000-acre Nawash reserve. They had 'decided' to 'surrender' (sell) their land. The decision wasn't so much a choice as much as it represented the culmination of the growing pressure being placed on them, similar to what the Credit River Mississauga had experienced (see Schmalz 1991:146). The town of Owen Sound was growing; some of the local townspeople were looking covetously at the 'Indian land' that surrounded them. The economic situation of the Nawash band, unique to being a Native community, was creating a financial, even a survival crisis for some of its members. This was especially true for those who had chosen to pursue a more traditional lifestyle of hunting, fishing and gathering rather than farming. From land sales previous to this, the people should have been relatively well off. The land had been sold for thousands of dollars. However, that money was held in trust by the government, and the people could not touch it. That money had a bad habit of disappearing, as similar funds had under Jarvis's mercenary care. Further, white settlers and land speculators owing money to the trust fund for land they had not completely paid for had their debts lowered considerably through government re-evaluation of the land. Sometimes those debts were even cancelled by a benevolent stroke of an official's pen. Officials themselves personally profited from this penmanship. What the Nishnabe received was pittance, some ten dollars a year each in annuities. Handing out such small payments was like providing water, a spoonful at a time, to a person dying of thirst (see Schmalz 1991:164-72).

Traditional decision-making was through consensus in council. However, government officials wanting land in Nawash just sought out those who might be vulnerable enough to be willing to sign in the hopes of bettering their own, not their band's, situation. The signatories that the officials recruited had no official authority within the band, nor were they representative of the people's opinion taken as a whole. According to a petition that Nah-nee was later to present to the Queen, the Indian Department appointed two chiefs "contrary to the unanimous vote of the General Council of the tribe; and these new chiefs... without the concurrence of the many of the tribe, surrender[ed] to the Government all the lands which had been reserved as a home for the Newash band..." (as cited in the *Friends' Review* 1860:10). Those without hard-worked-for-farms would support the surrender, probably figuring that some short-term gain might be more likely than the long-term government promises that seemed to mean little. Those who had cultivated their land and did not want to leave were forced off their farms. They had no choice.

That was the situation that greeted Catharine, William and their family when they returned to Nawash in 1857. Her beloved farm had been surveyed, divided up into town lots and put up for sale at public auction. The Suttons would not accept this loss without some sort of fight. They approached Richard Theodore Pennefather, the Superintendent of Indian Affairs, to see what they could do. They tried to get their land back on the grounds that the chiefs of the band had signed their 200 acres over to them; that attempt failed. Native common land hold was used against them. Pennefather told them that as the land had been held in common prior to the surrender, it could not have been divided before that time. Second, the Suttons tried to at least get Nah-nee's annuity payments for the period from 1852 to 1857, plus compensation for the improvements her hard labour had contributed to the value of the land. Other members of the band had received such annuities and compensation. This time her marriage and her missionary work were held against her. Pennefather denied her even this small amount of money, "on the ground of her having married a white man, and having been absent from the country during the time for which she claimed payment" (Smith 1976:591). The Indian Act had not yet been passed, legislation that would deny a woman her 'Indian' status for marrying someone (Native or non-Native) who did legally bear such status. She was still considered a member of the band by the other Nawash Nishnabe during the years she was away. But Pennefather, like other Indian Affairs officials before and after that day, had the power to arbitrarily decide what he liked, no matter what the legal technicalities.

Fortunately, the Suttons did have some money, so Nah-nee would try to buy some of the lost Native land when it was put up for sale at public auction. She would be bidding against anyone else who wanted to buy the land. She was on a level playing field with the newest immigrant to Canada. Money alone had rights. So, in September, 1857, determined to purchase a farm, Nah-nee went to the auction. She bid for four lots of the surrendered land. Nah-nee appears to have been a popular figure in the Owen Sound area at that time, for local emotions, white and Native, seem to have been in her favour. People refrained from seriously bidding against her. According to the historian Peter Schmalz (Schmalz 1977:108), Nah-nee was able to buy her 49.5 acres for only five dollars an acre, three to four dollars cheaper than the going price for the land at the auction.

After she was successful in the bidding, Nah-nee was given a certificate by the land agent. She probably clutched that paper close to her heart, as it was the first piece of paper certifying land ownership that she had ever held in her 33 years. There was a sad irony to this purchase. Here she was buying land, and the money would theoretically be going to the band she belonged to, money she could not share in.

It would be worse than that. This piece of paper proved as worthless as the promises made to her parents in earlier days along the Credit River. The Indian Agent disallowed her purchase on the simple discriminatory grounds that the lots were not to be sold to 'Indians,' their financial status notwithstanding. She was caught in a double bind. She could not receive annuities, nor money for the improvements she had made on her land because she was, by dint of marriage, 'not an Indian.' On the other hand, she could not buy the land she had successfully bid for because she was, by birth, an 'Indian.'

But Catharine Sutton was not one to accept defeat lightly, without a fight, verbal, written or legal. The fact that she gave birth to her fifth child, Mary Margaret or Sahsakahnooquay did not slow her down in this fight. Along with David Sawyer and Abner Elliot, two Mississauga in the same situation, she petitioned the provincial parliament in Toronto in 1858, with the assistance of John Sheridan Hogan, M.P.P. Her part of the petition read as follows:

> And that your petitioner, CATHERINE SUTTON and
> her husband be allowed to enjoy the benefit of the
> improvements they have made on the land, and also
> that they be allowed to retain for themselves and
> their family, the farm lots purchased at the sale
> September last, on the same terms that others
> bought, according to the conditions of the sale. And
> that your petitioner be permitted also to retain for
> her mother and her sister on the same conditions
> the lots purchased for them. (photocopy of petition
> in County of Grey-Owen Sound Museum)

Her band, then generally referred to as the Cape Croker Band after their new place of residence on the Bruce Peninsula, fought for her rights as well, declaring on September 4, 1858:

> She is entitled to the land she bid off, and we beg it
> may be granted to her. She is entitled to her
> improvement money as much as the rest of us. Mrs.
> Sutton stands as one of us; she is entitled to her
> rights as one of us, as she was adopted into our Band,
> and has a right of her portion to all our shares and
> complaints, as fully explained in our presence.
> (Schmalz 1977:110)

Her legal actions of 1858 failed. What could her next move possibly be? In July of 1859, at a general Indian council held at the Rama reserve by Lake Simcoe, Nah-nee was appointed to go to Britain on her people's behalf. Just as Peter Jones had done more than 20 years before, she was going to try to speak with the Queen. Her job, as stated in the *Colonial Intelligencer,* was to make known "to the British government the peculiar and oppressive circumstances under which the Indians in British North America are placed" (*The Colonial Intelligencer and Aborigines' Friend,* 1866:148). She would have loved to have had the advice and guidance of her unofficial adoptive father, but he had died in 1856.

It is all very well to be appointed by the general Indian council to embark on a great mission such as this, a different matter to be able to pay for such a mission and to have the connections necessary to get introduced to the ruler of the British Empire. With a few letters of introduction from politically minor players such as the local Methodist minister, she was off to New York to raise funds for her proposed journey across the Atlantic. During the long train ride to New York, she stopped in Rochester for a few days. This is possibly due to connections established through one of her former teachers, Sophia Cook,[19] who was from that city. Catharine was well received there. An article published in a local paper spoke of her being "removed from Paganism" through the work of Miss Cook, briefly mentioned the rights she was fighting for, discussed at great length the Native beadwork she brought with her and advertised a presentation she was making at a local church, saying, "Mrs S. is of noble or royal blood—being the lineal heir to the chieftaincy.... Go and hear her. She will have something interesting to say, and perhaps curious too." (*Union and Advertiser*, March 12, 1860)

The contacts she made in Rochester helped her on her way. According to one writer, "she was hospitably entertained and cheered by the friendly notice of several benevolent persons, one of whom accompanied her to the cars, and commended her to the care of an acquaintance going to New York, requesting him to take her to a suitable boarding house in the city, which he kindly did" (*Friends' Review* 1860:140). Despite this auspicious beginning, Nah-nee did not initially meet with success in New York: "The day after her arrival, she called on a person with a letter of introduction, but was coldly received, and lonely and sad, returned to her lodgings. Her faith was sorely tried, but she was comforted in prayer" (*Friends' Review* 1860:140).

Nah-nee was alone, without husband, children, relatives or friends; and she was pregnant. Many would have admitted defeat and gone home. Then, a young woman came to visit this self-described "lonely daughter of the forest." She told Nah-nee that some older men, Quakers, wanted to talk with her. This proved to be a significant turning point. The Quakers were very impressed with her devout nature and her strong desire to help her people. A series of presentations was arranged.

As can be easily detected from her writing, Nah-nee was good with words, if not always with spelling. Many writers weren't good spellers in those days. But what kind of impression would she make on the sophisticated society people of New York? A newspaper article written about some fund-raising event paints the following picture:

> Her appearance... was accompanied by much neatness. Her carriage as dignified, and though her

contenance is not beautiful, the expression is
intelligent and pleasing. Her flat beaver hat with a
profusion of cherry colored ribbons. She spoke with a
slight accent evincing education. (Croft 1980:79)

Although cultivating such an image would probably have brought
her greater financial returns in her fund-raising, Nah-nee refused to
capitalize on the then popular figure of 'Indian royalty' to which a
number of her supporters subscribed.[20] She didn't see herself as a
Nishnabe Pocahontas and didn't want anyone else to picture her
that way either. At one meeting, after she was introduced to the
audience, Nah-nee rose:

> ... and introduced her remarks by saying that she
> had heard that some of the papers had announced
> that an Indian queen was going to address them that
> evening. This was a mistake [she stated]; she was
> no queen, but only an humble Indian woman.... (from
> a New York Herald article quoted in the *Globe*, April
> 5, 1860)

She seems to have possessed a striking capacity to draw people
to her. Although admittedly from a biased source, her loving husband,
we have the following statement attesting to this capacity:

> I have known her to go on board a large steamboat
> where the large Saloon was full of Ladies and
> Gentlemen, and all entire Strangers, and in the
> allmost incredible short time she would become the
> Belle of the Saloon. There was something in her
> natural appearance that at once introduced her to
> the notice of all whom she came in contact. (Croft
> 1980:79)

In a letter from Robert Lindley Murray to his wife, we get a good
sense of how effective Nah-nee was during her presentations.
Speaking of a meeting of March 30, 1860, referred to above, Murray
wrote:

> She spoke in a touching strain for nearly an hour,
> giving a narration of the wrongs done to her tribe....

> After she had concluded, a committee was appointed to receive subscriptions to aid her in getting to England, and to provide her with proper introductory letters to enable her to find access to the Home Government.

Hats were passed round on the spot, and about $140 was collected. After this business had been concluded, the woman again came forward, expressing a wish to close the meeting with prayer. She knelt down, and in a melodious voice poured out a fervent petition for divine blessing for herself on her lonely pilgrimage, on the people of her tribe and on the white men their persecutors.

As for these last, broken with sobs, her prayer ascended, "Father, forgive them, for they know not what they do." The audience was moved to tears" (Murray 1876:75-76).

While the Quakers took Nah-nee's message to heart, back home in Ontario opposition was expressed in the *Globe* by its politically powerful editor, George Brown. After reporting what the *New York Herald* said about the meeting, the editor could not resist adding the following negative and generally uninformed commentary:

> We are astonished that the Friends [i.e., the Quakers], who generally mix prudence and shrewdness with their benevolence, should be so egregiously taken in by this "upright woman". Her statement of grievances is altogether false. There is no law or regulation which forbids Indians to buy land; on the contrary, they are encouraged to cultivate the soil. We have never heard in Canada of the appointment of "the upright woman" to the post of deputy to the Queen, and we believe that she is an arrant impostor, levying contributions from the charitable on false pretences. *Our Government have always dealt fairly and generously with the Indians, and if they did not, plenty of people would be found in Canada ready to contend for the redress of their wrongs.* (*The Globe*, April 5, 1860; emphasis mine)

Said then or today, both those latter statements are untrue.

Perhaps Brown took exception to Catharine Sutton's going to the United States to air Canada's dirty laundry. Fortunately, Brown's remarks did not affect the success of Nah-nee's mission. Sufficient money was raised for her to have first-class cabin passage aboard a ship sailing to Britain. She left on the steamer *Persia* on April 25, 1860. Something of Nah-nee's scrupulously honest character can be seen in what she did with the money. In a piece written in New York for the *Friends' Review* on April 30, we read that:

> After payment of her passage and other necessary expenses, about $100 remained of the money which had been collected by the Committee. So jealous was she, lest any should suppose the funds were applied by her for her individual benefit, that she refused to receive any of it into her own possession. It was therefore, remitted to a Friend in Liverpool, to pay her expenses on arriving there. (*Friends Review* 1860:588)

The Quakers also pressed into Nah-nee's hand letters of introduction that would link her with some very important people who belonged to the influential Aborigines' Protection Society. Included in their number were Robert and Christine Alsop, with whom Nah-nee would stay while she was in Britain. She early impressed them. In a letter of July 7, written after she had stayed with them for several weeks, Robert Alsop stated, "We are much edified by her Christian character, and feel it a privilege to have her under our roof" (*Friends' Review* 1860:789).

Nah-nee's first days of trying to gain an audience with Queen Victoria appear to have been somewhat frustrating. The colonial government of Canada probably saw to it that she would meet with substantial strands of bureaucratic red tape. We learn something of her frustration from a report of a presentation she made less than a month after her arrival in Britain. On May 23, Nah-nee addressed the annual meeting of the Aborigines Protection Society. The report appearing in the *Globe* of June 11, 1860, gives us a good, if indirect, sense of what she said:

> [S]he stated briefly the wrong under which the "poor Indian" suffered at the hands of the "Indian Department." When the white people first went over they spoke to the poor Indians of their great mother, the Queen, and she [Nah-nee] had been sent over to

> make their grievances known to her. But she found it
> very hard to get near her and where the door was to
> see her she did not know. Then again she had been
> told that Queen Victoria had very little power. Whom
> to apply to she did not know. Her heart was drawn
> after her people, and though she might lose her home
> and her all, she could not quench the feeling in her
> breast. She had rather suffer with her people than
> enjoy the pleasures of this life. (The *Globe*, June 11,
> 1860, p. 3)

Her presentation was a success. In a report written by the *Globe*'s
London correspondent on June 23, published on July 7, we read that:
"The touching speech made by Mrs. Sutton, at the meeting of the
Aborigines Protection Society,has gained for her cause many
sympathisers among our philanthropic men and women" (*The Globe*,
July 7, 1860).

Eventually the right contacts were made. These included
prominent reforming Member of Parliament John Bright, a Quaker,
and Henry Pelham, known more formally as the Duke of Newcastle
and as the Secretary of State for the Colonies (1852-54 and 1859-64).
They set up Nah-nee's meeting with the "great mother," and briefed
Her Majesty on the reasons why the Mississauga woman had asked
for an audience.

The fateful day when the two strong women would meet each
other came on June 19, 1860. We have two different accounts of the
meeting of the two, one from each of the two women. Nah-nee wrote
a letter to C.A. Jones, son of Sacred Feathers, which was later
published in the *Brantford Courier* of August 1, 1860. Nah-nee must
have worried about a number of things, both big and small, before
being presented to the most powerful woman in the world. How, for
example, should she curtsy when she was eight months' pregnant?
Should she try to hide her condition as much as possible, as Queen
Victoria, then the mother of nine was well known not to be too fond
of pregnancy, referring to it as the "shadow side of marriage." No
nervousness shows, however, in the following words from Nah-nee's
letter:

> So you see I have seen the Queen. The Duke went
> before us, and he made two bows, and then I was left
> in the presence of the Queen; she came forward to

meet me, and held out her hand for me to kiss, but I forgot to kiss it, and only shook hands with her. The Queen asked me many questions, and was very kind in her manners and very friendly to me.... (Sutton 1860)

After she wrote of John Bright and the Duke of Newcastle stating her purpose for seeking an audience with the queen, she tells us the following:

Then the Queen bowed to me and said, "I am happy to promise you aid and protection," and asked me my name. The Queen then looked at her husband, who stood at her left side, and smiled. She received me with much kindness as to astonish me, when I saw her come smiling and so good to poor Indians. (ibid.)

For the Queen, that was a day of meeting exotic people from faraway places. The same day she had two Maori chiefs presented to her. In her private journal, Queen Victoria wrote the following concerning her encounter with Nah-nee:

After luncheon the Duke of Newcastle introduced... an Indian Chieftainness of the Ojibeways, called Nah-nee-bah-wee-quay, or Mrs. C Sutton, as she is a Christian & is married to an English sailor. She is of the yellow colour of the American Indians, with black hair & was dressed in a strange European dress with a coloured shawl & straw hat with feathers. She speaks English quite well, & is come on behalf of her Tribe to petition against some grievances as regards their land. A worthy Quakeress, Mrs. Alsop, with whom she is living brought her. She seems gentle & simple. (Mackworth-Young 1960)

Nah-nee would ever after hold Queen Victoria in high esteem. We see this in an article entitled "Is there Hope for the Indians?" published in the *Christian Guardian* of May 28, 1862. After speaking disparagingly of officials who did not keep earlier promises concerning Native land rights, she said, "A shame on them, because they do it in the name of that noble lady the Queen, as though she approved of their wicked conduct" (Sutton 1862).

Another sign of her respect for Queen Victoria is the following poem, found in William Sutton's ledger, apparently composed by Nahnee, date unknown. Of especial interest is the fact that she refers to Queen Victoria as possessing the characteristics of her own name:

The daughter of a Chieftain, she stands before us now,
Her raven braids have mirrored no crown upon her brow;
Nor is she clad in royal robes of purple and of gold,
Nor has she other Herald, than the mission she told.
Yet beautiful, around her head, a halo bright is thrown
Of Faith, that in the darkest hours hath still more clearly [shown]
And, robed in its own dignity, her womans gentle heart
Grows queenly with the majesty her Nations wrong [impart]

God bless thee, Queen Victoria! may He thy spirit bless
To understand the Indians wrongs, and knowing, to red[ress]
Thy sister, of the forest wild, makes her appeal to thee
Oh, may'st thou as the name she bears, thyself deserving[ly]

That future ages may record of England's matron Queen,
A true and upright woman's heart in all her acts was seen
The Noble, and the Peasant poor, the Indian in the woods,
United all in loving her, "Victoria the Good."

> (William Sutton, ms, n.d.)

Once she had met the Queen, the next major item of Nah-nee's busy British schedule was to give birth to her sixth child, which she did at Stoke, Newington, on July 11, 1860. She showed gratitude to her benefactors in the naming of her newest son. He was christened Alsop Albert Edward Sutton. The Alsop was a respectful gift to her hosts. Albert, of course, was the name of Queen Victoria's beloved husband, Edward, the name of her eldest son.

Nah-nee made quite an impression on the British populace, as had her adopted father before her. An enthusiastic article published by the Aborigines' Protection Society even went so far as to state that, "Probably no Indian ever visited this country who excited more general interest than Mrs. Sutton" (*The Colonial Intelligencer*, 1866:155). While this may have been something of an exaggeration, her popularity in Britain is not to be doubted.

While part of her initial attraction for some Britons may have been to see a 'wild Red Indian' who could speak fluent and articulate English, Nah-nee refused to play the part of the side-show Indian. Her opinion on this subject, as well, perhaps, as her strong identification with some of the material and spiritual aspects of European culture can be seen in the following quote from the *Colonial Intelligencer*:

> And I have been asked by different people why didn't I fetch my Indian dress. I tell them I had none, this was my dress; this is the way we dress. I tell them we are not pagans, that we try to be like white people— to be clean and decent, and do what we can to be like the civilized people. (Sutton 1866:155)

At some point in Nah-nee's stay in Britain, she received a letter from her husband that suggests that the government in Canada (along with its representatives in Britain) was trying to undermine her criticism by saying that Natives could buy land. However, the conditions under which such purchasing was permitted were similar to those for Afro-Americans who were technically given the vote after the Civil War, but couldn't vote without passing literacy tests that most Southern whites couldn't pass. Nah-nee rightfully tore into such hypocrisy with the following words:

> [S]ince I have been here I have had a letter from my husband saying that we can purchase land—but on what conditions? Why, the Indian must be civilized; he must talk English, talk French, read and write, and be well qualified for everything before he can purchase land. Why, the poor Indians, none of them can go there. Poor things, how are they to get their education?... Why, I can tell you something. I have seen some people in our own country that came from your country that could neither read nor write; and they came to buy Indian land. But the poor Indian must be so well qualified before he can have a house of his own! (Sutton 1866:156-7)

What Nah-nee seems to have been referring to was part of the aforementioned Civilization or Enfranchisement Act of 1857. The landowning portion of that act determined that a qualified individual could have a maximum of 50 acres from the reserve lands. That piece of land could not be sold or passed down to the person's children. Upon death the land again became part of the reserve. To qualify for this 'step on the path to civilization,' a Native had to be:

> ... of the male sex, and not under twenty-one years of age... able to speak, read and write either the english or french language readily and well, and... sufficiently advanced in the elementary branches of education... of good moral character and free from debt. (Smith 1975:51)

No immigrating European settler had to meet such standards before buying Canadian land.

After her meeting with Queen Victoria, and despite the obvious appeal of speaking to large, receptive audiences, Catharine Sutton was anxious to return home. She began her voyage back on September 15, again on the steamer *Persia*. After arriving in New York, with stops at Rochester, Toronto and Collingwood, she travelled by trains, a steamer and finally a small boat. The reunion with her husband and children, who would be greeting both a long-time separated wife and mother, as well as a new child and brother, must have been something to behold. However, after the initial joy of those moments, and the thrill of telling scarcely to be believed stories to eager listeners, Nah-nee would have to renew the fight for her land and for the rights of her people.

Conditions in her home community when she returned were unsettled. Nawash was facing factionalism, in part brought on by the influx of American Catholic Potawatomi amongst the Canadian Methodist Ojibwa (see Schmalz 1991:200-2). The chief and some 20 families were threatening to leave; more disturbing was the situation concerning land rights. Some concessions had been granted while she had been in Britain, but they did not really amount to much. Her band at Cape Croker, for example, had been granted licences of occupation which could not be sold to those who were not members of the band. But they were only licences, not deeds of ownership.

A big disappointment was to come from someone she thought was an ally, the Duke of Newcastle. In a letter of March 26, 1861, Nah-nee bitterly wrote the following words telling of what she must have felt was his betrayal:

> [Queen Victoria] requested the Duke of Newcastle to investigate the wrongs complained of, upon his arrival in Canada…. He pledged himself to do so, and it appears the Duke professes to have discharged his duty in this respect, but how did he perform an investigation in which thousands of poor ignorant and deeply injured Indians have a great interest? The Indian Department, with the Governor General at its head, are the parties complained of, and the Duke made the investigation entirely through them; not a solitary friend of the injured party was allowed to be present to take part. I consider the Duke has no excuse for not allowing some of our friends the privilege of pleading our cause in presence of the Department; he was aware of a deputation which had been organized expressly for that purpose, which was composed of men of ability, influence and character. All the time allowed them for an interview was about five minutes, so that all they could do was to read over a list of the grievances and hand the papers to the Duke, who promised to write from Niagara and let them know the result, but failed to do so. (*Friends' Review* 1861:538-9)

As a person whose class and race insulated him from experiencing prejudice, the Duke obviously found it easy to buy the package of good-sounding intentions that the Indian Department was selling. He believed that the Superintendent of Indian Affairs was "kindly disposed towards the Indians, and would do all he could to benefit them." But Superintendent Bartlett was not "kindly disposed" towards Nah-nee, and he was manipulating the information that the Duke of Newcastle was receiving. In a letter of August 3 to W.J. Jones of Cape Croker, Bartlett wrote, "Discourage Mrs. Sutton's action of choosing others in whom she could place confidence to speak to Newcastle. You must tell Indians not to listen to her" (Schmalz 1977:110).

The Duke of Newcastle even accepted the obviously face-saving story that the department had concocted concerning why the government had disallowed her land purchase. According to an anonymous writer in the *Friends' Review:*

> The Duke stated that Nah-nee bought more than her
> own farm at the sale, and the agent she employed
> bought largely, which gave the idea that they were
> engaged in a land speculation, and therefore the
> government refused her money, and not because she
> was an Indian. (*Friends's Review* 1861:539)

The land she had tried to purchase was not just for her and her
husband but included lots for her mother and sister as well, not an
act of land speculation. What particularly hurt Nah-nee was that,
apparently because of all the work she had done to fight for the rights
of her family and her people, she seemed to be specially targeted to
be deprived of her heritage[21] and her home. In her words:

> The Duke says I am not an Indian, but a white woman,
> because I am married to an Englishman, and
> consequently can have no claim as an Indian. I am
> acquainted with quite a number of Indian women who
> are so married, but none of them have ever been
> troubled by the Department except myself—they have
> all their rights, but I am robbed of my birthright; the
> Great Spirit gave these things to my forefathers, and
> to me through them; now the Department withholds
> from me what the Indians themselves acknowledge
> to be our due, and request it to be allowed... and I
> am soon to be driven from my loved home with my
> family. (*Friends' Review* 1861:539)

In an almost identical letter of March 30, she expanded upon
this theme of special persecution by stating that: "Although I have
been married 21 years, it was not until the last four years that the
department has made this excuse for robbing me and my children of
our birthright" (*Friends' Review* 1860:120).

Her major concerns were for her husband, whose health worried
her,[22] and for her children.[23] The Owen Sound area was being cleared
of Natives. Without the farm, where would the Suttons live? Would
they have to move to a reserve populated by strangers? Or would they
be denied even that refuge, as the government was saying that she
was 'not an Indian.' She even considered moving to New York. What
kept her strong during those trying times, as always, was her faith.
In a letter of March 26, she wrote:

> If it had not been for my religion, I know not what I
> could have done in this trial. I have yet a home in
> heaven no earthly hands can sell, or withhold from
> me. May God give me grace and strength in every
> time of need. (*Friends' Review* 1860:539)

Later that year her prayers were answered. In September, 1861, she was finally paid compensation for the improvements she had made to the land she had worked for seven years. She received 60 dollars, a pittance. The annuities she would never receive despite her continuing membership in the Cape Croker band. More exciting was the news that she was finally permitted to buy the parcels of land that she had successfully bid for at the auction four years before. As mentioned above the four lots included land for her sister, Mary Sunego, and for her mother. The first instalment cost $402.52, the total cost came to $1610.00.

Perhaps one non-spiritual reason why the government reversed its position was that Nah-nee was dealing with a different level of government. Indian Affairs had been transferred to the provincial government of Upper Canada. Often such a power transfer is destructive to Native rights, a way for federal governments to avoid responsibility for agreements they have signed. In this case, at least for Nah-nee, the opposite seems to have been true.

A sour note was added to the song of celebration for this victory. No other Nishnabe was given the same right to purchase the land. David Sawyer, as we have seen (p. 167), had petitioned along with Nah-nee to receive land successfully bid for at the same auction. Sawyer, Sacred Feathers' cousin, and once a lay missionary, was a prominent, respected figure among his people and later became the chief of the Mississauga of the New Credit. Still he was denied the right to buy the land he wanted and should have been permitted to acquire, perhaps because he too was a thorn in the side of the government but hadn't acquired powerful friends.

The government seems to have been trying to buy Catharine Sutton off. If that is so, they did not know her very well. They could not buy her silence. She persisted in speaking with a strong voice in arguing for her people's rights. The same year that she was given permission to buy her land, she criticized the government's attempt to purchase Manitoulin Island for white settlers, land that had been promised in 1836 to remain forever in Native hands.

Recently published in Penny Petrone's book on Native literature is a good example of Catharine Sutton's capacity to speak up for her people. It is taken from a draft copy in William Sutton's ledger of what appears to be a letter to an editor who had written a particularly poisonous piece of anti-Native journalism. There is some question as to the date; Petrone claims it was written on September 8, 1864.[24] However, there can be no question as to the powerful and articulate nature of the writing. Appearing first in the journal was a hand-copied version of the piece in the paper that sparked Nah-nee's response:

> [O]n the shores of Goulais Bay Lake Superior and the neighbouring one of Batchawana, one of these publick nuisances—an Indian reserve was laid of a few years ago under Lord Elgin's Government the reserve covered a portage of 30 miles on the Lake with a sufficient depth into the country to make up an area of 300 square miles of land—some of the best land in the country and so situated as to block up the means of access to the entire regions lying in the rear of it and all this for about a dozen of the most wretched, squalid, miserable specimens of human nature that I have even seen: indeed *a close inspection of, and a little acquaintance with, these creatures leads one to doubt whether they are human, but whether they are men or monkeys, it matters not now, the present administration have found means to extinguish their title so far, that the country is now surveyed, and will soon be in market.* (Petrone 1990:66; emphasis mine)

Nah-nee picked up first on the original writer's reference to monkeys and skilfully used it to criticize him:

> I have lived for several years with in a few miles of Goulais bay and I have frequently seen those Indians aluded to but I never took them for Monkeyes neither did I ever hear such a thing hinted at by the white people I think they were allways, considered to be human beings, possessing living souls... [W]hen I was in England I went to the zoological garden were I saw a great maney monkeys and of various sises and kinds but I observed their was one trait coman to them all and *a close inspection & a little acquaintance with the Editor of the Leader has led me to the conclusion*

*that the same trait stands out prominently in his natural
disposition and character, and when I state what is the
nature of that trait so common to all the monkeys I ever
saw I will leave you to guess who is by nature verey
closly related to these four leged animals well I tell you
the trait wich I observed so comon to every variety of
monkeys was an entire absence of humanity.* (Petrone
1990:66-67, emphasis mine)

She then alluded to the possible benefits she felt the editor might
have been trying to gain for himself by siding with the views on Native
issues of a political party:

I have allso frequently seen the little trained monkey
exibited in our canadian towns and vilages with pants
red coat and cap... and I noticed that aftere he had
played [one] of his money anticks he allways went
round with his hat for a colection and as far as I can
learn this is just what a certen creature does after
he as performed something wich is pleasing to a
certen party he expects them in return to throw
something handsome into his cap. (Petrone 1990:67)

Her next criticism was for the land speculators who profited from
the weak position of Natives:

[W]hy are indian reservations aney more a publick
nuisance then large blocks of land bought and held
by speculators[?] I argue that Indians have a right to
be paid a fair valuation for aney lands wich they may
agree to surrender, I suppose the Leader would not
have a word to say if a dozen or two poor hard working
white men should get scatered through the Goulais
bay teritory, while all the remainder was bought up
and held by a few speculators untill those poor men
by hard persevering industry had cleared up their
lands and made roads and thus by the poor mans
hard labour raised the valued of the rich land
speculators property. (ibid.)

Finally, she discussed the deadly double meaning of the
'extinction' of Native title to the land and hinted at the possibility

that the military would bring about extinction in both senses of the word:

> ... the Editor of the leader states that the present administration have found means to extinguish their title, my english his so poor that I frequently have to consult Webster and I find the word extinguish means to destroy to put an end to; to extinguish a claim or title, a wonderful feat surely for the present administration to perform and for the Editor of the leader to brag of... our present administration can extinguish the red mans title at pleasure, what hope is their for the remnant that are yet left to whom can they go for redress who will help them or are they entirly without helper, I suppose Mr Linsey[25] will answer these questions when the present administration give him a commission to go to manitolin with soldiers to subdue the Indians or monkeys as he calls them. (Petrone 1990:67-8)

In 1863, Nah-nee contracted a severe case of asthma, probably related to tuberculosis, some time around the birth of her seventh child, Christine, named presumably after friend and hostess. Although this restricted her physically, it did not keep her from still doing what she could for her people. The summer of 1864 was hot and dry in Ontario, as the summer before had been, increasing the likelihood that fires would start, spread fast and be difficult to put out. So it is not surprising that fire struck both her farm and fields and the properties of other Mississauga living nearby. In a letter of August 14, 1864, she wrote the following concerning the effects of that fire:

> Some of the poor Indians have nothing left; all is gone by fire—nothing to live on for the coming winter; and, so all our little all will be gone. The fire has burnt most all we had. Last year's crops were destroyed with a little fly, so the crops were very light, and this year the fires have done their finishing work.... (Sutton 1864)

Despite the pressing needs of Nah-nee and her family, the 40-year-old woman shared as much as she could of the goods for which she had worked so hard. She knew more help was needed. On August 24, she wrote a letter to the Alsops asking them to set up an appeal in Britain to obtain funds and supplies for those who had suffered from the devastation of the fires. While it was not in her nature to ask for herself, she would try to use her connections to help her people:

> When the poor Indians come to my house to ask something to eat and to wear, and I see them half naked and hungry, how can I say no to them, though I know we have but little ourselves. Some are rich in faith, some know not the god we worship and love. I have been requested by some of our friends to ask this aid from my friends over the big water. You all know when I was with you I never asked anything from anybody. What you gave me you gave with a free good will, and I was thankful to you and to my heavenly father who careth for all. (Sutton 1864)

Perhaps the hard times brought on by drought and fire made her health worsen. She died only slightly more than a year after she wrote those letters. The following comes from the last paragraph of an obituary published on November 8, 1865:

> For several weeks before she died her health was greatly improved, and on the morning of the day of her death left home for Leith, six miles distant, in very buoyant spirits; on the way home she took bad and expired, in a few moments after being brought into the house. She died surrounded by her family and my colleague, Bro. Kidd, repeating these words, "Jesus, I want to love thee better." She died on the 26th of September, leaving a husband and seven children to mourn her loss. (*Christian Guardian*, November 8, 1865)

Her husband outlived her by some 30 years.

Today Nah-nee's grave lies in the land that she fought so hard to obtain. But will it stay there? In August of 1998 the 232-hectare piece of land that contains her grave, the stone foundation of the house that the Suttons built, and the lilac bush that she planted, was purchased by a developer for $900,000. He has upmarket plans for executive homes, championship golf courses, posh tennis courts and a marina. In a newspaper article published on December 12, 1998 (Smyth 1998), he was said to be "still deciding" on what to do with the grave and other physical remnants of Nah-nee's presence. Concerns about what will happen have been expressed by the Nawash band, historians, archaeologists and by Stephanie McMullen, a descendant of Nah-nee's, who states: "My fear is that when developers given any attention to a historical person they [*sic*] become a mascot, a sort of Laura Secord. I don't think she would be too pleased to become the mascot for a golf course" (Smyth 1998).

Appendix A: Mississauga Names and their Meanings

1) Mississauga

There are two main theories concerning the meaning of the word 'Mississauga.' One is that it means 'large river mouth,' with the -**missi**- having the same meaning as in Mississippi, 'large river.' The other is that Mississauga means 'many river mouths' (Smith 1987a:20 and see 266 fn 7). I prefer the former, as the prefix -**missi**-, in some dialects -**m(i)shi**-, typically means 'large' (see Rhodes 1985:253, **mshi**- and the words for lion, rough-legged hawk and apple; and Baraga 1878:252 Ojibwa-English). The latter is still a possibility, as the Mississagi River has more than one mouth.

2) Anishnabek

This word has been translated in a variety of ways. Among these are 'from whence man descended,' 'the good beings,' 'spontaneous man,' 'original human beings' and 'ordinary men.' Three contemporary Ojibwa interpretations of this term are the following:

 a) Ojibwa educator Basil Johnston wrote in a version of his people's origin myth that:

> The new men and women were called "Anishnabeg," beings made out of nothing, because their substances

were not rock, or fire, or water, or wind. They were spontaneous beings. (Johnston 1976:15; see also William Warren, *History of the Ojibway Nation*, 1970 (orig. 1852), Minnesota, Ross and Haines, p. 57).

b) Spiritual leader Edward Benton-Benai has written that after the Creator (Gitchie Manito) gave life to all things:

Gitchie Manito then took four parts of Mother Earth and blew into them using a Sacred Shell. From the union of the Four Sacred Elements and his breath, man was created.

It is said the Gitchie Manito then lowered man to the Earth. Thus man was the last form of life to be placed on the Earth. From this Original Man came the A-nish-i-na'-be people. In the Ojibway language if you break down the word Anishinabe, this is what it means:

ANI	NISHINA	ABE
From	Lowered	The Male
Whence		of the Species

(Benton-Banai 1988:2-3)
This is not a generally accepted etymology.

c) Nicholas Deleary, in his unpublished masters thesis stated the following:

Today's usage of the term "Ani-shin-a-bek"... conjures many interpretations and closely linked meanings. For example this term is used to make reference to a very ancient past, the beginnings of time and creation itself. In other usage, Anishnabek refers to one or many of the ancestral related and confederate tribal groups. In today's political arena, "Anishinabek" designates a Native lobby group. In another contemporary sphere, it could mean *all* aboriginal people of North and South America, a "Pan"-Indian usage. (Deleary 1991:12)

There is a slight exception to the use of the term '(A)nishnabek' by the Ojibwa. The speakers of Severn Ojibwe, people who live in the northwest of Ontario and across the border to Manitoba, use "Anihshininiwak" (Valentine 1995:62), which substitutes the morpheme (word part) -inini- 'people' for 'nabe.'

There is, then, no etymology of the word that is accepted generally by the Anishnabek peoples. What is of greater significance, however, is the point made by Roger Spielmann:

> The important thing to keep in mind, especially for non-cultural members, is that **Anishnaabe** is the term that people use to identify themselves, and that acknowledging and using the term is a show of respect for Anishnaabe people. (Spielmann 1998:241)

3) Nahnebahwequay

In Rhodes's modern *Eastern Ojibwa-Chippewa-Ottawa Dictionary*, he presents a contrast between the verb form "**niibwid**... stand" (Rhodes 1985:298) and the form created when the prefix **naa**- is added, making the verb "**naaniibwid**... stand up: (op. cit. p. 270). The older (and more complete) Baraga dictionary makes of this a distinction between 'to stand' (Baraga 1878:243 English-Ojibwa) and to 'stand here and there, in different places successively' (Baraga 1878:276 Ojibwa-English). I do not know which was the meaning attached to Catharine Sutton's name, although her interpretation of 'Upright Woman' suggests that 'to stand up' might be the more applicable translation.

4) Sunegoo

Rhodes gives "**san'goo**" as meaning "black squirrel" (Rhodes 1985:384 and 583). Baraga, however, presents "**Assanago**" as referring to "gray squirrel" (Baraga 1878:51, Ojibwa-English). Black squirrel is translated into Ojibwe as "**missanig**" (Baraga 1878:242, English-Ojibwa and 252, Ojibwa-English), meaning 'large squirrel.'

5) *The Sutton Children's Ojibwe Names*

The Ojibwe names of Nah-nee's children were presented as follows in the *Friends' Review* of 1860:539:

a) "Sah-gar-se-ga (rising sun) Joseph"

There is no -r- in this word, as there is none in the language. The same word appears with "gisiss" ('sun') as follows in Baraga's dictionary: "Sagassige gisiss. The sun comes out of the clouds" (Baraga 1878 Ojibwe-English, p. 360). The word appears to combine a morpheme -**saga**- referring to 'sticking out' (see saka- in Hewson 1993:171 and most words beginning with saga- in Baraga 1878, Ojibwe-English, pp. 359-60) and -**ssige**- referring to 'rising.'

b) "Nah-we-ke-gee-go-quay (blue sky) Catharine"

This is a difficult word for me to decipher. The -**(o)quay**- refers to 'woman' and the rest may relate in some way to a term for 'noon' (see Baraga 1878, Ojibwe-English, p. 279 and Rhodes 1985:529), but that is highly speculative.

c) "Nah-koo-quay (top buds of a tree) Sophia"

This word appears to combine -**nakoo**-, meaning 'to appear, be visible' (Baraga 1878, Ojibwe-English, p. 267 and Rhodes 1985:46) with -**quay**-, 'woman.'

d) "Sun-e-goo-nee (little squirrel) Wesley"

This is based on the term for 'squirrel' discussed above.

e) "Sah-sa-kah-noo-quay (little hail) Mary Marguerite"

This word is composed of a morpheme that Baraga presents as "sessegan," meaning 'it hails' or 'little hail" (Baraga 1878, English-Ojibwe, p. 124 and Ojibwe-English, p. 366, respectively).

Endnotes

[1] (Ellis 1995:xxxiii and 177). The first time I heard the story of the Iroquois and the Cree was in 1992, when Marcel Martin from Waswanipi on the east side of James Bay told me about an island near where he grew up where there were the bones and former possessions of the Iroquois who had once unsuccessfully raided the Cree.

[2] Fred, who combined a quiet politeness with a dry sense of humour, was also asked why the Ojibwa called the Iroquois by the same name that they used for a snake. His reply was, "It's the way they hold their heads up like this," and he proceeded to hold his head up.

[3] The military reputation of the Iroquois should not be too tarnished by reports of those times; they were outnumbered. The Iroquois Confederacy was somewhat overextended, attempting to stretch its influence far to the north, west and south of their traditional territory and power base. Their hearts might not have been as keen on defending this land as those of the Nishnabe were in acquiring it.

[4] Noteworthy is that the women of this nation, Nah-nee's predecessors, were not mere passive onlookers in the development of that reputation. Among other contributions, they played an actively supportive spiritual role. Reported in the somewhat negative language of French Captain Francois Pouchot, we hear of the women assisting their men out on a raid in the following way:

> These women assembled every evening to 'make medicine' one old woman singing, the others replying in chorus. It was reported in the fort that these women were working a spell of some supernatural sort, in accordance with ancient forms of their people, and the French officers from the fort went out to the scene of the strange ceremony and looked on. At the end of six or seven days, they inquired why they made no more medicine, when an old woman replied that their people had beaten; that she had juggled [i.e., performed a divination ceremony] and that they had killed many people. An officer... wrote down the spot, the day that she designated, and when the party returned, he questioned the Indians and prisoners, whose answers confirmed the old woman's account. (Schmalz 1991:52)

[5] See Isabelle Knockwood's *Out of the Depths* for a revealing book about some of the excesses of these schools. While the residential schools did involve good intentions and some individual successes, on the whole they were like a spiritual cavalry striking an unsuspecting Native camp. They wounded Native languages, tore families apart and attacked traditional religion. They left a shameful legacy of visible scars from emotional, physical, sexual and spiritual abuse that is still being felt.

[6] Ojibwa in the northwestern Ontario community of Lynx Lake developed an unusually high level of literacy in syllabic writing during the twentieth century through reading (and singing) their liturgical language of Cree in their community-run Anglican church (Valentine 1995).

[7] It excluded the considerable amount of land owned by the Hudson's Bay Company (all the lands drained by waters flowing into Hudson Bay), plus all the land then occupied by the French.

[8] According to Sir John Johnson, the idea that the Iroquois would be moving in close by "alarmed them greatly, as they apprehended it would be followed by disputes between them, and must terminate in One or the other leaving the Country" (Smith 1981:80).

[9] In Smith's words, "[W]hen the Mississauga learned in early 1784 that large numbers of white farmers intended to settle on their hunting grounds, they reversed their position and welcomed the Iroquois. At least the Iroquois, the old warriors reasoned, were fellow Indians with whom they might, if necessary, make common cause against the whites" (Smith 1981:80).

[10] *Indian Treaties and Surrenders* 1971, vol.1, p.5.

[11] See Introduction, p. 3.

[12] John Ferguson, 1794, as quoted in Smith 1981:74

[13] See Smith 1981:74 and 85.

[14] It was also recorded as Mes-sin-ninke. Early written renderings of Ojibwe names such as this were inconsistent.

[15] Smith 1987a:256-7 and Rhodes 1985:261 and 452.

[16] The scrupulous honesty of the Mississauga in this exchange was noted by the Englishwoman Anna Jameson, not always a sympathetic observer of Native people:

> This might seem a hazardous arrangement; yet I have been assured by those long engaged in the trade that for an Indian to break his engagement is a thing unheard of; and if, by any personal accident, he should be prevented from bringing the stipulated number of beaver skins, his relatives and close friends consider their honour implicated, and make up the quantity for him. (Clarkson 1967:16)

[17] His name is also recorded as Kineubenae and Quenebenaw.

[18] His name was written differently in different treaties. He was termed Acheton in the treaties of 1805 and 1820 and Adjutant in the treaty of 1818.

[19] Sophia Cook (1798-1849) taught at the Credit Mission school from 1832 to 1834 and later worked at the Alderville school for Mississauga children from 1840 to 1849.

[20] In the *Friends' Review* of 1860, Nah-nee was reported as being "one of the royal blood" (*Friends' Review* 1860:139). She was often referred to as an 'Indian Princess' by the Quakers, and other writers supportive of her cause.

[21] It wasn't until the 1869 version of the Indian Act that a Native woman could lose her 'Indian' status by marrying a man who did not have 'Indian' status.

[22] Nah-nee claimed at the time that: "During the last few years my husband's constitution has been broken by clearing new farms, so that his health is poor, and for that reason I thought we had better buy our own home" (*Friends' Review* 1860:120).

[23] In her words, "If I had no children I would say nothing, but I feel a mother's care" (*Friends' Review* 1860:120).

[24] Melba Croft claimed it appeared in a 1857 newspaper article (Croft 1980:66). A copy in the County of Grey-Owen Sound Museum has "c.1862?" at the top of the page.

[25] In one part of Nah-nee's letter, she makes mention of "Mr Charles linsey, the great Hearo who tried last fall to frighten the Manitoulin Indians out of their sences and their Lands..." (Petrone 1990:66). Later she refers to Natives being "at the mercy of such men as Mr Charles linsey" (Petrone 1990:67)

Bibliography

Notes on Sources

Many thanks to Christopher Densmore, Acting Director, University Archives, State University of New York, Buffalo for photocopies of articles from the *Friends' Review* and *Friends' Intelligencer*. Thanks as well to Donald Smith, who donated copies of those articles to the County of Grey-Owen Sound Museum and generously gave me copies of these and other works.

1) Newspaper Articles (No Acknowledged Author)

Christian Guardian Nov. 8, 1865

The Colonial Intelligencer and Aborigines Friend, 1859-1866 The Organ of the Aborigines' Protection Society, vol. 11, New Series, London.

The Friend Oct. 1, 1864

The Friends' Intelligencer June 2, vol. 17 #12, p182; July 21, vol. 17 #20, pp311-12; Aug.11, #22, pp343-4; Aug.25, #24, pp372-3; May 18, 1861, vol.18, #8, pp118-20

The Friends' Review 1860, May 26, vol.13 #37, pp587-8 ; Aug. 28, 13 #50, pp789-90

Sept.8, vol.14 #1, pp9-10, Nov.3, #9, pp139-41, and April 27, 1861, vol. 14 #34

The Globe, April 5, June 11, and July 7, 1860

Union and Advertiser (Rochester, New York), Monday, March 12, 1860

2) Catharine Sutton's Writings

1845 Letter published in the *Wesleyan Methodist Missionary Report of 1845-46*

1847 March 26, letter to Eliza Jones in Smith 1987a:148

1860 "An Indian Woman's Audience with Queen Victoria" in the *Brantford Courier* August 1

Letter of November 3 (in "Lo! The Poor Indian", in *The Friends' Review* , April 27, 1861 vol.14 #34, p538)

1861 Letter of March 3 (in "Lo! The Poor Indian", p538)

Letter of March 26 (ibid, pp538-9)

Letter of March 30, in "Nah-nee-bah-wee-quay" (*Friends' Intelligencer* May, 18, 1861, vol. 18 #8, p118-20.

1862 "Is there Hope for the Indians", in the *Christian Guardian* May 28

1864 Letters of August 14 and 24, published in *The Friend* October 1

1866 Speeches reported in *The Colonial Intelligencer* 1866, pp155-7

n.d. poem in William Sutton's Journal

Avery, Roberta. 1997. "Project cancelled to protect grave of "Indian Princess." *Windspeaker*, 15, (6):24.

Baraga, F. 1878. *A Dictionary of the Otchipwe Language*. Montreal: Beauchemin & Valois.

Benton-Benai, Edward. 1988. *The Mishomis Book: The Voice of the Ojibway*. Saint-Paul: Red School House.

Clarkson, Betty. 1967. *Credit Valley Gateway: The Story of Port Credit*. Toronto: Univ. of Toronto Press.

Copway, George (Kah-ge-ga-gah-bowh). 1972. *The Traditional History and Characteristic Sketches of the Ojibway* (orig. 1850). Toronto: Coles Publishing Ltd.

Croft, Melba Morris. 1980. *Fourth Entrance to Huronia: The History of Owen Sound*. Owen Sound: Stan Brown Printing.

Deleary, Nicholas. 1991. "The Midewewin: An Aboriginal Institution: Symbols of Continuity, A Native Studies Culture-based Perspective." Unpublished master's thesis, Carleton University.

Dickason, Olive. 1992. *Canada's First Nations: A History of Founding Peoples from Earliest Times*. Toronto: McClelland & Stewart.

Ellis, C. Douglas. 1995. *atalohkana nesta tipacimowina: Cree Legends and Narratives from the West Coast of James Bay*. Winnipeg: Univ. of Manitoba Press.

Fairley, Margaret, ed. 1960. *The Selected Writings of William Lyon Mackenzie, 1824-1837*. Toronto: Oxford University Press.

no author. 1971. *Indian Treaties and Surrenders*, 3 vols. (orig. 1891 and 1912). Toronto: Coles Publishing.

Hewson, John. 1993. *A Computer-Generated Dictionary of Proto-Algonquian*. Canada Ethnology Service, Mercury Series Paper 125. Hull: Canadian Museum of Civilization.

Johnston, Basil. 1976. *Ojibway Heritage*. Toronto: McClelland and Stewart.

Knockwood, Isabelle. 1992. *Out of the Depths: The Experiences of Mi'kmaw*

Children at the Residential School at Shubenacadie, Nova Scotia. Lockeport, NS: Roseway Pub.

Mackworth-Young, Robert. 1960. "Excerpt from Queen Victoria's Journal (unpublished)—June 19, 1860," in a letter from Mackworth-Young (Windsor Castle librarian) to Melba Croft, August 23, 1960. County of Grey-Owen Sound Museum.

McLean, John. 1970. *The Indians: Their Manners and Customs* (orig.1889). Toronto: Coles Pub.

Morris, J.L. 1943. *Indians of Ontario.* Toronto: Ont. Dept. of Lands and Forests.

Murray, Ruth. 1876. *Under His Wings:A Sketch of the Life of Robert Lindley Murray.* New York: Andson D.F. Randolph & Company.

Petrone, Penny. 1990. *Native Literature in Canada: From the Oral Tradition to the Present.* Toronto: Oxford University Press.

Rhodes, Richard. 1985. *Eastern Ojibwa-Chippewa-Ottawa Dictionary.* New York: Mouton.

Robinson, William, ed. 1891. *Friends of a Half Century; Fifty Memorials with Portraits of Members of the Society of Friends, 1840-1890.* London: Edward Hicks.

Rogers, Edward S. "Southeastern Ojibwa," in *Handbook of North American Indians* vol.15: *Northeast,* ed. by Bruce Trigger. Washington, D.C.: Smithsonian, pp. 760-1.

Schmalz, Peter S. 1977. *The History of the Saugeen Indians.* Toronto: Ontario Historical Society, Research Publication #5.

Schmalz, Peter S. 1991. *The Ojibwa of Southern Ontario.* Toronto: Univ. of Toronto Press

Smith, Derek G. ed. 1975. *Canadian Indians and the Law: Selected Documents, 1663-1973.* Carleton Library, no.87, McClelland and Stewart.

Smith, Donald B. 1976. "Nahnebahwequay," in *Dictionary of Canadian Biography*, vol.9. Toronto: University of Toronto Press, pp. 590-1.

Smith, Donald B. 1979. "Wabakinine," in *Dictionary of Canadian Biography*, vol.4. Toronto: Univ. of Toronto Press, pp. 755-56.

Smith, Donald B. 1981. "The Dispossession of the Mississauga Indians: a Missing Chapter in the Early History of Upper Canada." *Ontario History*, 73, (2):67-87.

Smith, Donald B. 1983. "Kineubenae," in *Dictionary of Canadian Biography* vol.5, pp. 466-7.

Smith, Donald B. 1986. "The Days of Wabakinine."*Horizon Canada*, 4, (48): 1136-1141.

Smith, Donald B. 1987a. *Sacred Feathers: The Reverend Peter Jones (Kahkewaquonaby) & the Mississauga Indians.* Toronto: University of Toronto Press.

Smith, Donald B. 1987b. "Ogimauh-Binaessih," in *Dictionary of Canadian Biography*, vol.6, p. 555.

Smyth, Julie. 1998. "Fighting for the grave of a princess." *National Post*, December 12, A3.

Spielmann, Roger. 1998. *'You're So Fat!':Exploring Ojibwe Discourse*. Toronto: Univ. of Toronto Press.

Sutton, William n.d. Journal m.s., County of Grey-Owen Sound Museum.

Valentine, Lisa Phillips. 1995. *Making It Their Own: Severn Ojibwe Communicative Practices*. Toronto: University of Toronto Press.

Warren, William. 1970. (1852). *History of the Ojibway Nation*. Minnesota: Ross and Haines.

Miss Mary McKee, of Anderson reservation, Essex county, Ontario, at the age of eighteen. (From a daguerreotype.)

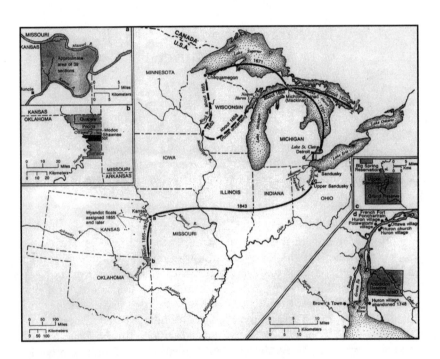

Wyandot travels. Tooker, Elizabeth. 1978. "Wyandot." In *Handbook of North American Indians*, vol. 15, *The Northeast*, p. 399. Washington, D.C.: Smithsonian.

5

Tarema (Carrying a Lake) or Mary McKee

[Mary McKee] has... been clamorous in assertion of her "rights", and her mother, at every pay-time... made a great disturbance on her behalf. (Mackenzie, March 31, 1877)

That Mary McKee's story has been chosen to represent the stories of all Wyandot women might seem strange. In a number of ways she was not typical. She was an only child, was raised by a single mother and never married. Yet, there are significant elements in her life that she shares with her countrywomen. Family was important, and not just the small slice of the family pie referred to in English as the nuclear family, but a larger, more generous helping (see Appendix A). 'Extended' family is only an extension when you think of something smaller as normal. Mary McKee would need all the family she could put on her plate. For, as with her mother and grandmother, and with a good number of mothers and grandmothers before them, her homeland was a moveable piece of property. An appropriate expression is one the Huron-Wendat used to describe their shared situation during the seventeenth century. For much of their history, the Wyandot were 'floating islands, drifting here and there.'[1]

Why, then, did I choose to write about Mary McKee? First, unlike the case for almost all other women of her nation, the fickle illuminating spotlight of the historical record shines on her and not on others. Second, in the disruption that caused her to move from her birthplace in Michigan to Kansas, Ontario and finally Oklahoma, her story follows the same itinerant plotline as the history of her people. Third, having seen her picture so often, I wanted to know her story.

The Wyandot

The Wyandot were formed in the 1650s from the disease and war-reduced ranks of three Iroquoian-speaking peoples termed in French the Petun, the Huron and the Neutre. The Petun, composed possibly of two related peoples, were the main group involved. Their eastern neighbours, the Huron-Wendat (see Appendix B), called them **Etionnontateronnon** ('People Where There Is A Hill'). The hill was Blue Mountain, near present-day Collingwood, by Georgian Bay. The French called them Petun ('tobacco'), but the Neutre ('neutral') to the south were the great growers of tobacco in Ontario. Like the Huron, they probably referred to themselves as '**Wendat**,' from which the word Wyandot was derived. Although various translations have been suggested, we still don't know what Wendat means (Steckley 1992a).

What caused the formation of the Wyandot? During the late 1640s and early 1650s, the then five nations of the Iroquois put together an almost unbroken string of military victories over the Petun, Huron-Wendat and Neutre, peoples already hard hit by disease. A decade before, the Huron-Wendat had lost close to half their number. The land of the ancestors had to be abandoned. Three paths lay open to them.

One led to the Iroquois. In 1651, the **Atahontayenrat** ('It Has Two White Ears') or Deer tribe of the Huron-Wendat petitioned the Seneca to live with them in peace. Magnanimous in victory, and needing to replenish their own disease and war-reduced ranks, the Seneca agreed. The Deer formed the base of the relatively independent village, Gandougarae ('At the Aspens'). In 1657, two other Huron-Wendat tribes, the Bear and the Rock, seeing that their French allies would not or could not protect them, linked up with the Mohawk and Onondaga respectively.

The second path led to Lorette. In 1650, the Huron-Wendat moved east to the area of Quebec City. When the Rock and the Bear left, the Cord remained as the nucleus of the people in a new land. After moving several times, they settled in 1697 in the place they live today, Lorette, a suburb of Quebec City.

The third path led to the birth of the Wyandot. On an Etionnontateronnon base, a new nation was formed northwest of Petun country. Sometime before 1652, the Wyandot set themselves up at Michilimackinac, where Lakes Michigan and Huron meet. No place remained home for long, which was especially hard on the Wyandot as they were sedentary farmers of corn, beans and squash. In 1652, the Wyandot moved to a small island near the entrance to

Green Bay in Lake Michigan. Sometime around 1658, they moved west to the Mississippi River, then to Black River, a tributary. By 1665, their community of some 500 people moved north to Chequamegon, along the southwest shores of Lake Superior. In 1671, made unwelcome by the powerful Sioux, they returned to Michilimackinac. In 20 years they had called six different locations home. For the next 30 years, they had the luxury of living in just one place.

At the end of the seventeenth century, a peace treaty was signed between the French, the Iroquois and the other Great Lakes Native nations, the most wide-scale agreement between Europeans and Natives to that time. **Kandiaronk** ('Rat'), a Wyandot leader, was a key player in obtaining this agreement (Steckley 1992b:48-9). Peace led to yet another Wyandot journey. From 1701 to 1704, they moved to the Detroit area.

Mary McKee's Family Tree

a) Mother's Family

Huron-Wyandot names belong to clans. They were passed down, as was clan identity, along the female line. The oldest recording of a name connected with Mary McKee's matrilineage was in the Jesuit Relation of 1642 with "Okhuk8andoron,"[2] written the next year as "Aotiok8andoron," both are references to a man of the Deer tribe of the Huron-Wendat.[3] His name, more accurately written as **Ayotiokwandoron**, means 'They are a valuable or difficult group' (i.e., to kill), referring to deer. It is one of the few Wyandot names whose rich heritage can be traced in the written record, although the wildly diverging spelling makes its path a difficult one to follow.

The next one known to bear the name was born in 1692. He was a prominent man among the Wyandot. In 1747, his name written as "otiok8andoron" and "hokoindoron," among other spellings (Toupin 1996:229 and 260), recorded that he was the leader of the **Ahtieronnon** ('People of Where There Is Basswood') or Striped Turtle clan of the Wyandot. Recorded as Odinghquanooron and Cuquandarong, we find him as a prominent chief signing a peace treaty in 1764 (Curnoe 1996:87-88).

On July 29, 1781, as an 89-year-old man whose name was given as "Tiockouanohon,"[4] he made a passionate plea for a replacement for the recently diseased Father Pierre Potier, the most recent in a long line of Jesuit missionaries to the Wyandot, the third that they called **Horonhiayehte** ('He Bears the Sky').

Tiockouanohan died the next year. He was some ancestor of Mary's, perhaps her great, great grandfather. The one to bring the name back to life, a short time later, was Mary McKee's maternal grandfather. The writing of his name was stripped down to the bare bones of **Quo Qua** or Kyukwe. The staunch Catholicism of both men would stay in Mary's family for at least two generations to come, despite the fact that the Wyandot were predominantly Methodist during the nineteenth century.

Quo Qua lived by the Huron River in Michigan. In 1806, on a trip to Ohio, his wife gave birth to Catherine, Mary's mother. In 1820, the family acquired what seemed to be secure rights to the land. They were granted a 50-year lease by the territorial governor of Michigan. They built a substantial home there (see Figure 1), intending to settle in long term. In two years' time it would be the scene of Quo Qua's funeral.[5]

Mary's mother remained in the home, alone. Charles Garrad, a leading Wyandot expert, creates an evocative word picture of Mary's mother that conjures up a kind of Wyandot Annie Oakley:

> His daughter, Katie To-ma-me Quo Qua (1806-1876), remained in the house alone, supposedly defending with a shotgun from intruding whites the house, property, a mysterious treasure, and her father's grave. (Garrad 1994)

The gutsy teenaged girl living on her own grew up to be a valued member of the Wyandot nation. Again according to Garrad, the mature Katie Quo Qua, "... was a confirmed traditionalist, and was revered as a native healer. Her obituary records that she was widely known for her skill with roots and herbs which she gathered from the wilds of Michigan" (Garrad 1994).

b) Father's Family

The mid-eighteenth century to the early nineteenth century saw a series of major conflicts between Euroamerican powers: the Seven Years War, the American Revolution and the War of 1812. No matter who won those confrontations, the Native nations always lost land. Most Native leaders did not want to sacrifice the precious lives of their warriors for 'foreign' causes. They preferred a balance of white power so that their people would not be dominated militarily or commercially by either side. Ultimately, however, they were almost always forced to take sides.

By the 1770s, a new split among people the Wyandot had thought were one nation was looming large on the horizon. As the two English-speaking forces drew up sides in the American Revolution, the Wyandot knew that they would have to choose their white friends wisely. Their homeland was at stake. One wise choice was Alexander McKee, Mary's great-grandfather on her father's side.

Alexander McKee was born around 1735, the son of an Irish trader and a woman who was either a Shawnee or a white woman adopted into the tribe. They were an Algonquian people from the east. Like the Wyandot, they had moved several times before taking up what they thought would be permanent residence in Ohio. McKee's heart seems to have been with his mother's people. His wife was Shawnee. As a trader and as an official Anglo-American contact with Native peoples in the area, he had proved to be a true friend to the Shawnee. He argued their case against the increasingly demanding American settlers who, despite official promises of permanent boundaries, were moving farther and farther west.

Once the American Revolution became an officially declared war, McKee had a difficult choice to make. Who could he trust to do what was best for the people of his mother and his wife? In 1778, disgusted with the American army's treatment of the Shawnee,[6] he defected to the British. There he quickly rose to a position of power. He was awarded charge of the Indian Department in the West (i.e., the western part of Ontario) and was promoted to the position of colonel in the militia by 1783.

The hard choices did not end with the war. Although the British government had lost the American Revolution, they wanted Natives living in the United States to keep up the fight. McKee was assigned the thankless and risk-taking task of encouraging Native people in the Great Lakes area to continue to resist the Americans. It was a rather one-sided deal, with the Natives taking all of the significant chances and the British supplying little more than grand speeches.

What further complicated McKee's life was that this same government wanted him to assist in a process that its American counterpart was also engaged in: getting Natives to give up land for white settlers. In southwestern Ontario, these prized citizens were called Loyalists, a term referring to people who had lived in the United States but had lost their land for supporting the King's cause in the American Revolution. The word was not applied to the Wyandot, who felt the same pressure to surrender their land, no matter what side of the border they were located.

On May 19, 1790, the Wyandot signed their first Canadian treaty. In return for giving up a substantial piece of land in the Windsor area, they were to receive £1200 worth of goods "delivered by the hands of Alexander McKee, Esquire, Deputy Agent of Indian Affairs." Further, some land that bordered on "the Indian Officer's" [i.e., McKee's] recently received property was to be reserved for their use (see *Indian Treaties and Surrenders* 1971, vol. 1, pp. 1-3).

Given the constraints under which he was placed, he must have dealt fairly with the Native people he contacted. They gave him the name White Elk (Curnoe 1996:64). According to award-winning historical novelist Allan Eckert, in McKee's honour, 16 months after Alexander McKee's death in January 1799:

> A great feast had been held first and then this was followed by the slow, intricate, methodical Death Dance in which more than two hundred Indians participated and that continued without pause for two full days and nights. This was an honor that had never before been bestowed upon a white man and only rarely for chiefs or warriors of uncommonly great distinction. (Eckert 1992:511)

Following his father's lead as a middleman between the British government and Natives was Alexander's son Thomas (1770-1814). Thomas was similar to his father in his knowledge of Native languages and customs and in his pro-Native sympathies. He firmly believed that "The Government should consult the Indians" (Clarke 1983:536). Thomas married Thérèse Askin in 1797 and they had three children (Farrell 1983:39). However, he also had a relationship with a Wyandot woman, Charlotte Brown (1781-1855). The exact nature of their relationship is not known. She was the daughter of Adam Brown (1747-ca. 1840), a white boy who had been captured at eight years old, was adopted into the leading Deer clan and eventually became chief. In 1800, Charlotte gave birth to Thomas McKee, named after his father. The boy would later become father to Mary McKee.

The War of 1812

Through the last two decades of the eighteenth century and the early 1800s, the Wyandot were compelled to sign treaties in which most of Ohio, some of Michigan and a good piece of southwestern Ontario were given up. Then came the War of 1812. Among the Wyandot leaders in Ohio, Michigan and Ontario, three different positions were taken, reflecting their geographical location. **Tarhe** ('Crane,' 1742-1818) of the Ohio Wyandot, after initially urging neutrality, eventually sided with the Americans, hoping to earn the respect of the encroaching settlers. **Myeerah** ('Walk in the Water,' 1748-1818) living on the US side of the Detroit River also wanted his community to remain neutral. He came, reluctantly, to support the British as the lesser of two evils, although he had signed an early, secret armistice with the Americans. Roundhead or **Hostayehtak**[7] ('He carries bark;' ca. 1750-60 - 1813) of the Canadian Wyandot, became a significant figure on the British side. Despite taking different political stances, the three Wyandot leaders had the same main goal: a home for their people for all time. All three would ultimately lose, even though after the war both British and American authorities promised that such residential permanence was possible.

Mary McKee's family seems to have sided with the British. In her words, "My Mother's father, Chief Quoqua, was Loyal to the British Crown, and during the War of 1812, fought on the side of Canada and the British forces" (McKee 1877).

Pressure on the Wyandot to Give up Their Land

The 1830s were tense times for the Wyandot. The US Congress passed the infamous Indian Removal Act, part of a determined effort to move all Native nations west of the Mississippi River. This included the Wyandot.[8] In 1831, 1834 and 1839, Wyandot delegates went west of the Missouri River to scout out the territory that would become Kansas. The people needed to know whether there would be sufficient good land in one block for all Wyandot to farm and live successfully as a community. Each time, the news the scouts brought back was far from positive. Prospects were grim. They did not want to leave. In 1832, some 16,000 acres of Wyandot land was sold in Ohio, in 1836 more yet. That same year, in what seems to be an effort for the Wyandot to 'appear more white' and therefore more acceptable, they replaced their centuries-old and efficient system of hereditary chiefs with an elected system. Revered names such as Ayotiokwandoron would lose a great deal of their significance.

In Canada, too, the roughly 150 Wyandot had to make land concessions during the 1830s. On September 20, 1836, Adam Brown (Mary's great-grandfather), the other "Sachems or Principal Chiefs" and the "Warriors" officially agreed to sell two-thirds of their Huron reserve in Anderdon township in the southwest corner of Ontario.

Mary McKee

Some time during the summer of 1837, one of the warriors who signed the treaty, a part-Shawnee/part-Wyandot/part-Irish man by the name of Thomas McKee, visited the shotgun-guarded Michigan home of Catherine Quo Qua. Thomas was 37 and Catherine was 31; neither was married. A fast-sparking, apparently just as fast-dampening attraction was felt between them. It is highly unlikely that they ever got married, even for a short time, as they appear to have avoided each other after the fateful summer. They seem just to have had a brief fling. In 1838, their baby girl Mary was born in Quo Qua's cabin. Mary was given the last name of her father, even though no marriage of her parents is on record. She was also presented with a Wyandot name, **Tarema**. The word is pronounced something like **Ta-ren-man**, with the last two vowels being nasal, spoken as if in French. Marius Barbeau, who recorded this name, suggested two possible translations. One is 'Carrying a Pond,' composed using the noun root -**ontar**- meaning 'lake' (as in Ontario, 'it is a large lake') with the initial -on- being dropped. The other is 'Carrying or Holding Mud,' likewise with the first vowel -a- of the noun root -**atar**- 'clay, mud, swamp' being lost. The verb in both cases is -**enman**- meaning 'to carry.' The first alternative is the more likely of the two, as in the baptismal record of 1734, the woman's name Maria-Magdalene Ontaren8a or Taren8a appears (Toupin 1996:835). With sound change in the language, the -nw- would become -nm-. Like her mother before her, Mary belonged to the Bear clan.

In young Tarema's early years, Native American children east of the Mississippi were hearing about and experiencing some very frightening situations. Ever since the passage of the Indian Removal Bill, horror stories had been making their way into the communities of the Wyandot, no doubt repeated within the children's hearing.

Three hundred Choctaw had died when the boiler of a steamboat carrying them west during the winter of 1831-2 exploded. In 1832, after roughly 1000 Sauk men, women and children attempted to return east to resettle on their old lands, most ended up being killed in what became known as the Black Hawk War (named after their leader, whose name is now borne by Chicago's NHL team). In 1834, the Wyandot's Michigan neighbours, the Potawatomi, were driven west. As told to an anthropologist approximately 100 years later by a Potawatomi elder raised on the stories:

> Each day of that hot summer travel, one or two Indians died. They were roped in, forbidden to step out to relieve themselves from morning to noon. Feces and urine were passed right inside the wagons; the dead Indians lay right in the filth. (Ruth Landes, "The Prairie Potawatomi," 1970, as cited in Vanderburgh 1977:239)

Perhaps the most horrible story concerned the Cherokee. Of the 14,000 or more Cherokee who were forced marched west by 7000 troops for 116 days during the hard winter of 1838-39, at least 4000 died of malnutrition, exposure and disease. They thereafter referred to that trek as Nunna daul Tsunyi, 'the trail where we cried,' known to history as the 'Trail of Tears.' Would the same fate pursue Mary and her people?

The Wyandot felt more and more unwanted where they were living. On December 4, 1839, **Summundowat**, who had earlier been the Principal Chief of the Wyandot, was murdered by white men, along with two members of his family. The murderers were taken, but the charges were dismissed.

In 1842, the Wyandot finally succumbed to the years of settler/land speculator/government pressure—forces stronger than the promises written in treaties and those spoken in treaty negotiations. On March 17, 1842, they signed their treaty of removal. The fatalistic reason why at least some agreed to the government offer can be seen in the following quote from Rev. James Wheeler:

> [W]hen the treaty was finally agreed to, I noticed that several voted in its favor who had always been on the other side. Among others, I inquired of one how he came to change his mind, and do so differently to

what he had always done before. "Well now," said he,
"I tell you. Suppose you have horse. Man come: say
sell your horse. You say, no: go away: I no want to
sell my horse at all: I wish you no say any more about
it. But he keep coming sixteen year, and you can no
make him stop any how you can fix it. You say, Yes,
take my horse, and go off, so I be troubled about it no
more." (Bland 1992:180)

They did not have to take the fateful trip until the next year—a stay of execution, not a pardon.

Historians sometimes use a strange word when they talk of treaties such as this, a word that modern journalists just as often employ when writing about more recent land agreements. They talk of the government 'giving' the Wyandot land, some 148,000 acres west of the Missouri. Consider, however, that they were in the same deal forced to surrender 110,000 prime acres of the Grand Reserve by the Sandusky River, plus other good land in Ohio and Michigan. This was country they had cleared and worked for several generations. Consider as well that the land to be 'given' to them was yet to be assigned, existing only on paper. It seems more accurate that the Wyandot were not 'given' anything, but were forced to 'trade down.' Compare this to being forced to leave a house your family built, improved, lived and died, to be given a house yet to be constructed in a neighbourhood yet to be specified, in a town you visited but did not particularly like.

Imagine this move from the perspective of the five-year-old Mary McKee. On July 12, 1843, a gathering of at least 664 Wyandot, over 600 from Ohio and a handful from Michigan and Ontario (25 and 30 respectively), are prepared, at least physically, to leave. All other Native nations in Ohio have already left; your people are the last to go. You and your single mother, known in the records of that time as Caty Cuqueh (i.e., Quo Qua), stand waiting amidst tears and sadness and a reluctance to leave. When you ask, "Where are we going?", the only answers you receive are vague ones. Even the elders do not know much more than you do. Before you leave, you hear the farewell address spoken by a Wyandot man known best as Squire Grey Eyes:

My people, the time for our departure is at hand.... It
remains only for me to say farewell. Yes, it is indeed
farewell.... Here our dead are buried. We have placed
fresh leaves and flowers upon their graves for the
last time. No longer shall we visit them. Soon they

shall be forgotten, for the onward march of the strong White Man will not turn aside for the Indian graves. Farewell—Farewell Sandusky River. Farewell—Farewell our hunting grounds and homes. Farewell to the stately trees and forests. Farewell to the Temple of the Great Spirit. Farewell to our White Brothers, and friends and neighbours.... (Marsh 1984:34)

Among the dead they were saying farewell to may have been the last Ayotiokwandoron. In the September 6, 1828 list of members of the First Missionary Society (Methodist) we find Hoocuhquondooroo (Marsh 1984:58). This is the last reference I have found to someone bearing the name; he was not mentioned in the muster roll of 1843.

Mary Goes to Live in Kansas

They loaded up the wagons to take them by land to Cincinnati, from where they would transfer themselves and their goods to steamboats headed west. But they would not travel alone. Whisky peddlers pursued them like a particularly aggressive pack of wild dogs. Wyandot without strong emotional and spiritual resources— Methodist, Catholic or traditional—became easy victims to these human predators. The whisky peddlers would get them drunk then return later to steal their provisions. Every night Mary and her mother would hear the loud talking and fighting that would inevitably follow the drinking. A good number of people lost possessions and heart during those first days and nights.

Also disturbing was the fact that they were treated like animals when they passed through white communities. According to Rev. Wheeler who travelled with them:

In ever[y] place through which we have passed since leaving Sandusky, there has been manifested a great anxiety to see the Indians; and although people meant no harm, yet their curiosity was of the kind that promoted them to crowd around the wagons in such a way as to cause the Indians to think that the whites were very poor hands to teach good manners. (Bland 1992:195)

On July 21, 1843, the travellers divided up into three groups in Cincinnati. Some of the young men took the horses west by land, while the remainder boarded two steamships, the ironically[9] named *Nodaway* and the *Republic.* This must have been a disturbing time for Mary. Shortly after they arrived two Wyandot died, one an old woman named Mrs. Bullhead, the other the sick child of a widow. The whisky sellers did not lose the opportunity to get some of the dislocated Wyandot drunk. One Wyandot man got so drunk that he fell off a boat and drowned. If Mary had heard the story of the Choctaw tragedy, she would step on board wondering whether she would ever set foot on land again.

We don't know which of the two vessels Mary travelled on, but it was probably the *Nodaway,* as that steamboat carried most of the Wyandot. If that was the case, she would have experienced the prejudice that the passengers on the *Nodaway* had to put up with from the captain and crew. The Wyandot were paying a considerable sum of money for their boat trip: $4500 for accommodation on both boats. They had arranged to pay the sum in three instalments. They had been treated fairly well up until the first payment. Then the situation changed. According to what Rev. Wheeler heard from the *Nodaway* passengers (he travelled on the *Republic*):

> The captain then seemed to become possessed with the apprehension that the Wyandots would ruin his furnishings. He therefore, ripped up the carpets and packed them away, put his patrons on short allowance, and otherwise imposed upon them, and made them uncomfortable. The worst of it, however, was yet to come.
>
> When the *Nodaway*... arrived at the intersection of the west line of the State of Missouri with the Missouri River, the sun was down and a heavy dew was on the grass. There was only one small house which could be occupied, and the captain was requested to allow his passengers to remain on the boat over night. He replied that he must go to St. Joe that night, and the Wyandots were turned out like sheep by a heartless shepherd. There was only a small spot which was treeless, and here the men, women, and children huddled together over night, Mr. Garrett and his family, Mr. and Mrs. J.M. Armstrong, and a

few others occupying the house. Early in the morning
the boat was still at the landing, the 'hands' having
spent much of the night in putting down the carpets
again, and 'putting things to rights.' (Bland 1992:204)

The boats arrived three days apart, the *Republic* on July 28 and
the *Nodaway* on July 31, near the confluence of the Missouri and
Kansas rivers. However, where the Wyandot were to live was yet to
be defined; meanwhile, they had to stay somewhere. William Walker,
a relatively well-to-do figure in the Wyandot community, clearly
expressed the situation and feelings of his people when he wrote to
a friend of his back in Ohio:

We have landed.... I have been employed busily in
collecting and getting under shelter my household
goods and in getting a house to live in temporarily....
My company are all above this place, some in tents,
some in houses, and some under the expanded
branches of the tall cottonwood trees. You cannot
imagine my feelings on landing... and hunting a
shelter for the family—faces all strange—we felt truly
like strangers in a strange land. (as cited in Jahoda
1995:284)

A few were able to rent houses. Mary, her mother and the majority
of the others stayed in temporary shelters and tents—most of which
were on swampy bottom lands by the river.

Months went by, and still no long-term home was found for the
Wyandot. If Mary had been in any way an adventurous child, there
would have been quite a few strange sights for her to discover. For
what was then called Westport, now Kansas City, was a gathering
place for a great variety of displaced Native peoples. According to one
author commenting at the time:

Westport was full of Indians, whose little shaggy
ponies were tied by dozens along the houses and
fences. Shawnees and Delawares, fluttering in calico
frocks and turbans, Wyandots dressed like white men,
and a few... Kansas Indians wrapped in old blankets,
were strolling about the streets or lounging in and
out of the shops and houses. (Bland 1992:207)

But Westport was also a dangerous place for Mary. As one observer put it, "Whisky... circulates more freely in Westport than is altogether safe in a place where every man carries a loaded pistol in his pocket" (Bland 1992:207). Worse, many of the small children were struck down by disease. According to Rev. Wheeler, the Wyandot experienced "the death of nearly all the younger part of their children" (Bland 1992:209). While they had been in Cincinnati, a curious onlooker, and a carrier of measles, came on board one of their boats. The disease—one of several going the rounds—spread with deadly effect in the camps by the Missouri River. It was not long before the newly consecrated Wyandot cemetery would contain 60 bodies, many of them young children.

Eventually land was found for the Wyandot through their Native contacts. Past kindness was remembered and rewarded. The Delaware, who in 1756 had been given permission by the Wyandot to stay on Wyandot land in Ohio when they had been forced off of their own land farther east, returned the favour. They sold the Wyandot some 36 sections of land, and, unlike the American government, they actually gave the Wyandot some land. The following is taken from the article of agreement between the Wyandot and the Delaware, dated December 14, 1843:

> The Delaware nation of Indians, residing between the Missouri and Kansas rivers, being very anxious to have their uncles, the Wyandots, to settle and reside near them, do hereby donate, grant and quitclaim forever, to the Wyandot nation three sections, containing six hundred and forty acres each, lying and being situated at the point of the junction of the Missouri and Kansas rivers. (as transcribed on the Kansas Wyandot website, 1995)

That did not bring an end to the Wyandot's problems. Rain began to fall in May 1844, and the downpour didn't stop for six weeks. From June 13th to 16th, much of what is now Kansas City was covered with a reported 14 feet of water. Many Wyandot homes were flooded. With the floods came cholera, a dreaded killer in North America during that period. Wheeler claimed that he had heard "there was not a single well person in the nation by the latter part of the fall of 1844" (Bland 1992:215).

The next year there were also floods. Again, following the flood came disease. By September of 1845, the death toll of the Wyandot since arriving out west rose to over 200. One of their number was Thomas McKee. What this meant to Mary is not known. Did she know her father? Did her mother or someone else point him out to her as they travelled west and pitched their tents? Did he ever talk to her during the trip or afterwards? We cannot be sure.

Mary Moves to Canada

For Caty and Mary this tragic land was not to remain their home for long. Their next move, however, was not a forced one; it was their own decision. They had a chance to go back east, and they didn't let it slip through their fingers. Caty had received some small financial compensation for land she had surrendered by the Huron River in Michigan and for giving up her family's 50-year lease. With that money she took advantage of an opportunity to purchase land in Anderdon to set up a farm in Ontario in 1846.

There was land pressure there too, although not yet quite so forceful as in the United States. On July 19, 1853, the "Chiefs and Principal Men" of the Canadian Wyandot, led by Joseph White or Mondoron, signed a provisional agreement, later ratified on April 28, 1854, to sell yet more of the land that had been reserved for their use in 1790. The wording of the document suggests that some mistrust of government officials existed at that time in the minds of the Wyandot leaders. There wasn't a McKee that they could believe in and trust as one of their own. The treaty contained these words: "the monies arising therefrom to be appropriated to the use and benefit of the said Indians and *for no other purpose whatsoever*" (Indian Treaties and Surrenders 1971, vol. 1 p. 192; emphasis mine).

Mother and daughter had to work hard to survive. They grew crops, gathered berries, roots and herbs for food and medicine. Caty made and sold beadwork and baskets. Life, however, was not all work for this energetic woman in her early 40s. There was romance as well nearby. Their neighbour was James Clarke, a single man (one of the "Principal Men"), a Wyandot, two years older than Caty; they met, fell in love and got married.

How did Mary feel about her stepfather? She and her mother had been alone all Mary's life. Was there some jealousy? Did Mary sometimes feel like an unwanted outsider around a pair of middle-aged newlyweds? Traditional stories of the Wyandot include a number in which stepfathers were villains, mistreating their stepchildren, who were made to feel ashamed or punished for their acts. One of the stories that Mary provided the anthropologist Marius Barbeau with in 1911 began with her saying the following words, "In the beginning, the step-fathers and step-mothers were known to be without love for their step-children" (Barbeau 1915:102).

Eventually, Mary moved out. But it might well have been more pull than push that caused the move. Mary and her stepfather seemed to have formed a close relationship. After her mother died, Mary took care of him, and she attributed part of her knowledge of traditional stories to his teaching. In 1877, Mary claimed that she had left Anderdon in order to receive an education. Maybe, however, her decision to leave was mainly a response to an exciting offer that Mary received from a relative that non-Wyandot might call distant.

Mary's father had a cousin in Anderdon, named Mary Williams, who as a 13-year-old had travelled west of Kansas in 1843. Maybe Mary Williams had acted the part of an older sister to the only child at some point. If she had been the daughter of Thomas's father's brother or his mother's sister, then Thomas would have addressed her by a term that would be a rough equivalent of the English word 'sister.' By extension, this could have made the relationship between the two Marys to be that of aunt and niece, a close tie in traditional Wyandot culture. Whatever happened during the trip, or whatever their exact kinship link, some connection must have been established between the two. Mary later referred to the older woman as her 'aunt.'

By 1853, Mary Williams had married into money. Her husband was Isaiah Walker, or Taorhense ('Dawn of Day'). He was the nephew of William Walker, the first Wyandot to be elected head chief, a man who became a provisional governor of Kansas-Nebraska when they were one territory. In 1854, the young couple had built a three-storey house named "Turtle Hill," after one of their clans. The house was also referred to as the "Walker Mansion" because it was made out of brick rather than the more usual wood, contained a grand piano, a marble mantelpiece, carved stairways and was surrounded by a terrace garden. All of this would have been very tempting to a girl not yet in her 20s.

Mary Moves Back to Kansas

In 1856, Mary moved in with her 'uncle' and 'aunt' in their mansion in Kansas. Maybe it was at Turtle Hill that Mary acquired the nickname **Ngyawich** ('Turtle') that she was recorded as having as an old woman.

But wealthy relatives and the elegance of a fine home did not necessarily bring with them acceptance to a young woman of the American West who was not white. Kansas territory had been opened up in 1853 to non-Native settlers even before treaties had been finalized with the Native nations who still were endeavouring to put down roots in their new country. Many whites thought of Natives, no matter how well established, as barbaric impediments to civilization—human underbrush to be cleared away from the pathway of progress.

One who did not feel this way was a young white man (name forgotten) who proposed to Mary McKee and received a positive response. His family, of German heritage, thought differently. Apparently, they would have none of their son's marrying an 'Injun' and the wedding was cancelled. There is some question as to whether her fiance's relatives did this or whether Mary herself called the wedding off when she learned of their disapproval, an effort on her part to salvage some pride. She would never marry.

We have a picture portrait of Mary in 1856 (Figure 2). It is an ambrotype, then state-of-the-art photographic technology. As Charles Garrad, the man responsible for rescuing this historical treasure, perceptively expresses it, this picture reveals:

> a beautiful eighteen-year-old girl in the flush of youth
> (and possibly romance) with poise, natural elegance
> and fashionable dress revealing an upbringing of
> schooling, culture and... refinement. (Garrad 1994)

But if you look carefully at the picture, you may also detect a slight look of sadness, or is it worry? Does this picture hint at Mary's great secret at that time? She was pregnant. Like her mother (and apparently her paternal grandmother) before her, she was with child but without husband.

Devastated by the heart-rending and socially deadly combination of losing a fiance while carrying his child, Mary locked herself in her room at elegant Turtle Hill with the intention of committing suicide. Isaiah Walker had to crash through the locked door to stop her.

Isaiah and Mary Walker had a traditional Wyandot love of children, as well as a great deal of compassion for their teenaged 'niece.' They did not cast her out. Mary's daughter, named Catherine after the child's grandmother, was born at Turtle Hill.

One of the gaps that exist in what we know about Mary's life concerns the fate of her child Catherine. Shundiahwah or Cecile Wallace, the granddaughter of Isaiah and Mary Walker, claimed that Catherine died young at Turtle Hill and was buried in Kansas at the age of ten, another tragedy added to Mary's growing list. The Wyandot Tribal Roll of 1867 has an entry with her name on it, her being at that time around ten. It also states that both Mary and Catharine were living in Canada. Further, in Caty Clarke's obituary of 1876, we read that she was survived by "an only daughter... and a granddaughter" (Garrad 1994) to whom she bequeathed her land. Catherine would then have been around 20. Further, in a letter that Robert MacKenzie, an Indian Affairs official, wrote on March 31, 1877, to the Minister of the Interior, he claimed that in 1867 she brought "with her a child whose father was, she says, a German" (Mackenzie 1877).

Like so many mixed-heritage Native women, then and later, Mary's rejection on account of her Native background caused her, at least temporarily, to deny that vital part of her self, to want to cut it out like a cancer. She began to pretend that she was Mexican, not Wyandot. She was trying to pass into 'civilized' society by presenting herself as being what she was not.

Citizens and Indians

Civilization was closing in on Mary and her people in Kansas during the mid-1850s, much as it had in Ohio when she was a small child. The Wyandot in Kansas were under official government attack. For 200 years the Wyandot, as a nation and as individuals, had drawn strength and support from the tribal nature of their people. Land was held in common; major decisions were made in a true democratic fashion based on the consensus of discussions held in council meetings. Even with a moveable homeland, as long as the tribe held together then Wyandot identity was reasonably secure, their sense of community strong. The American government knew that Natives could be more easily manipulated—their much-coveted land made more vulnerable to acquisition by white settlers—if they could divide and conquer each tribe. In addition, there were the increased taxes that government officials could apply and derive large sums of money from, if the tribes were divided. If individual Wyandot families could not pay these taxes, there would be white settlers waiting in line to take their land.

That was what was done to the Wyandot in Kansas when they signed a new treaty on January 31, 1855. They were to "relinquish and release" all their rights and claims flowing from previous treaties; in the words of the treaty, giving up everything "of a national character" (Kapler 1904) in exchange for a series of three payments. Their land was divided up into separate allotments. Enabling Wyandot to become 'full-fledged citizens' meant disenfranchising them from the social entity that had the most meaning and use for them: the tribe.

The process was undertaken clumsily. Some Wyandot were made 'American citizens,' others were given an at least temporary reprieve. By 1857, the allotment process was set into motion. Then the Wyandot were swarmed by tax-grabbing government officials, unscrupulous land speculators and financial tricksters that seemed to follow treaties like hyenas do fresh kills. Many lots of Wyandot land would be sold, some for debt from bad deals hastily made, some to pay for the sudden flood of newly imposed taxes. The people seemed doomed to disappear like the then-vanishing buffalo.

However, there was a distinct group of Wyandot who opposed the 1855 treaty and were seeking an alternative. They were headed by **Tauromee**, one of the leading Wyandot from the early 1840s, and principal or head chief beginning in 1853. He and 68 of his fellow members of what was to be called the "Indian Party" deferred becoming American citizens. Their solution to the proposed dissolution of their nation was to travel to Indian territory (later named Oklahoma) and remain as a tribal unit. They would receive land from a branch of their one-time enemy, the Seneca. As was the case with the Delaware, this Seneca band had once been beneficiaries of Wyandot land-sharing in Ohio. They invited the Wyandot to move to part of their reservation in northeast Oklahoma. Negotiations went on until November 22, 1859, when the Indian Party Wyandot and the Seneca signed an agreement that would give the former 33,000 acres of Seneca land in Indian territory.

The 1860s did not begin well for Mary and her fellow Wyandot living in the United States. They were beginning to feel crowded out in Kansas. In 1855, there were reportedly 555 Wyandot in that state. The census of 1860 recorded their being 107,206 people in Kansas. In

June of 1861, the Kansas legislature passed a resolution requiring Wyandot land to be taxed, in violation of the terms of the 1855 treaty. Then there was the American Civil War. The Wyandot seem to have supported the Union or Federal side. Their first Methodist preacher, of revered memory, was a black man, John Stewart. A number of Wyandot were the descendants of African-Americans who had been kidnapped and adopted into the tribe. In 1862, Confederate forces drove the Wyandot out of Indian territory.

In February, 1867, a treaty was signed by Tauromee and John Kayrahoo of the Indian Party that arranged for the Wyandot to resume tribal status in Oklahoma, with land purchased from the Seneca. Individual Wyandot had important decisions to make. Did they want to live in Oklahoma under tribal organization and relatively free from the incoming white settlers? Or would they opt to hold on to what they had built up in Kansas?

Mary McKee Returns to Canada

There was a third possibility open to Mary McKee. She could go to Canada and return to the home she had shared with her mother back in Anderdon. This she did that same year.

Leaving would bring with it a sad farewell. For the Walkers had been very kind to her, like a true traditional Wyandot aunt and uncle. But it seems that they were undergoing increasing housing constraints. In the Wyandot Tribal Roll of 1867, they are listed as having seven children. That would not leave much room for Mary and Catharine McKee. Mary and Isaiah Walker (and their many children) would later become part of the migration south. In 1874, the Walkers left their mansion of Turtle Hill, and moved to the Wyandot Reservation in Oklahoma. There they built a new house, this time smaller and of wooden frame, not brick. Somewhat appropriately, they named this dwelling "Last Chance" (Figure 3).

Although Mary McKee and perhaps her daughter seemed to have been received well enough by her mother and stepfather back in Canada, she was not made as welcome, officially, as she might have wished. Mary had walked into something of a wasp's nest at the Canadian reserve at Anderdon that would make her rejoining her band and receiving her rights quite difficult. The community was split as to their position on enfranchisement and the attendant dividing up of their commonly held land and tribal monies held in trust by the federal government. There was one faction, apparently the most powerful one, led by Head Chief Joseph White (1803-1885), his sons Solomon (a barrister-at-law) and Joseph Jr. (who ran several business concerns in the reserve). The other side was headed by the writer Peter D. Clarke, James Clarke (Mary's stepfather) and Joseph Warrow. The white faction were all for immediate enfranchisement, immediate division of land and funds. They certainly knew how to play a tune that the government officials wanted to hear. The following is an excerpt from their petition of September 16, 1873:

> We your Indian children recognizing the urgency of the demand of our white neighbours, and believing that we are sufficiently enlightened and advanced in civilization to secure to us the end hereinafter mentioned, beg to authorize our chief and two other members of our Band to accompany him for the purpose of negotiating a treaty with our Father in Ottawa with the view of changing our present position to that of the other subjects of Her Majesty our Great Mother:—first representing and seeking an adjustment of those matters of grievance which we believe ourselves to labour under, then to ask for and obtain a division of a sufficient portion of our Reserve to secure to each of our male members one hundred acres of land, and twenty-five acres for the females, as well as a division of all monies as soon as may appear practicable, and to propose to sell or surrender for sale, for our benefit, the residue of our lands en block for cash to enable the desired end to be carried out as early as may be convenient, and generally to act in the matter as may appear to them, meet and consonant with our wishes.
>
> Your Indian children respectfully submit that their present advanced state, and social position, entitled them to the consideration they seek to have extended to them by their Father. (Indian Affairs RG10, volume 1911, file 247311)

The names Peter D. Clarke, James Clarke and Joseph Warrow are conspicuous by their absence from this list. They sent petitions of their own in which they stated that they were in favour of the sale of some lands and properties and the enfranchisement of those both willing and able to do so. However, in a petition dated February 16, 1874, they wrote:

> We are decidedly opposed to having the "residue" of our lands "sold en bloc" to any individual or company for speculation. And we, the undersigned, believe that there are some of our band who are not fully competent to take charge of their portion of land and "monies" if handed over to them, as proposed in said petition. They may be dissipated and reckless yet they have a permanent home, but if each of such was to get a deed in fee simple for their allotment of land, the most, if not all of them would sell to *designing persons (both within and outside our band)* in less than six months and become homeless and destitute. (Indian Affairs RG10, volume 1911, file 2473, emphasis mine)

The "designing persons" that they suspected doubtless had the last name White. In a personal petition of 1874, Peter D. Clarke questioned the mercenary motives of Joseph White, or did they stem more from the chief's lawyer son, who seems to have been quick to calculate what any situation meant in terms of his personal financial loss and gain. We can see the implications of this concerning Mary's application to be readmitted to the band in the followings words from Clarke's petition:

> With an eye to their own interest, it has always been the sole aim of Joseph White and sons to have the whole control of our Tribal affairs, and he—the father—claiming to be the principal chief arrogate to himself the right to say who has a right and who has not, in our Band. "My Money" he would say whenever a re-admitted (by the Government) member of our band received his share of our semi-annual income. "You steal it, my money," says he. (ibid.)

A word of caution is necessary here. It is easy to follow Peter D. Clarke in vilifying Joseph White and his sons. While there is good reason to suspect that they were artful entrepreneurs, not averse to using political position for financial gain, we must keep several thoughts in mind. One is that there was a sense in which Joseph White was right. The law was such that added membership did diminish the value of monies doled out to individuals. The situation itself created conflict. The governments holding Native monies for land sales 'in trust' kept strict control over the large sums involved. The chief and band council were restricted from investing the money in collective projects that would benefit all, projects in which added band membership would not appreciably diminish the benefits received by each band member.

Second, living in highly populated southern Ontario in small numbers, the Wyandot were inundated with the individualistic thinking that was prominent during the nineteenth century. As well, the Wyandot would have often heard the social Darwinism catechism of the inevitable 'evolution' of their Native ways into those of the 'more advanced' Euroamerican society. The principles of collective good that were such a source of strength and adaptability in tribal beliefs and practices would have been hard-pressed to survive in the minds and actions of more than a minority of the Wyandot band.

And all the members of the Wyandot community could, like the Whites, feel "the urgency of the demand of our white neighbours."

Mary had to fight for her rights when she first returned to her Anderdon home. Mary and her mother worked together in this fight. Robert Mackenzie, an Indian Affairs official, rather negatively stated that Mary "has... been clamorous in assertion of her 'rights,' and her mother, at every pay-time... made a great disturbance on her behalf" (Mackenzie, March 31, 1877). Mary was to lose both her greatest ally plus rights to 50 acres of land when her mother, Caty Clarke, died at age 70 on September 7, 1876. The valued Wyandot elder was buried in an unmarked grave in the Huron cemetery at Anderdon.

The circumstances surrounding how Mary lost 50 acres show us an only too clear view of the level to which Wyandot politics had descended. Mary had still not been accepted as a legal member of her band by 1877, even though she had been living back in her former home at Anderdon since 1867. She argued her case in a petition of January 13, 1877:

> I did not leave my Mother, nor go to the United States,
> for the purpose of leaving the Wyandotte tribe, or

band, for it was understood by my Aunt and Mother
that I was to return to her, my Mother, after I had
been done with my school, which I did.... (McKee 1877;
for entire petition see Appendix C)

Since returning to live with her mother, Mary had received only a
single annuity payment of 21 dollars. She was only able to obtain
that small sum in 1875 because Robert Mackenzie had requested the
band to do so. When a non-Native working for Indian Affairs is more
generous to you than your own band is, then you know that you are
in trouble (although it should be kept in mind that he had nothing to
lose by his generosity).

According to Mackenzie, the Wyandot band council, led by the
Whites, was refusing to grant her band membership because "it would
be the opening of a door to others who would then assert their claims
to similar privileges" [i.e., receiving annuities and an allotment should
the band enfranchise] (Mackenzie, March 31, 1877).

The year before (i.e., 1876) the federal government passed the
Indian Act. Contained within that act was a section that provided a
way for 'Indians' to disappear legally, rights and all: enfranchisement.
Native people didn't exactly rush to the Indians Affairs office to take
advantage of this offer. Only 102 people enfranchised from 1876-1918
(Frideres 1993:33). The only tribe to do so was the Wyandot, led by
the White family. The allotment assignment process had begun in
1876, with rules that men would be allotted 100 acres, women 50. On
December 21, 1877, Solomon White, his wife and his brother Joseph
Jr. received separate lots of land carved out of formerly communal
Wyandot territory. In what appears to have been the product of some
manipulation, Solomon obtained three lots, of 67, 100 and 50 acres,
more than his share. On May 7, 1879, the Wyandot lawyer received
yet another piece of land out of the communal pot.

Mary McKee stated her position on the rights of her family in a
petition of 1877 (see Appendix C) to the Minister of the Interior:

[O]ur family has been living on two hundred acres,
known as Lot Number Seven, in the Third Concession
of the Township of Anderdon in the Indian Reserve,
for the last... Thirty years, and that we have been to
great expense, and labor, in fencing, and other
improvements, on said Land.

> And your petitioner would Humbly pray that she
> may be allowed her fair share of the Reserve, to which
> she is duly and lawfully entitled to, and be placed on
> the same footing as the other Members of the
> Wyandotte Tribe or Band of Indians, of the said
> Township of Anderdon, in addition to, any with the
> land that was allotted to my Mother in her lifetime,
> and that the two Hundred Acres may be left to my
> stepfather James Clark, and myself, that is one
> hundred acres, to Mr. Clark, fifty that was allotted to
> my Mother, and fifty my own just share, making two
> hundred acres, which would leave the land held by
> our family for the last thirty years in our rights, and
> which is now in our possession. (McKee 1877)

Timing seemed to be against Mary. According to Mackenzie, he
wanted to have the allotments declared at a time of the fall payment
of annuities, when Caty Clarke was still alive, but because:

> it was inconvenient to some members of the members
> of the Band to have a second days sitting at that
> time, I agreed, at their request, to return some day
> in December to attend specially to that business,
> and in the interim Mrs. James Clark died, rather
> suddenly, I believe. (Mackenzie, March 31, 1877)

Was it coincidence that the Wyandot band council which had
opposed Mary McKee's return to band status also decided that Mrs.
Mary L.White, wife of Solomon White was given 50 of the 200 acres
that had been in Mary's family for 30 years?

To put the Wyandot band council in a more positive light, one
reason given both by Peter D. Clarke and Mackenzie for the delay of
Mary being granted membership status in the band was that:

> [T]he Wyandot Council (at the instance of Sol White)
> objected because—as they said—the Department
> decline confirming the grant which they had made to
> the five women, members of the Band, fifty acres each
> out of the residue of our Reserve, on account of their
> being married to white men. (Clarke 1877)

The Indian Act included a sexist aspect that continued until 1985 and the passing of Bill C-31. A status Indian woman marrying a non-status man (no matter what his genetic heritage) lost her status as a legal Indian. No matter who a status Indian man married, he always kept his status. On May 7, 1879, the same day that Solomon White was granted his fourth piece of land, five women who had married non-status men were allotted 50 acres each (Treaties and Surrenders 1971 vol.3, pp. 85-6). Had the White family and other leading Wyandot preserved enough of their traditional tribal sense that they wanted to take care of women they felt were still members of the band, despite loss of Indian status through marriage? This is possible with a traditionally matrilineal people. However, such a charitable act seems to go against the band council's actions concerning Mary McKee. Maybe the Whites had left band politics once they had received what they wanted. Perhaps there was some way the Whites profited financially by this apparent favour. There might have been some kind of trade off that resulted in Solomon White's receiving the extra land. These questions may reflect the fact that my source material is somewhat biased, being the writings of Peter D. Clarke and Mary Mckee, and not of the Whites. That being considered, my suspicions still remain.

Mary did not own her land until February 24, 1887, when she was permitted "absolute purchase" of 50 acres, her aforementioned "own just share," for the token price of one dollar. The property was named Walnut Hill.

Through the 1880s, little piece by little piece, the remaining Wyandot land was signed away. The Clarke faction appears to have taken over what remained of their people, but they could not stop the inevitable disappearance of their nation in Canada. Mary's stepfather's name was the first to appear in the second and third last agreements of 1886 and 1889 respectively. In the final treaty of November 2, 1892, in which the last land of the Wyandot was signed away, the first two names written were Joseph Warrow and James Clarke. The fourth was Peter D. Clarke. By 1914, everyone in the band had become enfranchised. According to Laurie Leclair, "A 1914 report noted that the seventy-year old Mary McKee remained 'the only person with exception of Harriet Laforet that shows any trace of Indian blood'" (Leclair 1988:86[10]). As a private citizen, Mary McKee still owned land in what had been the Anderdon reserve. However, with the legal evaporation of her people in Canada, it would seem that another home, one social and spiritual, had been taken away from her. She would remain in Anderdon only a few more years.

Mary McKee:Culture Bearer and Key Informant

Despite the powerful acculturative influences of living in an increasingly populated southwestern Ontario, Mary McKee still appears to have maintained a strong connection with her traditional culture. When Caty Clarke died in 1876, her broad knowledge of Native medicines and culturally rich traditional stories was missed by the people, but not completely lost. Along with inheriting her mother's material possessions, Mary McKee became heir to her mother's ample storehouse of old ways, learning both when she was growing up and when she as an adult living with and taking care of her mother.[11] Women were responsible for planting and maintaining crops in Wyandot culture. So it is not surprising to discover that Mary learned from her mother the traditional women's wisdom of the story of "The Old Robin." She told the following tale in 1911:

> The old Robin was very late in making her garden. She went to see her neighbour, "Have you got any seeds to sow—corn or something?" asked she. "We have had such a splendid time and had such fun dancing that there was no time left for gathering seeds, and I have nothing to sow." And she added, "What a fine time we had! there could be no time left for gathering seeds."
>
> When some of their neighbours asked for seeds, the old Wyandot women used to say, "That's always the way. There has been so much dancing that there was not much time left for gathering seeds. It was the same way with old Robin." (Barbeau 1915:209-210)

The land and the stories were linked in ways that made both meaningful to Mary. They would help give her an all-important sense of connectedness with the past of her people. Lore and land, past and present were linked for Mary McKee in stories such as the following. One seventeenth-century, Huron-Wendat story told of a large feline associated with water (*JR* 10:177 and 325 fn 17). The cat's name, **'Ontarayenrat,'**[12] probably means 'It is a White Lake'. White Lake was a source of dances, songs and medicinal talismans to those brave enough to seek communication with this spirit cat. Speaking in 1911 of the area in which she lived through most of her life, Mary said:

> There used to be a spring between the second and third concessions of Anderdon, near the present schoolhouse. A long time ago a monster lived in that spring, and many people were injured by him, some of whom died of their injuries. (Barbeau 1915:95 fn1)

Despite its fearsome nature, this spirit was said to have originated the songs and dances performed by the members of what anthropologist Marius Barbeau called the "Lion Fraternity" (Barbeau 1915:95 and 1960:12). We can see, indirectly, that Mary McKee may have perceived the creature as being a spirit guardian for those Wyandot who had come before her. Edward Grondin, a white settler of Anderdon township, reported to Barbeau:

> Many old people, including... Mary McKee, have told me about it, although the monster had been seen long before their time. The Wyandots used to communicate with him, as he was their protector. He would then come out of the ground and speak to his friends. His advice was concerning the future, and what they had to do in case of danger. (Barbeau 1915:95 fn 1)

As she grew older, Mary seems to have drawn more and more upon her Wyandot heritage as a source of comfort and strength. Her days as a Mexican were over. In her petition of 1877 to the Minister of the Interior, Mary even went so far in the other direction as to make the exaggerated claim that "I am a full bread Wyandotte, that my father, and Mother, was full bread Wyandotte, and with the exception of Mr. and Mrs. Diver, I know of no other in the band" (McKee 1877). Mary may have believed in there being a spiritual significance of being a "full-bread" Wyandot. She was quoted as saying that in the opinion of some old Wyandot, "a full-blooded Wyandot was never struck by thunder" (Barbeau 1915:47).

During the summers of 1911 and 1912, Mary greatly contributed to the recorded preservation of the language, stories and culture of the Wyandot. She did this through Marius Barbeau, one of the most influential Canadian academic writers of his time. He listened to and learned from elders belonging to a number of Native nations across Canada. Particularly valuable are his two collections of the traditional stories of the Wyandot and the Huron-Wendat, published in 1915 and 1960. If it weren't for these publications, as well as his wax cylinder recordings and unpublished writings, we would know only small scraps of the language, songs, stories and general culture of the Wyandot. My own 25-year study of the language of these people began with Barbeau's linguistic field notes—several boxes of file cards.

Barbeau had been influenced by the Huron language early in his life. When in 1895, as a nervous 12-year-old scheduled to sing a song at his school, he had the following experience, remembered vividly 70 years later:

> I sang my little song and I was almost frightened when coming into the wings to see an Indian, although he was a priest. Abbe Prosper Vincent, a Huron priest of Lorette, near Quebec.... He went on stage and I was struck! He sang **Wenia** (running after the enemy to take his scalp) and other old Huron songs. That's all I remember there, but that was my beginning. This opened the door for what would happen later. (Nowry 1995:32)

Barbeau began his anthropological fieldwork at Lorette in 1911 with Abbe Prosper Vincent, but the aging priest was not quite as Barbeau remembered him. Vincent was more a performer in the language than a good informant. While he was a great source of Huron songs (57), Vincent appears not to have been fluent in the Huron language. In referring to his meeting with Mary McKee later that same year, Barbeau wrote: "I heard for the first time the Huron language spoken by an old woman named Mary McKee" (Nowry 1995:104). When he sought out other informants, he received Mary's name from her cousin B.N.O. Walker, then Chief Clerk at the Quapaw US Indian Agency in Oklahoma. In June, Barbeau went to the Windsor/Detroit area. His initial attempts to speak with someone knowledgeable in the ways of the Wyandot were frustrating. This frustration ended, however, as soon as he encountered Mary McKee. He wrote back to his mentor, the famous anthropological linguist Edward Sapir, that "Miss Mary McKee is really about the best informant I have struck so far" (Nowry 1995:104).

How good an informant was Mary McKee? On the one hand, she did seem to know a good number of stories.[13] She told Barbeau stories about seven brothers who became seven stars in the sky, about animals such as the powerful Big Turtle and the always joking Raccoon. One of the longer tales she told was about the traditional spirit snake, pieces of whose dead body provided powerful talismans.

On the other hand, Mary had experienced a great deal of exposure to cultures, both Native and non-Native, other than her own. From the footnotes in Barbeau's publications, we learn that the traditional stories she told him, in Wyandot and in English, were often not in the extended versions given by some of the Oklahoma-based informants.[14] Mary, in her 70s, would sometimes apologize to Barbeau for the gaps in her memory. Further, Barbeau was somewhat critical of her ability with the songs:

> Unfortunately she does not remember many songs, I have recorded about three so far closely resembling those I have secured at Lorette. Although she understands and speaks Wyandot, she could not translate and understand (the songs), a word here and there. (Nowry 1995:104)

One should not read too much into this. I have worked with transcriptions of some of the songs that she had a hard time trying to "translate and understand." I have had similar difficulty. Those songs had obviously been long sung by those who did not totally comprehend what the words meant. The transcription of the lyrics has suffered accordingly. Only after playing with their written form for some time have I been able to connect some of the recorded lyrics with real Wyandot words. Further, Mary's area of greatest expertise was not with songs or stories. Her real strength as an informant lay in other areas. According to Charles Garrad:

> She contributed far more to Barbeau's research than he mentions. She provided Wyandot words and grammar, posed for many photographs, danced and recorded songs and stories on his wax-cylinder Edison

phonograph (which may still be seen in Ottawa). She demonstrated the making and use of a number of artifacts and showed him the ambrotype of herself as a young girl, which he copied, mistakenly calling it a daguerreotype. Mary, in Anderdon, was also the key to Barbeau's research in distant Oklahoma. The people he interviewed there were mostly relatives of Mary's among them her aunt Mary (Mrs. Isaiah) Walker and Uncle Bertram Walker. Barbeau boarded at the Walker family home "Last Chance". (Garrad 1994; cf. Nowry 1995:104)

We also see that Mary had retained a sense of humour despite the hardships she had endured. Before he left for Oklahoma, Mary told him: "The love medicine is a secret for the Huron-Wyandots; and I would not dare to go to Oklahoma if I knew that you were going to mention it" (Nowry 1995:105).

Barbeau returned to visit with Mary in July of 1912, to corroborate the information he had received from the people in Oklahoma and to purchase her collection of Wyandot artefacts for $60.

Mary Moves to Oklahoma

With the breakup of her people in Anderdon, Mary's heart and spiritual home were in Oklahoma. She travelled there by train every summer that she could, first with her stepfather James until his death in 1895, then alone. In 1918, she sold her property to a woman whose maiden name was the respected Wyandot name of Splitlog. Mary insisted that the land must remain in 'Indian' hands. She did not want this former home to disappear totally from the Wyandot. That had been the fate of the home of her birth in Michigan and of 'Turtle Hill,' a place of pleasant and sad memories to her. Turtle Hill had been purchased by Dudley E. Cornell in 1876, a non-Native man who had met his future wife at a Walker family party there.

Perhaps Mary wasn't just repeating an old story (shared by Natives and Europeans alike), but was at least in part expressing her opinion especially concerning the moral of the story when she told Barbeau the following tale:

> When the white man was first seen here, in the old
> time, he began to barter with our ancestors. Nowhere
> could he step without coming across some red man....
> The stranger came forth with a cow's hide, saying
> that he wanted a piece of land. The Indian, thinking
> that it was all about a piece of land the size of a
> cow's hide, agreed to the barter. The other fellow,
> however, cut the cow's hide into a string [wherewith
> to measure a large domain]. The Indian remarked,
> **"This is the way the white man does. He cheats
> the Indian**." And he had to give away the land which
> the string had measured. (Barbeau 1915:271,
> emphasis mine)

Mary headed south to live in Last Chance in Oklahoma, Mary Walker's home until her death in 1915. There Mary stayed in the same second floor room where Barbeau had boarded while engaged in his research. Taking care of Mary at Last Chance was Shundiahwah or Cecile Wallace, the granddaughter of Isaiah and Mary Walker and principal informant for Charles Garrad (whom she adopted and named "Tauromee" after the traditional chief).

In 1922, Mary McKee died of stomach cancer. It is noteworthy that Mary had been the last survivor of the 1843 migration to Kansas. Like her mother before her and in common with earlier generations of her family since the first Jesuit missionaries came to Ontario, she was buried with the rites of the Catholic church. Her unmarked grave is in the Walker family cemetery.

Not long after Mary's death, Last Chance was lost to the Walkers and to the Wyandot through a legally slippery mortgage plan. The last known fluent speaker of the Huron-Wyandot language, Mary Logan, died in 1949 at 86. That same year, in an article entitled "Famed Tribe Slowly Dying Out," in the *Windsor Daily Star* (Douglas 1949), it was noted that Walnut Hill was the last piece of land remaining in Anderdon township that was still held by a Wyandot descendant, Norman Gibb, who had received the property from his mother who had purchased it from Mary.

In 1959, 29 neighbours of the abandoned Turtle Hill petitioned for the former mansion's demolition. A *Kansas City Star* article documented the run-down condition of the house and property:

Every window has been broken. The yard is a jungle.
Transients move furtively past the empty windows.
They have chopped up ornate mantlepieces and carved
stairways for firewood on chilly days. Rats and mice
thrive undisturbed. (Lapham 1959:16A)

In 1972, Turtle Hill was finally demolished. In 1999, Mary's
Anderdon house, Walnut Hill, remained intact but was no longer
owned by a Wyandot family. Little physically remains of Mary McKee,
a few pictures and an unmarked grave, but the stories continue.

Appendix A: Family among the Wyandot

There are two words that mean family in the Huron-Wendat
language. One is -**hwatsir**- which means matrilineage (see above p.
38; and Potier 1920:447). This includes multiple generations, even
extending to those in the distant past and those yet to be born. More
significant is the verb root -**yentio**- meaning 'to be of a matrilineal
clan' (Potier 1920:391). To get some sense of how someone might feel
connected to clan as a kind of immediate family, look at the following
description of who would be a particular young girl's fellow clan
members in a Wyandot longhouse of 1747 (Toupin 1996:208-9).

In 1747, **Agnes Tandoyares** was seven years old. She lived in a
longhouse to which a census taker, Jesuit Father Pierre Potier, had
assigned 40 names. Most of the people in her house were related in
some way to Agnes.

The first name mentioned on the list of the people living in Agnes's
house was her mother's mother. She belonged to the Striped Turtle
clan, as did her daughter, the clan elder who was Agnes's mother.
While it is not possible to determine the clan membership of everyone
in the house, we know that at least 16 of them were Striped Turtles.
In addition to those mentioned there was an old woman from the Fox
tribe that Agnes's grandmother adopted, her grandmother's niece, a
100-year-old man named Jacob Tehatontaratase ('He bends the lake
in two'), a younger man who would receive his name when the old
man died, Agnes's mother's three brothers and one sister, an
unmarried man with no known family connection, and Agnes's two
brothers and two sisters. The following is a list of their names:

Striped Turtle Clan Members in Agnes's House

1) Dorothy Skwatandik	- her grandmother (mother's mother)
2) Marie Ndatiohaon	- her grandmother's adopted sister
3) Joseph Handiayenhwi	- her uncle (mother's brother)
4) Marie Yaennench	- her mother, clan elder
5) Nicholas Iwatenta	- her brother
6) Marie Tsuskwa	- her sister
7) Jean Baptiste Tehatat	- her brother
8) **Agnes Tandoyares**	
9) Marie-Louise Yannieneronnon	- her sister
10) Pierre Sarenhes	- her uncle (mother's brother)
11) Baptiste Horonhiate	- her uncle (mother's brother)
12) Therese Tsuteharinnon	- her aunt (mother's sister)
13) Catherine Tekwena	- herr grandmother's niece
14) Jacob Tehatontaratase	- 100-year-old man
15) Martin Sawendwat	- clan elder, next Tehatontaratase
16) Joseph Taronwe	- clan member

Appendix B -The Term 'Huron'

'Huron' is a French term. Like many outsider-imposed names for Native nations, it is insulting, as the following discussion from J.N.B. Hewitt demonstrates. I use the cumbersome 'Huron-Wendat' to avoid confusion with 'Wyandot':

> *Huron* (lexically from French *hure*, 'bristly,' 'bristled,' from *hure*, 'rough hair' (of the head), head of man or beast, wild boar's head... and the suffix *-on*, expressive of depreciation and employed to form nouns referring to persons). The name *Huron*, frequently with an added epithet, like *vilain*, 'base,' was in use in France as early as 1358... as a name expressive of contumely, contempt, and insult,

> signifying approximately an unkempt person, knave, ruffian, lout, wretch. The peasants who rebelled against the nobility during the captivity of King John in England in 1358 were called... *Hurons*....
>
> But Father Lalemant... in attempting to give the origin of the name *Huron*, says that... when these people first reached the French trading posts on the St. Lawrence, a French soldier or sailor, seeing some of these barbarians wearing their hair cropped and roached, gave them the name Hurons, their heads suggesting those of wild boars.... But it certainly does not appear that the rebellious French peasants in 1358... were called Hurons because they had a similar or an identical manner of wearing the hair; for, as has been stated, the name had long previous to the arrival of the French in America, a well-known derogatory signification in France. (Hewitt 1971:205-6)

Appendix C: Mary McKee's Petition of 1877

To the Honourable, the Minister of the Interior, Ottawa

The Petition of the undersigned, a daughter of the late Kitee Clark, wife of James Clark, one of the Wyandotte band of Indians in the Township of Anderdon in the County of Essex;

Humbly sheweth that her Mother departed this life on the 7th day of September last year, at her late residence in the Township of Anderdon, and before her death she requested all her worldly goods should be allowed to me, her only child; that I have lived with my Mother, and taken care of her for the last nine years at her late home on the Wyandotte Reserve; that, when young, I left home with an Aunt of mine, and lived with her in Kansas, the U.S., and returned to the Wyandotte Reserve in the year 1867, and has lived with my Mother ever since up to the time of her death; that I did not leave my Mother, nor go to the United States, for the purpose of leaving the Wyandotte tribe, or band, for it was understood by my Aunt and Mother that I was to return to her, my Mother, after I had been done with my school, which I did, and as the Wyandotte Tribe has not since my return from the United States *readmitted me into the Band, for what reason I cannot tell*, nor have they in any way made provision for me in the distribution of the reserve, to which I am *intitled*, but they at different times have offered me half share, which I always refused, at one time since my return the Band paid me one full share amounting to $21.00 this was about two years ago.

I would further state that I am a full bread Wyandotte, that my father, and Mother, was full bread Wyandotte, and with the exception of Mr. and Mrs. Diver, I know of no other in the band.

My Mother's father, Chief Quoqua, was Loyal to the *British Crown*, and during the War of 1812, fought on the side of *Canada*, and the *British forces.*

I would further state that our family has been living on two hundred acres, known as Lot Number Seven, in the Third Concession of the Township of Anderdon, in the Indian Reserve, for the last (30) Thirty years, and that we have been to great expense, and labor, in fencing, and other improvements, on said Land.

And your petitioner would Humbly pray that she may be allowed her fair share of the Reserve, to which she is duly and lawfully entitled to, and be placed on the same footing as the other Members of the Wyandotte Tribe or Band of Indians, of the said Township of Anderdon, in addition to, any with the land that was allotted to my Mother in her lifetime, and that the the two Hundred Acres may be left to my stepfather James Clark, and myself, that is one hundred acres to Mr. Clark, fifty that was allotted to my Mother, and fifty my own just share, making two hundred acres, which would leave the land held by our family for the last thirty years in our *rights*, and which is now in our possession.

And now your petitioner as in duty bound will ever pray

Dated at the Township of Anderdon
in the County of Essex, this 13th day of
January A.D. 1877
Mary McKee

Endnotes

[1] In the Jesuit Relation of 1648, a Huron-Wendat speaker summed up the perilous position of his people and of their dependence on the French with the following image: "This country is an Island; it has now

become a floating one, to be overwhelmed by the first outburst of the storm. Make the floating Island firm and stationary" (*JR* 33:237-9).

A number of seventeenth century dictionaries of Huron have an entry such as the following: "**hoti8enda,rak** les hurons, les insulaires [the islanders]" (FH1697:97). The noun root in this word is -8end- signifying 'island,' and the verb root is -a,ra- signifying 'to float.'

[2] This suggests that at least some of this clan had originally come from the Deer tribe.

[3] The '8' represents a -w- sound.

[4] This chief and gifted speaker used wampum belts to represent his words and their sincerity. With one belt he addressed Bishop Briande of Quebec:

> My father, in the name of God and of all the Huron [Wyandot] Nation, help us in our urgent need of a missionary. The loss of Father Potier has plunged our village into a general grief which will not cease until he is replaced by another. Instructed from childhood in the principles of the Christian religion, we follow them faithfully under the direction of our spiritual leaders. But what will become of us now? The souls of our warriors will tremble henceforth at the thought of the death that awaits them at every moment; the blood of our old men and of our women runs cold at the approach of the last moment of their lingering lives; the mothers are distressed at the fate of their children; in any case, your charitable zeal, more than our words, will lead you to act in our behalf. (Lajeunesse 1960:125)

[5] According to Charles Garrad, a leading Wyandot expert:

> His burial place was marked with an engraved headstone. This was developed into, of all things, a cemetery, and incorporated into a monument to "the last reservation of the Wyandot Tribe of Indians in Michigan Occupied 1818-1842." This monument, a concrete replica of an inappropriate teepee, much vandalized, still stands in Willow Metropark. (Garrad 1994)

[6] Perhaps the strongest recorded statement of that disgust came later, in 1794, when he said:

> the American Army have left Evident marks of their boasted Humanity behind them, besides scalping and mutilating the Indians who were killed in Action, they have opened the Peaceful Graves in different parts of the Country, and horrid to relate have with unparalled barbarity driven stakes through them... (quoted in Allen 1992:89)

[7] Much of what has been written about Bark-Carrier is suspect because writers have mistakenly linked his Wyandot name with Te(y)ata(k), which has a different meaning (see Curnoe 1996:133).

[8] The pressure placed on the American Wyandot to move west was formidable. The tactics employed by those commissioned by the government to obtain a treaty were often underhanded. This can be seen in the following excerpt from a letter written on August 29, 1837, by John Armstrong, a white man adopted into the tribe some years earlier. Armstrong is referring to what the commissioners did after a vast majority of the Wyandot had voted against the treaty offer in a public meeting of the tribe:

> This did not satisfy them. They had represented to the department that a large proportion of the Wyandots were in favor of emigrating. A gross misrepresentation in order to obtain their commission. They have now drawn up articles of a treaty, and are obtaining individual signers. And it is an absolute shame to the civilized community to witness the manner in which they obtain them. They have for these two months been tampering with offscourings of the nation. If nothing else will do they get them drunk and then obtain their names. Such has been the fact and after they have become sober again all their attempts are in vain to release themselves. When once there, it must stay, interferance of the Chief of the nation are fruitless. Some worthless vagabonds sign their names for the sake of a little provision, and yet these enlightened men are not ashamed of having to do with such individuals. In order to obtain numbers all are put down, women and children and individuals who have been dead these ten years. One of the selling party will come and sign for several individuals beside himself whether he knows their sentiments or not and yet all are received. If they would stop here, and let us alone we could well spare these classes of our nation, but such is not the intention. The avowed object of the selling party now is to get as many names as possible and go on to Washington and sell the whole or half the reservation. They have not got the names of one third of the nation nor anything near it fairly gotten. Yet from the currupt state of the present administration we have no doubt that a treaty could be effected for the whole reservation even with this small number. (Armstrong 1837)

[9] This is ironic, as the name for the boat that was taking them from their country was cognate with that which the Nishnabe called the Iroquois, who drove the ancestors of the Wyandot out of their country.

[10] Leclair was citing P.A.C. RG 10 (Red) Series vol. 6829, file 503-4 Pt. 1. Statement Submitted in Connection with final report of Wyandott funds, March 3, 1914.

[11] Her stepfather James Clarke seems also to have taught Mary some of the stories (Barbeau 1915:72-3 and 262).

[12] This word was presented as **"Ontarraoura"** in the *Jesuit Relations* (*JR*10:176-7), but as "Ti ontara,onra" in the more accurate dictionaries also written by the Jesuits (FH1697:231). The verb root -**,enrat-**, 'to be white,' combines closeness and appropriateness of meaning enough to suggest that it is the correct translation here.

[13] See Barbeau 1915: 181, 189, 192,194, 210, 250.

[14] See Barbeau 1915:59 fn1.

Bibliography

no author. *Agreement with the Delawares and Wyandot*, 9 Stat. 337, signed on December 14, 1848, on Kansas Wyandot website.

Allen, Robert S. 1992. *His Majesty's Indian Allies: British Indian Policy in The Defence of Canada, 1774-1815*. Toronto: Dundurn Press.

Armstrong, John M. 1837. Letter to Lucy Armstrong, ms., August 29.

Barbeau, Marius. 1915. *Huron and Wyandot Mythology*. Can. Dept. of Mines, Geol. Survey, Memoir #80, No.11, Anthro. Series. Ottawa: Govt. Printing Bureau.

Barbeau, Marius. 1960. *Huron Wyandot Traditional Narratives*. Ottawa: Nat. Museum of Canada Bull. 165.

Barbeau, Marius. n.d. *Huron-Wyandot dictionary* m.s.

Bland, Bill. 1992. *Yourowquains, A Wyandot Indian Queen: The Story of Caty Sage*. Elk Creek: Historical Publications.

Brown, Jennifer S.H. and Vibert, Elizabeth. 1996. *Reading Beyond Words: Contexts for Native History*. Toronto: Broadview Press.

Clarke, John. 1983. "Thomas McKee." *DCB*, 5:535-6.

Curnoe, Greg. 1996. *Deeds/Nations*. London: London Chapter, Ont. Arch. Society.

Douglas, Ted. 1949. "Famed Tribe Slowly Dying Out." *Windsor Daily Star*, Feb. 19.

Eckert, Allan W. 1992. *A Sorrow in Our Heart: The Life of Tecumseh*. New York: Bantam Books.

Farrell, David R. 1983. "John Askin." *DCB*, 5:37-39.

FH. 1697. *French-Wendat Dictionary*, m.s., John Carter Brown Library, Brown University, Providence, RI.

Frideres, James S. 1993. *Native People in Canada*. Scarborough: Prentice Hall.

Garrad, Charles. 1994. *Mary McKee (1838-1922)*. ms.

Garrad, Charles and Heidenreich, Conrad E. 1978. "Khionontateronon (Petun)" in *Handbook of North American Indians*, vol. 15, *The Northeast*. Washington: Smithsonian Institution, pp. 394-97.

Hancks, Larry K. 1993. *The Emigrant Tribes: Wyandot, Delaware & Shawnee, A Chronology*, ms.

Hewitt, J.N.B. 1971. "Huron," in *Handbook of Indians of Canada* (orig. 1913), ed by F.W.Hodge. Toronto: Coles Publishing.

no author. 1971. *Indian Treaties and Surrenders*, 3 vols., (orig. 1891 and 1912). Toronto: Coles Publishing.

Indian Affairs, RG10, col. 1911, file 247311.

Jahoda, Gloria. 1995. *The Trail of Tears: The Story of the American Indian Removals 1813-1855* (orig. 1975). New York: Wings Books.

Kapler, Charles J., ed. 1904. "Treaty of Washington, D.C. with the Wyandot on January 31, 1855," in *Indian Affairs, Laws and Treaties*, Vol.II: Treaties. Washington: Government Printing Office (as transcribed on the Kansas Wyandot website).

Lajeunesse, Ernest J., ed. 1960. *The Windsor Border Region*. Toronto: The Champlain Society, Univ. of Toronto Press.

Lapham, Jim. 1959. "Poor Time to Raze an Old House." *Kansas Star*, June 7, 16A.

Leclair, Laurie. 1988. *The Huron-Wyandotte: A Case Study in Native Adaptation 1701- 1914*. Unpublished M.A. thesis, History, University of Windsor.

Mackenzie, Robert. 1877. Letters to the Minister of the Interior: March 31, April 10, and July 16, RG10, volume 2004, file 7719.

Marsh, Thelma R. 1974. *Moccasin Trails to the Cross: A History of Mission to the Wyandot Indians of the Sandusky Plains*. Upper Sandusky: United Methodist Historical Society of Ohio.

Marsh, Thelma R. 1984. *Daughter of Grey Eyes: The Story of Mother Solomon*. Upper Sandusky: United Methodist Historical Society of Ohio.

McKee, Mary. 1877. Petition to Minister of the Interior, Jan.13, RG 10, vol. 2004, # 7719.

Morris, J.L. 1943. *Indians of Ontario*. Toronto: Ont. Dept. of Lands and Forests.

Nowry, Laurence. 1995. *Man of Mana: Marius Barbeau*. Toronto: NC Press Limited.

Peers, Laura. 1996. "'The Guardian of All': Jesuit Missionary and Salish Perceptions of the Virgin Mary," in Brown and Vibert, pp. 284-303.

Potier, Pierre. 1920. *The Fifteenth Report of the Bureau of Archives for the Province of Ontario*. Toronto: C.W. James.

Steckley, John L. 1988. "How the Huron Became Wyandot: Onomastic Evidence." *Onomastica Canadiana*, 70, (2):59-70.

Steckley, John L. 1992a. "The Wendat: Were They Islanders?" *Arch Notes* 92-5:23-26.

Steckley, John L. 1992b. *Untold Tales: Four 17th Century Huron.* Toronto: Ass. Heritage Pub.

Stevenson, Winona. 1996. "The Journals and Voices of a Church of England Native Catechist: Askenootow (Charles Pratt), 1851-1884," in Brown and Vibert, pp. 304-329.

Sugden, John. 1998. *Tecumseh: A Life.* New York: Henry Holt and Company.

Thwaites, Reuben G. (JR). 1959. *The Jesuit Relations and Allied Documents.* New York: Pageant Book Company.

Tooker, Elisabeth. 1978. "Wyandot," in *Handbook of North American Indians,* vol. 15, *The Northeast.* Washington: Smithsonian Institution, pp. 398-406.

Toupin, Robert s.j. 1996. *Les Écrits de Pierre Potier.* Collection Amérique Française N° 3, Les Presses de l'Université d'Ottawa.

Trigger, Bruce. 1976. *The Children of Aataentsic.* Montreal: McGill-Queen's Univ. Press.

Vanderburgh, Rosamond M. 1977. *I am Nokomis Too: The Biography of Verna Patronella Johnston.* Don Mills: General Publishing Co.

Zane, Holly. 1996. "Trespassers Beware." *Yale Journal of Law and Feminism,* 8, (1):15-30.

6

Conclusions

Neither Princess Nor Squaw

What can we conclude from biographies as diverse as these? First, of course, is the realization of the diversity itself. The lives of all of these women differed significantly from the familiar, stereotypical roles of Indian princess or squaw. Although all of them at some point had close working relationships with white men, they at no point acted merely as tools of those men, with no consideration for their own goals or for the good of their people: Kateri sought her own spiritual path, taking extreme steps even her missionary mentors would not follow; Thanadelthur worked for her people to stand as equal partners with the English, using the guns obtained to stand up to the better armed Cree; Nah-nee would not let her devotion to the white man's faith keep her from fighting government and powerful newspapermen; Mary McKee used her role as anthropological informant in the presentation of a story to criticize how the white man took Native land away. None of them were drudges, controlled by the men of their own culture: Kateri ran away from her powerful uncle; Thanadelthur chastised Chipewyan men who acted to jeopardize the trade; Mary McKee fought for and won her rights to be reinstated into the Anderdon band despite opposition from the chief and the powerful men who were of his party.

We should also note that colonialism was responded to in different ways by these five women. It is easy for ostensibly sympathetic writers to portray Natives as hapless, helpless victims of the forces of colonialism. Shanawdithit has been portrayed that way in the past (Winter 1975), and it would not be difficult to depict Kateri in such a way. I thought of her in that way before I wrote my first biography of her. This undervalues the dynamism of the response and the abilities of the responders. It overlooks what is coyly termed 'Native Agency' (word play on Indian agent), when Natives do not merely react to colonialist tools but, to use an overworked but still appropriate term, are proactive in their response, showing initiative, imagination and exercising a certain degree of free will.[1]

As Brownlie and Kelm note in their cautionary article "Desperately Seeking Absolution: Native Agency as Colonialist Alibi:"

> The argument for Native agency is now nearly twenty years old in the writing of Canadian history and its use in understanding Aboriginal roles in the fur trade, for instance, is virtually undisputed. (Brownlie and Kelm 1996:211)[2]

A growing literature suggests that in a good number of historical circumstances Native women acted as 'agents' and were proactive in a variety of different ways. In the introduction to her collection of readings that provide examples of these ways, Nancy Shoemaker states:

> The four-hundred-year period covered by this volume reveals surprising continuity in native women's experiences. Where scholars have previously seen a history of decline and increasing marginality, these articles show that native women actively, creatively, and often successfully resisted marginality. In responding to the changing world around them, Indian women did not conform to the Euro-American gender ideal. Sometimes native women were forced to adapt to Euro-American gender expectations, but more often they sought alternatives and created a new understanding of their roles by merging traditional beliefs with cultural innovation. (Shoemaker 1995:20)

As we have clearly seen, Thanadelthur's life story provides a good example of Native agency in the fur trade. Once a captive of a people better armed than her own because of contacts with the trade, she played a leading role in obtaining the trade for her people. The one-sided nature of the battles between the two peoples came to an end.

More slow to develop, but gaining acceptance, is the literature about Native agency exhibited in the interaction between Christianity and Natives. Good examples come from Donald Smith's continuing look at Mississauga Methodists (see Donald Smith 1987). Christianity has been a tool—more like a weapon—of colonial oppression. It would be wrong to overlook or downplay that salient fact. Brownlie's and Kelm's caution is wisely taken here. In their article they rightly criticize four authors writing about Native responses to the oppressive banning of the potlatch ceremony in British Columbia:

> [T]hey go beyond the argument for the recognition of Native agency to one that uses evidence of Native resilience and strength to soften, and at times to deny, the impact of colonialism, and thus, implicitly to absolve its perpetrators. (Brownlie and Kelm 1996:211)

However, in some circumstances Native agency has exerted itself through the medium of Christianity. This is seen in "'The Guardian of All': Jesuit Missionary and Salish Perceptions of the Virgin Mary" by Laura Peers, and in "The Journals and Voices of a Church of England Native Catechist: Askenootow (Charles Pratt), 1851-1884" by Winona Stevenson, and two articles appearing a recent innovative collection of historical interpretations entitled *Reading Beyond Words: Contexts for Native History*, edited by Jennifer Brown and Elizabeth Vibert (1996).

When Natives are secure in their identity and have positions of authority in the church, Native agency can be quite strong. One of the best modern illustrations of that is found in Lisa Philips Valentine's illuminating study of a Severn Ojibwe community in northwestern Ontario, *Making It Their Own: Severn Ojibwe Communicative Practices* (Valentine 1995). In an excellent chapter that discusses this process, "Church, Discourse, Church Discourse, and Discourse about the Church," she states:

> In Lynx Lake, Christianity has become the primary religious paradigm through which the spiritual world is addressed, owing in no small part to the efforts of two generations of strong, local leadership.[4] Religious discourse in Lynx Lake is free from concerns about 'living like Whitemen,' 'turning from the old ways,' or any of the other reactionary themes that might be

expected given the presentations of religion in the area by outside researchers. Lynx Lake has been designated by scholars and religious agencies in northwest Ontario as the heart of the 'Anglican North' and as is known as a community which allows only one church so that its spiritual and social unity might not be broken. Through representative discourses, we hear the voices of a people committed to a strong Christian world-view not expected of those whose Native identity is so unquestioned. (Valentine 1995:165-66)

We have seen two good examples of Native agency in response to Christianity in this book. Through the medium of her faith, Kateri Tegakwitha became a major figure in New France, a Canadian Joan of Arc in the late seventeenth and early eighteenth century, who continues to stand tall today. She will rise to become an even more influential 'Native agent' when, eventually, she attains her sainthood. It will enable Natives to take a more complete political role in the Catholic church in the Americas. Nah-nee took her Methodism and used it as a source of strength. Along with her secure roots in her culture and the support of her family and people it enabled her to fight and win her battle for land against daunting odds and opposition.

Endnotes

1 See Covey 1989:68-92.
2 The examples in the literature that they cite are: R.A Fisher, *Contact and Conflict: Indian-European Relations in British Columbia, 1774-1890*, Vancouver, University of British Columbia Press, 1977; A.J. Ray, *Indians in the Fur Trade: Their Role as Hunters, Trappers and Middlement in the Lands Southwest of Hudson Bay, 1660-1870*, Toronto, University of Toronto Press, 1974; A.J Ray and D. Freeman *"Give Us Good Measure": An Economic Analysis of Relations between the Indians and the Hudson's Bay Company before 1763*, Toronto, University of Toronto Press,1978; J.S.H. Brown, *Strangers in Blood: Fur Trade Company Families in Indian Country*, Vancouver, University of British Columbia Press, 1980; S. Van Kirk *Many Tender Ties: Women in Fur Trade Society*, Norman, University of Oklahoma Press, 1980; B. G. Trigger *Natives and Newcomers: Canada's "Heroic Age" Reconsidered*, Montreal and Kingston, McGill-Queen's University Press, 1985.

[3] A somewhat appropriate analogy here is found in Covey's discussion of how Jewish psychiatrist and writer Victor Frankl developed a strong proactive response to living in Nazi concentration camps (Covey 1989:69)
[4] This was personified in Judas and William Pipoon, two generations of Anglican preachers in one family (Valentine 1995:129 and 140).
[5] This is as opposed to a 'personality ethic' in which success: "became more a function of personality, of public image, of attitudes and behaviors, skills and techniques, that lubricate the processes of human interaction" (Covey 1989:19).

Bibliography

Brownlie, Robin and Kelm, Mary-Ellen. 1996. "Desperately Seeking Absolution: Native Agency as Colonialist Alibi" (orig. in the Canadian Historical Review 75 (4) 1994:543- 546), in *Out of the Background: Readings on Canadian Native Agency*, 2nd ed., ed. by Kenneth Coates and Robin Fisher. Mississauga: Copp Clark Ltd., pp. 210-222.

Covey, Stephen R. 1989. *The Seven Habits of Highly Effective People: Restoring the Character Ethic*. New York and Toronto: Simon and Schuster.

Peers, Laura. 1996. ""The Guardian of All": Jesuit Missionary and Salish Perceptions of the Virgin Mary."

Smith, Donald. 1987. *Sacred Feathers: The Reverend Peter Jones (Kahkewaquonaby) & the Mississauga Indians*. Toronto: University of Toronto Press.

Stevenson, Winona. 1996. "The Journals and Voices of a Church of England Native Catechist: Askenootow (Charles Pratt), 1851-1884."

Valentine, Lisa Philips. 1995. *Making It Their Own: Severn Ojibwe Communicative Practices*. Toronto: Univ. of Toronto Press.

Winter, Keith. 1975. *Shananditti: The Last of the Beothuck*. Vancouver: J.J. Douglas Ltd.

Index of Native Nations
and Language Families

Erie: ('It Has a Long Tail', i.e., a cougar), an Iroquoian-speaking nation that formally ceased to exist as a people after 1654. – 27

Huron-Wendat: an alliance of Iroquoian-speaking tribes that in the seventeenth century consisted of the Bear, Cord, Deer, Rock and the Bog; for a discussion of the name see – 7-9, 15-17, 22-23, 26, 29, 30, 36-37, 63, 63, 141, 196 passim

Inuit: ('people', 'men', singular is **Inuk**) a people living across the north from Alaska to Greenland, formerly often known as the 'Eskimo', based on the Micmac word for eating meat or blubber raw. – 71, 89, 91, 104-105

Innu: ('people','men'),an Algonquian-speaking nation living in Labrador and Quebec. Often referred to as Montagnais or Naskapi. – 91, 100, 103-104, 130-131, 134

Iroquoian: a family of Native languages comprised of two branches: northern including Huron, Mohawk, Oneida, Onondaga, Cayuga, Seneca and Tuscarora; southern branch now only including Cherokee. – 15-6, 27, 33, 63, 91, 197

Iroquois: the Confederacy of Iroquoian-speaking peoples, originally five, later six, known by those people by a name (in Mohawk 'Rotinnonhsionni') meaning 'they build or extend a house' (a different verb is used in different languages). – 15, 18, 22-24, 31, 34-36, 42, 44, 48, 52, 54, 58, 60, 62-3, 140-42, 147, 161, 187-189, 197-98, 233

Micmac: an Algonquian-speaking people living in Newfoundland, Nova Scotia, Prince Edward Island, New Brunswick and Quebec. – 16, 62, 100-103, 112, 116, 119, 121, 123, 130-31, 134-35

Mississauga: an Ojibwa band from the north shore of Lake Huron who moved to Southern Ontario, where their name was applied to all local Ojibwa. – see chapter four

Mohawk: the easternmost of the nations that formed the Iroquois Confederacy. In their own language they are called '**Kanyenkehaka**' or 'People of Kanyenke'. – 2, 5, 10-11, chapter one (especially 14-31), 91, 146-47, 197

Mohican: ('wolf'), an Algonquian-speaking people who fought against the Mohawk, and who came to symbolize the 'Vanishing American' in the nineteenth century. – 24, 79, 103

Montagnais: an Algonquian-speaking nation, the southernmost of the two groups now usually called the Innu. – 16, 40-1, 61, 91, 103, 135

Naadawe, an Ojibwe word making reference to snakes, and an unflattering reference to Iroquoian and Siouan speakers. – 15, 142

Naskapi: an Algonquian-speaking nation, the northernmost of the two groups now typically called the Innu. – 91, 103

Neutral: a collection of Iroquoian-speaking people living in southern Ontario, some of which were to join the Seneca, others the Wyandot. – 142

Nishnabe: a word used by the Algonquian-speaking Mississauga, Saulteaux, Ojibwa, Odawa and Potawatomi, to refer to themselves and to Native people generally. – 9, 91, 142-44, 163-66, 169, 179, 184-86, 233

Ojibwa: (Ojibwe for the language) a term used to refer to an Algonquian-speaking nation living in from Quebec west to B.C. and from Michigan to Minnesota. – 7, 9, 16, 57, 63, 91, 132-34, 141-42, 160, 184-89

Oneida: a nation of the Iroquois Confederacy, living west of the Mohawk. – 15, 22, 29, 34

Onondaga: a nation of the Iroquois Confederacy. – 15, 48, 50, 197

Petun: an Iroquoian-speaking people who lived by the shores of Georgian Bay, in Southern Ontario. They were to form the nucleus of the Wyandot. – 8, 142, 197

Rock: (Arendaenronnon - people at the rock), a member of the Huron-Wendat alliance. They eventually joined the Onondaga. – 197

Seneca: the westernmost of the members of the Iroquois Confederacy. – 15, *23*, 62-63, 197, 214

Shawnee: an Algonquian-speaking nation originally from near the Atlantic. – 134, 200, 203, 208

Slavey (from Cree **Awokanak**): a Dene people living in the Northwest Territories – 70, 91

Tuscarora: an Iroquoian-speaking nation that early in the eighteenth century became the sixth member of the Iroquois Confederacy. – 15, 63

Wyandot: an Iroquoian-speaking nation formed from the southern Ontario peoples – see chapter five

Yellowknife: a Dene group living west of the Chipewyan – *4*, 70, 75, 92

Index of People

This will include a brief description for historical figures, particularly those who are Native.

AGMV Marquis

MEMBER OF SCABRINI MEDIA

Quebec, Canada
2002